Modernizing Racial Domination

SOUTH AFRICA'S POLITICAL DYNAMICS

Modernizing Racial Domination

South Africa's Political Dynamics

Heribert Adam

UNIVERSITY OF CALIFORNIA PRESS

BERKELEY · LOS ANGELES · LONDON

1971

University of California Press, Berkeley and Los Angeles
University of California Press, Ltd., London
Copyright © 1971
by The Regents of the University of California
ISBN: 0-520-01823-0
Library of Congress Catalog Card Number: 75-132422
Printed in the United States of America
Designed by Dave Comstock

FOR KOGILA

Contents

Preface

THIS STUDY IS BASED ON FIVE YEARS OF CLOSE OBSER-
vation of South Africa beginning in 1966 with six months of
field research, mainly in the African territories and at five non-
White universities. This was later followed by a one-year teaching commitment in Sociology at the University of Natal in Durban which afforded opportunities for further acquaintance with
the local conditions for another year. From this ensued a systematic analysis of the domestic and international context of
the South African conflict. It included the regular reading of
South African newspapers, journals, and all other available
material relevant to the racial question. The qualitative content
analysis of the editorials, particularly in the Afrikaans-language
press, constitutes one of the major sources of data for this study.

I am indebted to South African acquaintances from all ethnic
groups and political convictions. Although many generous Afrikaner hosts in Pretoria will probably find their efforts to
convince the ignorant foreigner of the correctness of their policy
have failed, they did indeed give me valuable insight into the
Afrikaner personality and attitudes. This experience undoubtedly contributed toward a realistic assessment of the political
trends. I have benefited from almost daily discussions with my
colleagues at the University of Natal, especially Fatima Meer,
Tony Mathews, and John Torres. Above all, my friend Hamish
Dickie-Clark has influenced my perspective with his sceptical
sensitivity, rational argument, and considerable experience.
Many talks with Jack Mann and informed criticism by John
Blacking proved very useful. However, this study is, for the
most part, a critical discussion of the work of the two socio-

logical giants in this field: Leo Kuper and Pierre van den Berghe. And it proved to be impossible to always distinguish which ideas from their perceptive analyses have influenced my own arguments.

From the vast political literature on southern Africa this study differs in perhaps two respects: (1) by its focus on the political economy and the specific dynamics of the South African scene, and (2) in that it tries to avoid the tone of moral indignation frequently present in writings on South Africa. To be sure, there can be no neutrality on the question of racial discrimination, and the argument that it could be worse is indeed a poor rationalization. On the other hand, emotional abhorrence, derived from deep commitment to universal ethics, seems understandable but is no substitute for realistic analysis. The dedicated activist too frequently suffers from illusions arising from wishful thinking.

The failure of moralism against an overwhelmingly stronger reality and the ambivalence of pragmatic survival within it was for me the most striking aspect of the South African experience. My wife, herself a member of the South African subordinate group, has above all helped to clarify my perspective on this crucial question. My contact with her vulnerable Indian community in Durban has most contributed to my understanding of South Africa's ethnic problems.

I am greatly indebted to Sylvia Hale for proofreading and for valuable suggestions to improve my style. I am grateful to the editors of the University of California Press, especially William McClung, for conscientious criticism and careful editing. Bonnie Braaten, Chris Stamelias, Jan Inouye, and other staff members of the Political Science, Sociology and Anthropology Department at Simon Fraser University typed the manuscript patiently and conscientiously. Finally, I have benefited from the challenging questions posed by many thoughtful students during courses on southern Africa and comparative race relations.

Some initial chapters of this study have been published in German by Suhrkamp under the title: *Südafrika: Soziologie einer Rassengesellschaft* (Frankfurt, 1969).

Grants from the *Deutsche Forschungsgemeinschaft* and the President's Research Fund at Simon Fraser University are gratefully acknowledged.

Heribert Adam

I

South Africa's
Stalled Revolution

IN THE PRESENT WORLD SYSTEM OF ECONOMIC RELA-
tions, the southern African complex has significance for Western nations as a rapidly expanding trading market and as a
so-called peripheral center of mineral exploitation. Moreover,
with the abundance of relatively cheap labor in a developed
infrastructure of transport, communications, water supplies,
and education, profits for private investments in an advancing
secondary industry are among the highest in the world. However, despite her close economic ties with European countries
and some international corporations, South Africa is no neocolonial satellite of a distant metropolis. Her early independence under the control of a minority against an antagonistic
majority has not only led to progressed capital formation but
also to a distinct political structure which now runs counter
to the dominant trends in the rest of the world. In terms of the
competition between capitalism and socialism, the colonial
south of Africa constitutes an embarrassing ally for Western
political leaders as well as a potential risk area.

In the context of sub-Saharan Africa, the economic and military power of the developed south occupies such a position of
dominance as compared with the underdeveloped north, that
South Africa has already succeeded in surrounding herself with
a ring of more or less dependent satellite countries, in spite of
the almost universal ideological opposition against her internal
political system. This internal structure resembles in many

ways the well-known relations between colonizer and colonized, between a rich metropolis and an impoverished hinterland under its direct or indirect control. There is, however, one important difference in this comparison. South Africa represents both metropolis and colony in geographical unity and inseparable economic interdependence. The country's hegemonic group, therefore, cannot follow the example of the European nations in granting full political independence to the conquered territory as a whole. South Africa's colonizers have no homeland overseas to which they could return. They are as much indigenous inhabitants as the subject population with whom they persistently refuse to share civil rights. In this social system all colonizers live in close contact with the colonized. As many authors on southern Africa have indicated,[1] all members of the colonizing group (not merely a few traders, missionaries, and civil servants) share the infrastructure with their subordinates and rely on the same resources. The key social feature of this "settler colonialism"—as compared with a mere territorial exploitation by a distant metropolis—is the unique relationship of domination that develops from simultaneously living together and maintaining extreme social distance. This settler domination is maintained by a complex system of interwoven coercive, economic, and ideological controls, which has been labeled domestic or internal colonialism.

In spite of this economic and geographic interdependence of the dominant settler minority and the subordinate majority, the South African "metropolitan" government emulates the political and territorial pattern of separation practised by European colonial powers. According to the proclaimed goal of "separate development," the subordinates will be able to change their political status gradually through self-determination in a system of nine politically independent states linked economically to the former metropolis as surrounding satellites. Increased economic integration and reliance on the cheap labor of the subordinates are countered by enforced political, social, and economic segregation by the dominant sector. Above all, the

1. See especially Leo Marquard, *The Peoples and Politics of South Africa* (Cape Town: Oxford University Press, 1960), p. 235.

rulers fear the growing conglomeration of a proletarianized peasantry in the cities and attempt to fragment these rightless masses as far as the dependency on their labor permits.

In contrast to the Portuguese or French colonial policy, South Africa's domestic colonialism uses not cultural but racial criteria for separation and social stratification. The ruling 3.8 million whites, comprising 17.5 percent of the population, divide the 17.7 million non-whites into three racial groups, each subject to varying degrees of control on their economic and geographical mobility: 2 million Coloureds stand at the top of the hierarchy of the colonized; followed closely by 0.6 million Asians, predominantly of Indian descent; and 15.1 million Africans (70 percent of the population) stand at the bottom and are subject to the harshest restrictions.[2]

Some authors intent on finding revolutionary tendencies have tried to categorize relationships between these groups in terms of Third World peasant revolts or of an advanced European

2. Figures from the preliminary results of the 1970 census. The frequent use of racial categories in this book reflects, of course, the South African reality. The choice of names of the different groups, in itself an indication of a specific political outlook in South Africa, is not intended to prejudge an analysis here. Names have been chosen according to the dominant preference of the respective group, not according to the official designation. The term African (in former times, "Kaffir," "Native," now officially "Bantu") does not imply that members of other ethnic groups are not also African citizens by descent or naturalization.

South African "Coloureds" distinguish themselves from the Africans, in contrast to the Anglo-American meaning of the word. They are descendants of unions between whites (both English and Dutch) and slaves (from the East Indies or Madagascar), Hottentots, or Bushmen. The term "Negro" is not used in South Africa. "Europeans" comprise all whites, including white Americans and Australians. "Asians" or "Asiatics" refer mainly to Indians. The few hundred Japanese in the country have been declared "honorary whites" except in the case of intermarriage with whites, which is forbidden. The official status of the small Chinese community (9,000) remains undefined in various respects.

While this analysis attempts to avoid usage of the many terms which have a colonial bias, it is hardly possible to exclude all controversial categories, such as "homelands" or "white areas," "freedom fighters" or "terrorists." However, when used, it is in the sense advocated by their proponents and does not necessarily represent the author's identification with the concepts.

proletariat. These frequently contradictory interpretations are indiscriminately applied to a unique historical situation. Little account is taken of the complexity of this "very strange society"[3] whose rate of economic growth and industrialization has been among the fastest in the world, and whose particular social, political, and economic institutions have emerged in relative isolation from other Western nations. Technological modernization has been accompanied by retarded political development and the refusal of the dominant group to accept values universally endorsed. At first sight South Africa displays the classical Marxian prerequisite of a prerevolutionary situation: an extreme gap between advanced forces of production and obstructive modes, held together by the chains of an outdated political superstructure.

Of all nondemocratic regimes the South African system of domination by a privileged minority is the only one in the world officially based on color. In an era marking the end of political colonialism and the beginning of the emancipation of subject peoples all over the world, a white minority has set out to rule an economically interdependent industrialized society. Hence, almost all critical analysts of South Africa have predicted that the Apartheid endeavor would inevitably fail. No country in the Third World, it is said, either in Latin America or among the feudal states of Asia, has been riper for a violent revolution, certain to take place in the foreseeable future. The magnitude of this revolution has been viewed as likely to exceed all other colonial revolutions because of the severity of suppression, the technological development of the country, and the divergent interests at stake for the two uncompromising antagonists. In addition, many foresee far-reaching consequences of this conflict for Western powers, especially with respect to their relationships with the developing countries and their positions in the cold war.

Before setting out the perspectives and central questions of this study, it seems useful to summarize the existing literature of South Africa. This literature provides the essential elements

3. The title of a lengthy report by Allen Drury (New York: Trident Press, 1967) about "a journey to the heart of South Africa" which gives rather superficial impressions of the country.

for an understanding of the South African system, and it is against the background of the strengths and shortcomings of these studies that a more adequate analysis can be developed.

The frequent prediction of revolution is based on elementary insights of political sociology. In South Africa domination is easily recognizable as direct personal exploitation. The rulers are not hidden behind a sophisticated ideology or an anonymous bureaucratic apparatus. On the contrary, they are definable as a precise group visible even to the most politically naïve. In contrast to Western countries, domination has not been transformed into subtle manipulation but is experienced in daily and vivid humiliations. Consequently, there are few incentives for subordinates to identify with their rulers.

The crude distinction between privileged white and under-privileged non-white, it is argued, diminishes the ethnic cleavages among the non-white groups: Coloured, Indian, African, and their various subgroups. In the face of unifying hate against white rule and in a common state of subordination, class as well as educational differences among the ruled would seem irrelevant; structural change appears to be in the interests of even the small non-white middle class, which in other countries has obstructed the realization of the colonial revolution. The more the machinery of law and police interferes with the chances of the masses, the more it would seem to reinforce the revolutionary potential, not only in terms of the subjective preconditions of a revolution but also by the increased objective gap between advancing levels of production and retarded modes of production.

Most critical analysts stress the industrialization achieved up to this time as the safest guarantee for the quick abolition of race separation. While South Africa has only 4 percent of the continent's territory and 6.5 percent of its population, nearly one-third of all commodities produced for the market in Africa stem from this area. An economy which was based almost entirely on agriculture and the export of mineral products prior to World War II has expanded since the late fifties into a diversified secondary industry. Although the country still supplies 74 percent of Western gold, gold exports account for only roughly one-third of South Africa's foreign exchange. With the free market price likely to rise well above the monetary price of

$35 a fine ounce, the predicted rapid decline in gold production seems far off. The increasing export earnings from other scarce minerals with which the country is richly endowed, such as diamonds, copper, iron ore, manganese, and above all chrome, in addition to the rapid growth of industrial exports, seem to guarantee a favorable balance of payments under almost any circumstances, even if gold output declines. Economists predict that the country could, therefore, increase its imports substantially over the 1969 figure of 2.137 million rands in the seventies.

In the late sixties, the gross domestic product rose on the average by 6 to 7 percent, outstripping the 5.5 percent target rate of the five-year economic development plan. With a population growing at the rate of nearly 3 percent a year, economic growth has, nevertheless, progressed even faster. During the sixties, this resulted in an annual increase in real income per head, of all race groups, on an average by about 3.5 percent. With a continued expansion at this pace, the standard of living would double in less than twenty-five years.

Some of this wealth has also filtered down to those whose contributions toward these economic advances are least rewarded. Africans are on the whole materially far better off in South Africa than in the rest of the developing, newly independent African states. A comparison between these different economies is frequently used to legitimize the political stratification in South Africa by indicating its higher living standards.

The rapid industrialization of the country has created a permanent urban proletariat, which now comprises roughly one-third of the 15 million Africans. The other two-thirds are in approximately equal numbers rural workers on the white-owned farms and the inhabitants of the overcrowded reserves, with the traditional subsistence economy barely supporting a standard of living frequently below the bread line. Because of low wages, urban Africans are also largely excluded from enjoying the consumption level of the whites. The apportionment of income by racial group as estimated by market research institutes, gives the following picture.

Compared with the economic incentives to be gained from the struggles for independence in the ex-colonies, the prospects for Africans in South Africa are much more promising after a

INCOME BY RACIAL GROUP

	Percentage of Total Population	Percentage of Income (Estimate)[a]
Whites	17.5	73.4
Coloureds	9.4	5.4
Asiatics	2.9	2.4
Africans	70.2	19.8

[a]According to Wally Langschmidt, Managing Director of Market Research Africa, as reported in *STATS* (Johannesburg) 1 (February 1969):903. The estimates are derived from the 1967/68 National Readership Survey, the research report "An African Day," and survey reports of The Bureau of Market Research of the University of South Africa.

political change. In most former colonies only a small group of African civil servants directly benefited from the transfer of power, while the economic situation of the population as a whole hardly changed. By contrast, a redistribution of accumulated wealth in South Africa could fundamentally change the life style of every African.

Over and above the fact of material inequalities, the specific political contradictions in South Africa would seem to intensify these general revolutionary conditions. Rapid industrialization and concomitant growth in urbanization and increased education appear to favor and even require a nonracial society. Yet the more the different segments of the population have adjusted to this common industrial culture, the more the ruling group has emphasized and legalized ethnic distinctions at every level of social organization and in every sphere of life chances. Above all, the ethnic groups so defined have been prohibited from competing in organized form for a more equitable share of the national product: this is distributed according to the sole and unchallengable decision of the white minority. Prohibited from unionizing effectively and from striking, denied any political rights at their homes or places of work, and subjected to white control in their geographical mobility through rigid pass laws, the African workers have in effect the status of serfs whose life chances depend on racialist white unions rather than on the divergent interests of their employers.[4] Accordingly, organized multiracial contact in public has been outlawed, and all private

4. On the economic contradictions within the ruling group, see Chapter 6.

contact between whites and non-whites has been institutionalized and segmented by a variety of laws. The greater the number of Africans who became "detribalized" through permanent
instead of temporary stay in the urban areas, the more the system emphasized racially defined barriers. Apartheid can best be
understood as the systematic attempt to reverse economic integration as much as possible by legislating social barriers in order
to channel the inevitable political consequences of African
economic advancement in the interests of the privileged whites.

The numerical weakness of the dominant white group, and
even more their traditional prejudices, have militated against
the development of an institution which in other industrial
societies has most effectively paralyzed revolutionary consciousness for collective action: the transformation of class-based political aspirations into individual expectations, permitting the
rise of a few token individuals into the ruling class as an example
of such possibilities. South Africa has her collaborators but no
"Uncle Toms," "assimilados," or black directors with formally
the same privileges as their rulers. Individual mobility which
could cut across the ascribed race barriers is legally excluded
in the castelike race structure. Here, however, the "programme
of separate development," as Apartheid is now euphemistically
called, is supposed to provide unlimited opportunities in the
"homelands." Thus far, apart from some churches, there exists not a single role in the society of 21 million inhabitants in
which a single member of the non-white majority exercises any
authority over a member of the white minority. From the perspective of maximizing productivity, the system incurs great
waste in leaving the potential talents of 80 percent of its population untapped. In addition, not all senior positions can be
filled adequately because only a limited reservoir for white
recruitment is available. While, on the one hand, the achievement principle for the non-white majority is forcibly suspended
by denial of opportunity or rendered impotent by transference
to a fictitious "homeland," the system ensures, on the other
hand, that no member of the ruling group can descend to an
unprivileged stratum, regardless of his capacities. Race and class
criteria are thus almost synonymous in South Africa.

It is true that in each of the three non-white groups there are a few persons with considerable wealth, and there still exists a strata of so-called "poor whites," but these exceptions do not matter as far as their control over the relevant means of production is concerned. Class or status structures within each group seem to be of secondary importance, since the ascriptive criteria of race determines overall life chances. The achievement principle, however, does apply within the racial segments, although probably with a greater significance among non-whites.[5] Since they face greater obstacles in acquiring a higher education or a comparable white income level, the prestige attached to this rare achievement is also relatively higher. In the case of those few who reach the top of their respective racial group, the discriminatory limitations are particularly felt when compared with the privileged whites of lower educational status. This status incongruity is a primary source of tensions.

With respect to differences of rank among the three subordinate groups, the objective and subjective level has to be clearly distinguished. The boundaries of domination are most obvious when class membership in South Africa is defined in terms of access to political decision-making and authority over whites. In this respect all non-whites are equal in that they exist, in a way, outside the central political system. From the perspective of most authors on South Africa, two apparently diametrically opposed race or class castes face each other in visible polarization: white and non-white, ruler and ruled, privileged and underprivileged, exploiter and exploited, a numerical minority against a four-times stronger majority which has the support of an almost unanimous world opinion and is backed by the historical tendencies of a declining colonial era.

This "world opinion," represented for instance in the debates and voting results of the United Nations or in press reports, is more outspoken against the South African race system than in the condemnation of more momentous injustice, greater exploitation, or direct physical extermination in other parts of the world. A partial explanation for this situation might be that South Africa is the only state in the world that has legalized

5. Leo Kuper, "Structural Discontinuities in African Towns: Some Aspects of Racial Pluralism," in Horace Miner (ed.), *The City in Modern Africa* (New York: Praeger, 1967), p. 132.

race criteria while the continuing race discrimination in other countries is supposed to be prevented by laws or is at least camouflaged by other criteria. Such world opinion seems to mirror, somewhat late, the uneasy feelings of liberal imperialists who see their outdated practices continuing in South Africa, its exploitive features revealed, bare of any missionary ideology. Members of either world group, white or black, feel more challenged by South Africa than by a conflict between two nations or political systems in which oppression allows a neutral noncommitment.

The South African race conflict is distinguishable from all other ethnic frictions or colonial wars in that it is a situation which seems to allow no compromise for either antagonist. The 3.8 million whites living in the country for three centuries cannot return to a "motherland" as the French settlers did after the Algerian war. Ideas that the South African whites could be resettled in Europe or Australia are as unrealistic as suggestions that American blacks return to Africa. What has been the logical consequence of independence for temporary settlers and colonial officers in other parts of Africa is not possible in a case where whole population groups have acquired a "home-right" through acculturation or generation-long stay. It is, therefore, not the right of the white tribe to live in South Africa that is questionable, but its privileged political and economic status compared with the majority of the country's population, and a policy that aims at ensuring its continuation.

In this respect, the South African situation differs from the conflict between Israel and her Arab neighbors. African leaders inside and outside the country have repeatedly declared that they would accept the existence of the whites and that their hostility is not racially motivated. In the Lusaka Manifesto, fourteen East and Central African countries stated that their rejection of racialism did not imply "a reversal of the existing racial domination. We believe that all peoples who have made their homes in the countries of Southern Africa are Africans, regardless of the colour of their skins; and we would oppose a racialist majority government which adopted a philosophy of deliberate and permanent discrimination between its citizens on grounds of racial origin."[6] Similarly, Nelson Mandela, the leader of the African National Congress, stated in his speech from the dock before his lifelong jail sentence in 1964: "The African National Congress has spent half a century fighting against racialism. When it triumphs, it will not change that policy."[7]

However, the major fear of the whites—their continued survival if they were to give up their power—is in itself a political factor, regardless of the justification of this anxiety. Colin Legum states: "On objective grounds, no one can honestly say that such fears are entirely groundless. After the kind of treatment Black South Africans have received over three centuries, why should one suppose they will behave any better than White South Africans?"[8] Yet even though there are no guarantees, apart from the assurances of African leaders, these prophesies of black suppression are questionable because they overlook the changed conditions of legitimation which would accrue after a successful African revolution. The status of the white *Herrenvolk* is based on the underprivileged position of the majority: an African majority government, however, would need only a transfer of political power as a means for a redistribution of the accumulated wealth. A material equality of chances as a basis for its existence, not a continued political suppression of a group, would be required after such a change. Tens of thousands of remaining whites in the independent African states today feel no desire to emigrate; many have settled there after independence.

Nevertheless, the fear of the South African whites is realistic insofar as they will have to lose their privileged position. In this regard, their "racialism" differs from other well-known forms of race prejudice. In anti-Semitism or prejudice against any outgroup, the individual components of the authoritarian char-

6. *New Statesman,* 30 May 1969. The policy in East Africa of Africanization at the cost of Indians, even those with African passports, undermines the credibility of the statement in the eyes of many South Africans.
7. Quoted in Julius Lewin, *The Struggle for Racial Equality* (London: Longmans, 1967), p. 90.
8. Colin Legum, "Colour and Power in the South African Situation," *Daedalus* (Spring 1967):484.

acter play a dominant role, the outgroup functioning as a scape-goat for various frustrations. But if the whites of South Africa were to change their attitudes toward the objects of their preju-dice, they would certainly face the loss of their supremacy. In the other situations, such a change of mind would remain with-out political consequences; in South Africa it would alter the social structure.

This structural situation, which seems to exclude compromise unless the ruling group were to commit a "voluntary suicide," is augmented by immediate emotional incentives for revolution-ary change. With 600 daily arrests of Africans violating the pass laws in Johannesburg alone,[9] there seems no need for a unifying ideology to create revolutionary awareness among the masses. "Nobody needs to read Marx to react with hostility to brutality," comments the sociologist J. C. Davies.[10] According to his widely accepted theory of revolution,[11] the rapidly increasing gap be-tween rising expectations and their fulfillment in reality would seem responsible for the outbreak of revolutions. The theories of other authors with more complex explanations of revolutions seem also to be applicable to South Africa. "Exigency," the cen-tral category in the model of Zollschan and Willer—defined as a feeling of unease in a person and unrest in a collectivity stem-ming from a differential between definition of the relevant sit-uation as it is and as it should be—would seem to exist in South Africa as well as the "articulation" of such "needs."[12] Charis-matic leaders of the African resistance have raised their voices since 1912, when the African National Congress was founded, to articulate cautiously the hopes and demands for equal rights and gradual assimilation into the white society. In contrast to the other African colonial areas, the south had a relatively large

9. *The Star* (Johannesburg), 8 August 1968. If not stated otherwise, the weekly airmail edition of this paper is quoted.
10. J. C. Davies, "The Circumstances and Causes of Revolution," *Journal of Conflict Resolution* 11, 3:255.
11. J. C. Davies, "Toward a Theory of Revolution," *American Sociological Review* 27 (February 1962):5–19.
12. D. Willer and George K. Zollschan, "Prolegomena to a Theory of Revolution," in G. K. Zollschan and W. Hirsch (eds.), *Explorations in Social Change* (Boston: Houghton Mifflin, 1964), pp. 125–51. See also Chalmers Johnson, *Revolutionary Change* (Boston: Little, Brown, 1966).

number of university graduates much earlier, detribalization and acculturation had progressed further, and through the migratory labor system the more traditional groups in the reserves had also come into early contact with Western ideas and life styles.

Those struggles for racial equality and integration reached a climax and temporary end in the Passive Resistance Campaign of 1952 and finally in the Anti-Pass Demonstrations of 1960, when the more militant Pan African Congress was founded, and gradually turned away from the old goal of a nonracial democracy to be achieved only by peaceful means. The total suppression of non-white opposition organizations after a series of "treason trials" excluded the possibility of a legal change of power. Since then, it is argued, all the prerequisites for revolutionary change are present. The opposing blocks of African and Afrikaner Nationalism have become increasingly polarized, and both display readiness to use force. An end of communication between the antagonists parallels a refusal to compromise and negotiate; a lack of consensus about the rules of the game accompany the mutual denial of legitimate right to power; gradual reform, instead of revolution, is thus ruled out by the South African political system according to these analyses. Hence, almost all social science studies on South Africa published during the sixties have predicted violence, bloodbath, unrest, and upheaval for this polarized situation. The following selection presents an overview of the most common perspectives in the analyses of South Africa:

> A numerous and well-armed ruling class, partly fortified by the religious sanctification of Apartheid, may be expected to fight for survival with great determination and ruthlessness. As for the non-Whites, the systematic oppression creates a situation in which they begin to feel that only the most radical measures will effect change. And so the conflict moves continuously to greater extremes.—Leo Kuper[13]

> I am afraid that what does seem the most probable outcome is the very gradual building up of a kind of Algerian situation which is horrible to contemplate.—Robert Birley[14]

13. *An African Bourgeoisie: Race, Class, and Politics in South Africa* (New Haven: Yale University Press, 1965), p. 392.
14. Interview with *The Observer*, 22, April 1967.

Furthermore, the risk that violence might erupt during the movement toward non-racialism would need to be weighed against the near certainty of eventual racial violence if South Africa persists in its present course.—Gwendolen M. Carter et al.[15]

. . . and the future would appear to promote turbulence and violence until this accommodation is reached.—Sheila T. van der Horst[16]

There remains also the possibility of a sharp intensification of racial conflict inside the country, in spite of the activity of security police and laws prohibiting sabotage and subversion. In the event of widespread disturbances, the stability of the present regime would be demonstrably shaken to an extent that South Africa could fairly be described as a threat to world peace.—G. V. and M. P. Doxey[17]

The likelihood of revolution seems high. Mounting internal strains and external pressures doom White supremacy and racial segregation within the near future; the entire evolution of race relations since Union, and even more since 1948, excludes the possibility of a peaceful and gradual reversal of the present situation. Far from making any concessions, the government moves faster than ever in the reactionary direction, and becomes more and more repressive. This course is, in fact, the only one left to Nationalists in order to prolong their stay in power. Any retreat would precipitate the crisis, but every new repressive measure, while postponing the explosion, also increases its potential violence.—Pierre van den Berghe[18]

It took a world war and the loss of 30 million lives to dispose of the Nazi menace—simply because those who had the power refused to use it in time to stop Nazism from overrunning Europe. Let us hope that the cost of ending Apartheid will not be so great.—Brian Bunting[19]

15. Gwendolen M. Carter, Thomas Karis, and Newell M. Stultz, *South Africa's Transkei: The Politics of Domestic Colonialism* (Evanston: Northwestern University Press, 1967), p. 182.
16. "The Effects of Industrialization on Race Relations in South Africa," in G. Hunter (ed.), *Industrialization and Race Relations* (London: Oxford University Press, 1965), p. 139.
17. "The Prospects for Change in South Africa," in *The Year Book of World Affairs, 1965* (London: Stevens & Sons, 1965), p. 88.
18. *South Africa: A Study in Conflict* (Middletown: Wesleyan University Press, 1965), p. 262.
19. *The Rise of the South African Reich* (London: Penguin, 1964), p. 325.

On the other hand, the apologists of Apartheid think in strategic terms; they frequently end their writings with threats and exhortations to stand firm:

> If and when the bogey of a world colour war is recognized as such, and the cold ideological war against Southern Africa is desperately warmed into action, it would be well for its enemy to reflect that the land has great economic strength and ties, plus a virile stock which has so often proved its die-hard grit, and would be more resolute than guerrillas in a jungle because of a more inspiring cause, the cause of a people who have their backs to the wall of their civilized existence.—H. F. Sampson[20]

In contrast to these predictions, this study attempts to show that revolutionary change in South Africa—with mutual use of force exceeding the degree of coercion implicit in repressive laws—is unlikely to occur in the near future. Actual developments in recent years as well as new forms of dictatorial domination, which hamper revolutionary change precisely where it seems theoretically most likely, support this view. It departs from the above-quoted studies, written under the impression of widespread unrest in the fifties and early sixties, which underestimated the effects of an increasingly streamlined and expanding system of sophisticated dominance.

A central question posed in this study is: What apart from naked coercion enables a society ridden with such deep-seated conflicts to continue to function? Pierre van den Berghe has commented: "That South Africa has survived so long in such an acute state of disequilibrium is indeed highly problematic for sociological theory."[21] As a near ideal type case in the Weberian sense, it permits the basic question of the limits of suppression to be studied, an issue Dahrendorf regards as the fundamental problem of politicial sociology. Dahrendorf presumes that in a totalitarian system "restrictions of the possibility to realize interests collectively are feasible only within certain temporal and substantive limits."[22] While such vague general-

---

20. *The Principle of Apartheid* (Johannesburg: Votrekkerpers, 1966), p. 119.
21. van den Berghe, *South Africa*, p. 213.
22. Ralf Dahrendorf, *Conflict After Class: New Perspectives on the Theory of Social and Political Conflict* (London: Longmans, Green, 1967), p. 18.

izations cannot be readily tested, totalitarian regimes today seem to practice forms of domination which seriously challenge this presumed relation between the suppression of interests and the jeopardizing of the system's existence. The interests of the suppressed are obviously manipulated to an extent frequently underestimated. South Africa, with its openly opposing interests and extreme degree of suppression, would seem to represent a society in which these new forms of manipulated domination are more evident than elsewhere. The Apartheid system has been viewed as simply the most outdated relic of a dying colonialism, yet possibly it is one of the most advanced and effective patterns of rational, oligarchic domination.

To explore this central hypothesis, it is necessary first to consider how fruitful a comparison between the Apartheid system and the other well-known forms of colonial and fascist rule can be. If the thesis proves correct that the system of domestic colonialism has discovered ways to prevent or delay its collapse in spite of inherent contradictions, then perhaps more general inferences could be drawn with respect to the relationship between modernization and racialism. An analysis of a society in which all the prerequisites for revolution seem to exist might well shed light on a vital and related question: Is it realistic to expect revolutions generally in the Third World, especially through guerrilla warfare, and what kind of counterrevolutionary techniques will these forces have to overcome?

For a sociological study it is necessary to analyze rather than merely condemn Apartheid. This requires study of the interests implicit in the policy. Much of the polemical literature on South Africa, however, merely denounces the Apartheid system and expresses disgust. The local liberal critique which continually proves that the country has turned into a police state and that basic civil rights, as announced in the "Human Rights Charter" of the United Nations, are violated, remains ineffectual because the alternative of a bourgeois state of civil liberties, in which civil rights of all people are expressions of mighty interests, has never existed in the colonial situation, except in the form of philanthropic branches.

Apart from moral descriptions of South Africa, there are four main, not necessarily mutually exclusive, conceptual schemes with which to analyze the Apartheid system: (1) the concept of cultural pluralism, (2) the theory of colonial imperialism, (3) the theory of totalitarianism, and (4) various theories of fascism, especially as far as they focus on the race ideology of National Socialism.

In a critical comparison the weaknesses of these perspectives for an analysis of the South African situation will be illustrated, this leading into the consideration of "pragmatic oligarchy" as a key concept in the understanding of the Apartheid system. Its analysis, although for the most part descriptive, attempts to be theoretical in the sense that it explains and predicts, to a certain extent, the direction in which settler colonialism is likely to develop. A realistic and detailed analysis of the existing situation seems to be a prerequisite for any question as to how change in South Africa might be instrumented. The final chapter of the study raises this complex problem by critically evaluating the shortcomings of past responses to South African racial policies in light of the changed internal and international context.

In doing this, one has to take into consideration an insight many authors critical of colonialism emphasize; rather than treating colonialism as a problem of the colonized, as the "white man's-burden" notion and similar ideologies suggest, the key to the problem is the colonizer. This study is thus more concerned with the rulers than the ruled, since the experience of the latter, a European can hardly share.

2

Racialism and Colonialism: Conclusions from the Economic History of South Africa

APART FROM VARIOUS TYPOLOGIES OF RACE RELATIONS, such as paternalistic and competitive interactions, there are basically three, not mutually exclusive, theories about the origins of racial or ethnic discrimination, emphasizing different facets of the problem.

The first, mainly psychoanalytic interpretation, focuses on personality dynamics and deficiencies. Hate toward outgroups is interpreted as projection of the suppressed drives of the "authoritarian personality." According to this scapegoat theory, the bigot is characterized by a weak ego, due to a harsh socialization process. Fear of sexual inferiority seems an important part of a general anxiety.

The second explanation focuses mainly on economic frustrations as the reason for racial hate. The prejudiced person is concerned about his status; he feels threatened by competition, marginal position, and "status inconsistencies."

A third theory attempts to get away from personality components and emphasizes racial attitudes as results of conformity to one's group; racialism is viewed as a socially prescribed mode of behavior; races are seen as culturally accepted definitions of the situation according to group interests; race relations, therefore, are explained as part of the distribution of power in the social structure.

These theories implicitly recognize that it is not the presence of physical differences between groups but the perception of such differences as socially important, that creates a racial problem; yet despite this, many sociologists still neglect to analyze the historical and social context from which visible or imagined group distinctions derive their significance. There is a certain reluctance to treat racial ideologies as a part of power conflicts which cannot be separated from the economic criteria of stratification. Raymond Aron, for example, expresses this view: "The main principle of social distinctions is not economic but religious or racial. It would be absurd for instance not to realize that in South Africa racial differences determine the entire organization of society."[1] Others concede the connection between race discrimination and fear of competition, but they too refuse to view racialism mainly as a product of other social circumstances without a significance of its own. Hence, Leo Kuper comments in a review of a book which contends that "the essence of Apartheid is not race discrimination but class domination":[2] "This may be so, but it is not easy to abstract the economic from the racial, and I would suppose that the racial differences have facilitated the economic exploitation, and that racism has its own quite independent vitality."[3]

It would indeed be absurd not to see that in South Africa class conflicts are secondary to race conflicts. Even the South African Communist Party once rallied behind the slogan: "Workers of

1. Raymond Aron, *La Lutte de Classes; Nouvelles Leçons sur les Sociétés Industrielles* (Paris: Gallimard, 1964), p. 356.
2. Alexander Hepple, *South Africa: A Political and Economic History* (London: Pall Mall, 1966).
3. Leo Kuper, *Race* (July 1967):114. In a later article, Kuper explains that racial differences as such have no intrinsic significance, which derives from their associated cultural meanings and institutional use made of racial identity by the colonizers. "It is by reason of cultural emphasis and structural elaboration that racial difference now appears to assume independent significance as a major determinant of social relations in white settler societies." Leo Kuper and M. G. Smith (eds.), *Pluralism in Africa* (Berkeley: University of California Press, 1969), p. 171.

the world unite, to defend a White South Africa!" Yet, nevertheless, one deals only with epiphenomena so long as racialism is analyzed in isolation from political economy. An analysis of racialism is sociological only if it probes into the historical dimension of racial attitudes, thereby explaining and elucidating racialism in its entanglement with the social structure. In short, racialism is an expression of specific interests.

The extent to which such a perspective has been successfully applied to the analysis of colonial situations has become one of the central arguments in the dispute about the usefulness of a "pluralist approach."[4] While the idea of cultural pluralism has merit as a set of sensitizing concepts with which to view the perseverance of cultural entities, it has serious shortcomings. First, there is hardly any useful consensus among its leading proponents, as the most sophisticated formulation amply documents.[5] It is not only the diversity of societies with which one has to cope, but with a matching diversity of definitions. Kuper himself refers to the "embarrassing riches of choice"[6] among conceptual frameworks and categories. Vague jargon frequently becomes an end in itself instead of adding new insights through

4. Among the vast body of literature on cultural pluralism, the more important sources are J. S. Furnivall, *Netherlands India: A Study of Plural Economy* (Cambridge: Cambridge University Press, 1939) and *Colonial Policy and Practice: A Comparative Study of Burma and Netherlands India* (Cambridge: Cambridge University Press, 1948); M. G. Smith, "Social and Cultural Pluralism," *Annals of the New York Academy of Science* 83, 5 (1960):763–77; Kuper and Smith, *Pluralism in Africa*; Vera Rubin (ed.), "Social and Cultural Pluralism in the Caribbean," *Annals of the New York Academy of Science* 83 (January 1960):761–916; Pierre van den Berghe, *Race and Racism: A Comparative Perspective* (New York: John Wiley, 1967); John Rex, "The Plural Society in Sociological Theory," *British Journal of Sociology* 10 (June 1959):114–24. "Perhaps the first full-length critique of the 'pluralist' approach to the study of change and conflict in Africa" (van den Berghe) is: B. Magubane, "Pluralism and Conflict Situations in Africa: A New Look," *African Social Research* 7 (June 1969):529–54. Pierre van den Berghe has replied to Magubane in *African Social Research* 9 (June 1970): 681–9.
5. Kuper and Smith, *Pluralism in Africa*.
6. Ibid., p. 469. It is suggested here that the theory has survived the constant barrage of criticism chiefly by virtue of the fact that its main tenets are so vaguely stated as to become irrefutable, in that no empirical observation could constitute a negative case. At this level, it becomes merely semantic wrangling, reified vocabulary.

the interweaving of theoretical and empirical analyses of colonial societies.

From this point of view, it seems understandable that impatient critics of colonial ideologies, such as Ben Magubane, lash out against the colonial biases of many traditional anthropologists who see ethnic cleavages as a static, almost innate characteristic of African societies; tribalism rooted in primordial identities instead of historical conquest and its consequences. The central shortcoming of the "pluralists" is seen in their failure to apply a perspective that truly integrates the analysis of cultural rivalries and segmentation with political economy. Ethnic conflicts are often viewed as being unrelated to questions of material well-being, equal opportunities for all, justice, and discrimination. In short, the economic sector, the changing mode of production, is largely excluded from the analysis or at best added as another variable and not seen as a constituent of ethnic cleavages. Ethnocentrism is seldom seen as a rationalization or substitute for other frustrations, but as constituting a force in its own right. Hence, the analysis rarely focuses on the objective and psychological roots of strong ingroup feelings but on its manifestations.[7]

However, the critics of the pluralist approach tend to overlook the fact that many of their alleged opponents concur with the assessment of colonialism and its impacts but frequently express this in a rather abstract and neutralizing terminology. In this sense van den Berghe's reply to Magubane, though overreacting, is correct insofar as he in particular, and also Kuper, have shown great sensitivity toward the historical and structural factors of racialism. However, when one reads that "racial differences derive social significance from cultural diversity"[8] and that "racial and ethnic sentiments . . . seem to be autonomous, subject to their own laws, gathering their own momentum,"[9] then it becomes apparent that the focus on cultural diversity as

7. On the concept of ethnocentrism, see J. Levinson in T. Adorno et al., *The Authoritarian Personality* (New York: Harper & Row, 1950), p. 102.
8. Kuper and Smith, *Pluralism in Africa*, p. 13. The opposite perspective would stress the fact that Negroes were scarcely made slaves because they were culturally different from white Americans.
9. Ibid., p. 485.

the outcome of other forces is indeed neglected. It would seem more fruitful to analyze *why* "politicians readily find in racial and ethnic cleavages a resource for political exploitation?"[10] If one is not to presuppose inherent aggressive tendencies among members of different racial stock, then the struggle for scarce resources among segmented groups has to be seen as the decisive reason for ethnic strife. As long as an equal share of these scarce goods or equal opportunities to acquire them does not exist; as long as there is, in Smith's terminology, "differential incorporation," or "differential access of these social or racial sections to the institutions of the common public domain,"[11] ethnic conflicts will not disappear, as Smith himself acknowledges in his concluding remarks. Kuper similarly points to the dialectical tensions associated with "depluralization." He suggests that, for ethnic identity to be transcended, it must first be asserted so that the deep-rooted humiliation and lack of self-respect of the colonized mind can be overcome. Hence, depluralization would paradoxically seem to take place through a process of increased racial polarization, as Kuper aptly speculates.

To conclude: instead of reifying cultural heterogeneity as a quasi-natural state of affairs, ethnic identifications should be seen as the result of efforts by underprivileged groups to improve their lot through collective mobilization or, conversely, the efforts of a superordinate group to preserve the privileges they enjoy by exploiting subjected groups. The basis of group unification may vary according to historical circumstances: a common language or religion as well as race can provide the collective bond. Racial tensions arise when members of a traditionally subordinate racial group become politicized and aware of discriminatory practices. Conflicts tend to result from the dominant group's feeling that former subordinates are beginning to compete in areas where they have prior and superior claims. In addition, the rigidity of prejudiced attitudes, or their resistance to change, is intimately related to the degree to which they have become integrated into the life styles of individuals as a legitimation for behavior that protects their material interests. Historically, the climax of black-white racialism coincides with

10. Ibid.
11. Ibid., p. 431.

colonial expansion in Africa and the slavery debates in the south of the New World.[12]

The history of South Africa best illustrates the economic basis of race discriminations. In 1652 Jan van Riebeeck established with a few Dutch soldiers a refreshment station at the Cape for the ships of the Dutch East India Company. A few years later slaves from other parts of Africa and Asia were imported for the manual work in the colony's vegetable gardens. Soon the first "free burghers" quit the service of the Company, which was in any case more concerned with the profits of its shareholders than the proper administration of its African colony. After about 1700 *Trekboers* left the Cape Town area for the interior where they lived as seminomadic pastoralists. The historian Leonard Thompson, commenting on the economic attitudes of this phase, states: "Therefore, the free burghers were never an autonomous community but a community dependent on non-White labour. Like other slave-owning communities, they despised manual and domestic work as servile work; and they did not generate an artisan class."[13]

Nevertheless, in the first decades of the colony, it was common practice for some Hottentots to become fully accepted into the white society through Christianizing and marriage with white settlers. It was only later that religious barriers were replaced by racial criteria. Promiscuity between the races continued, however, with the not insignificant motive of adding to the otherwise expensive slave supply. "The Dutch ladies," an early nineteenth-century traveller remarked, "have no reluctance to their slave girls having connection with their guests, in hopes of profitting by it, by their being got with child. I, myself, know instances where they have been ordered to wait on such a gentleman to his bedroom."[14] By the end of the eighteenth century, a

12. See Michael Banton, *Race Relations* (London: Tavistock Publications, 1967), p. 12. Banton's review is one of the most comprehensive studies in this field.
13. Leonard M. Thompson, "The South African Dilemma," in Louis Hartz (ed.), *The Founding of New Societies* (New York: Harcourt, Brace & World, 1964), p. 183.
14. Robert Percival, *An Account of the Cape of Good Hope* (London: Baldwin, 1804), p. 291, quoted in Ronald Segal, *The Race War* (London: Johnathan Cape, 1966), p. 45.

new society had developed under the new African circumstances, clearly distinct in custom and language from its Dutch origin.

Some years after the Cape was taken over by England in 1795 and again in 1806, the first sizable contingent of 5,000 British settlers arrived in 1820. In contrast to the unregulated streams of British immigrants to the United States and Canada at that time, these settlers were selected from 90,000 applicants and subsidized by the British Government. They differed from the preindustrial homogenous Boers in the heterogeneity of their professional qualifications as well as their religious and political attitudes. Disgruntled by British rule even more than by the Company's regime, and above all dissatisfied with the philanthropic abolition of slavery in 1836, about 12,000 Boers left the colony in the Great Trek and founded new independent republics in the interior and in Natal. This province was soon also occupied by the British and the Boers trekked back over the Drakensberg into the Transvaal. The aim of this British move and the systematic settlement along the coast was twofold: to bar the Boers access to the Indian Ocean harbors and to curb the African pressure on the frontier of the Cape.

The settlers encountered three different groups of the indigenous population:[15] (1) The Hottentots in the Cape, originally nomadic pastoralists who, together with the imported slaves, became the servant strata of the colony, the descendants of whom are nowadays referred to as "Coloureds." (2) The Bushmen,

---

15. For most authors the history of the country starts with the landing of van Riebeeck and develops into a struggle between a culturally superior white civilization and backward Bantu tribes. The first volume of *The Oxford History of South Africa*, published in 1969 and edited by Monica Wilson and Leonard Thompson, constitutes the first attempt by historians and social scientists to explain South Africa's past essentially as conquest and colonization of indigenous people who lived in various parts of the Republic's territory long before the arrival of the settlers. Stone-walled settlement sites throughout the Transvaal and the Orange Free State may be attributed to prehistoric Bantu occupation, some of them as early as A.D. 1060, according to radio carbon dates found by archaeologist R. Mason (*The Star*, 6 January 1966). For a short comprehensive review of historical research on South Africa see: D. M. van der H. Schreuder, "History on the Veld: Towards a New Dawn," *African Affairs* 68 (April 1969): 149–59.

scattered hunting tribes, whom the Boers viewed "as little different from vermin," shooting them at sight, since the Bushmen
retaliated with cattle raids. "That a few thousand Bushmen did,
in the end, manage to survive," Segal comments, "must be attributed less to a lapse in settler ferocity than to the capacity of the
Bushmen themselves to retreat into desert regions, like the Kala-
hari, where they were unlikely to be followed by any but the
most fervent anthropologist."[16] (3) The Bantu-speaking Africans, cattle-pastorals like the *Trekboers*, highly organized in
complex nations, and much less manageable than the Hottentots and Bushmen, in spite of the Boers' advantage in having
rifles and horses. The more the *Trekboers* moved toward the interior, the more frequently they clashed with the Bantu, and
for a long time a series of so-called Kaffir wars resulted in a vir-
tual deadlock with regard to the frontier in the Eastern Cape.
Due to the increasing lack of pastoral space, there were, at the
same time, wars among the African tribes themselves in the
1820s, largely dominated by the Zulu dictator Shaka, whose con-
quests restructured the South African tribal map as much as the
intervening white powers. After several hundred expanding settlers had been killed, Boer rifles finally defeated the Zulu power
in 1838 in a major battle at the "Blood River."[17]

A decisive turning point in South African history was then
the discovery of diamonds (1869) in Kimberley and shortly afterwards of gold in Johannesburg. Attracted by those developments was the most ruthless branch of British imperialism,
which defeated the two Boer-Republics in the so-called Boer
wars at the turn of the century and incorporated them as British
Colonies in the Treaty of Vereeniging, 1902. In 1910 they were
granted independence in the Commonwealth as "Union of
South Africa," together with the two other provinces, Cape and
Natal.

From this point up to today three groupings have been decisive for the internal development of the country: (1) The Afrikaner, initially active only in the agricultural sphere and later
comprising most of the urban White proletariat. (2) The interests of the British-owned mining industry. (3) The rather pow-

16. Segal, *Race War*, pp. 45–46.
17. Ibid.

erless mass of African laborers and migratory workers, as well as a permanent urban proletariat.

Under the stimulus of production for an urban market a change in the agricultural sector took place with consequences in South Africa similar to those in Europe earlier. With increased subdivision, droughts, and antiquated methods, farms were unable to provide a sufficient living for the owners together with numerous "bywoner" and black workers. From this situation a rural proletariat evolved which became the reservoir for the growing urban worker masses. In South Africa, this stratum of unskilled white laborers drifting toward the cities was mainly Afrikaans-speaking and later became known as "poor whites."[18] Faced with the conditions of a laissez-faire economy and competition from less fastidious black workers, the "poor whites" could expect improvement of their lot only through state protection, since neither qualifications nor private capital enabled them to compete on the market.

The same was true for the older Afrikaner activity. The farms, rendered unprofitable partly through geographical conditions and partly through mismanagement, were kept going by subsidies. Horwitz writes: "In the South African experience not all farmers were politicians but from the beginning nearly all politicians were farmers."[19] Both groups could achieve economic security only through a collective effort aimed at compensating an unfavorable market position with political decisions.

The Afrikaner nationalist movement—exceeding in intensity, totality, and finally in success similar tendencies in Europe during the nineteenth century—has to be explained in the light of its historical-economic origins. The strength of Afrikaner nationalism was based on its numerical majority in the white electorate, on ideological unification through a new language and an Old Testament religion, and on the backing of dozens of specifically designed folk institutions in the economic and educational sector. It triumphed ultimately in achieving exclusive

18. See report of the Carnegie Commission, *The Poor White Problem* (Stellenbosch, 1932).
19. Ralph Horwitz, *The Political Economy of South Africa* (London: Weidenfeld & Nicholson, 1967), p. 9. Even today, 37 percent of the members of parliament elected in 1970 are farmers.

political power in 1948, thus providing more opportunity to expand the Afrikaner economic position as well. Whereas nationalism elsewhere was a prerequisite for economic development in the early phase of competitive industrialization, the Afrikaner ideology can be viewed as a means for an economically handicapped group to catch up with the privileges of industrialization.

The decisive conflict between the British-imperial mining tycoons and Afrikaner nationalism took place during the depression of the twenties, when the Afrikaans-speaking proletariat was under the particular competitive pressure of cheaper black labor. With strikes and political pressure, the white unions enforced a "civilised labour policy" which legally confined the Africans to unskilled jobs and reserved the better-paid skilled jobs for whites only.[20] On the surface, the Afrikaner rise to power has almost all the classical attributes of a Marxian revolution. A subordinate laboring class achieves political domination through collective mobilization and annexes economic enterprises to the state. Yet, they lack unifying interests with their fellow workers. Even though they exist by selling their labor—or rather *because* of this fact—their objective class interest sets them against all other laboring masses. Given the relative scarcity of employment opportunities with adequate wages under the capitalist conditions, job openings themselves become scarce resources which people have a vested interest in monopolizing. Thus, the Afrikaner proletarian government, far from spreading the economic resources equally, developed a vested interest in using political control to monopolize these assets in favor of a labor aristocracy, composed of their own group members only.

The mining capitalists, on the other hand, were more interested in the concept of economic integration, to enable the use of the cheapest labor for all jobs. Because of the fixed gold price, cheap labor constituted a productive factor as important as the gold ores themselves for the profitability of the mines. A general characteristic of colonial exploitation has always been to provide this labor supply. When Lord Shepstone first designed na-

20. A comprehensive and informative source on job reservation is G. V. Doxey, *The Industrial Colour Bar in South Africa* (Cape Town: Oxford University Press, 1961).

tive reserves in the middle of the nineteenth century, it was his intention not only to curb the African pressure through partition but also to provide rural workers. The destruction of the traditional subsistence economy, either through the colonial takeover of the land or through tax bills, forced the native population to look for cash income in the money economy. What is nowadays often mentioned as proof of a relatively humanitarian past; namely, that the indigenous population in South Africa was not exterminated or culturally destroyed as in America, was in fact an economically useful policy under these special circumstances. Govan Mbeki's description of the function of the reserves emphasizes this aspect: "From the outset the purpose of maintaining the reserves was to provide a source of cheap labour for White agriculture, mining and industry. On the one hand, the reserves have served as mating camps for the production of migrant labourers, while on the other, they have proved suitable dumping grounds for the physical wrecks whom industry discards in the same way as waste fibre is thrown away after its juice has been extracted."[21]

With the abundant supply of both non-white and white cheap unskilled labor, the qualified expert jobs in the mines still had to be done by trained European immigrants. The wage gap between both groups was then indeed in accordance with market demands and supplies. This wide discrepancy between black and white wages subsequently developed into a sacred and legally enshrined principle of South African working conditions, since the Afrikaner proletariat was not willing to compete with black labor on the market. The enforced cooperation of the English industrialists was compensated for by dropping earlier demands to nationalize the mining industry.

This unique historical situation—the complete separation between imperial private economy and domestic political power— was subsequently paralleled by a growing economic activity of the state.[22] Through the "Industrial Development Corpora-

21. Govan Mbeki, *South Africa: The Peasants' Revolt* (Baltimore: Penguin, 1964), p. 67.
22. For a basic review of the South African economic structure, see D. Hobart Houghton, *The South African Economy* (Cape Town: Oxford University Press, 1967).

tion," founded in 1940, the Afrikaans-speaking public sector now controls huge steel mills (ISCOR), oil refineries (SASOL), and fertilizer plants (FOSCOR). Of all domestic investments between 1961 and 1965, only 57.5 percent came from the private sector, 36.1 percent directly from public sources and 6.3 percent indirectly from state controlled corporations. South Africa thus practices a state capitalism, unparalleled in its extent in any other major capitalist society.

The economic activity of the state, at first considered only as counter policy to solve the "poor white" problem in the face of the laissez-faire policies of the Chamber of Mines, subsequently acquired strategic relevance,[23] enabling the government to make full use of all the long-term advantages of a planned economy.

Furthermore, South Africa has been able to build up her productive forces largely from her own resources. This was based not only on the mineral wealth of the country which guaranteed a favorable trade balance, but above all on the political subjugation of 80 percent of the population, which made it possible to ignore their consumption demands and employ them at a relatively low wage level. The high growth rate stems partly from the fact that economic planning hardly ever had to take into account the consequences of a temporarily low level of consumption, and instead could concentrate all efforts on the growth potential of the system, the yields of which are now being harvested.

The example of South African domestic colonialism further

23. The strategic significance of South Africa's state capitalism became clear during the state of emergency in 1960. The racial crisis after Sharpeville, together with South Africa's withdrawal from the Commonwealth, resulted in an outflow of foreign capital and a domestic economic crisis. A sharp decline in confidence was clearly reflected in a net outflow of private capital of about 194 million rand (one rand = $1.4) during 1960. The foreign reserves dropped from 250 million rand in March 1960 to a low of 175 million in May 1961. Through strict financial regulations and mobilization of domestic reserves, the crisis soon turned into a boom. At the end of 1968, the country's total reserves stood at more than one thousand million rand, compared with 564 million rand at the end of 1967. Precautionary measures against potential sanctions constitute, of course, a major aspect of the state's economic planning.

confirms the proposition that nowadays economic processes are more than ever politically mediated. Contrary to a vulgar Marxist assumption, the political decisions in this country are not based monocausally on economic interests of big business, but rather the process of production and distribution is largely determined by the polity in which the white, particularly the Afrikaner, interests are embodied. In conclusion, this relative dominance of the political sphere results from the specific heterogeneity of white material interests: on the one hand, the British mining capital, relying on the cheapest labor available; and, on the other, the Afrikaner proletariat, which tried to improve its lot by pursuing a policy at the cost of its black competitors.

The common Marxist theory of colonialism, as applied to a case such as South Africa, obviously needs revision. In this context, it seems meaningful to distinguish two different types of colonies:[24] (1) *Colonies of exploitation* in which the climate does not encourage a very large European settlement. Few colonists occupy or lay claim to the foreign territory except temporarily. In this case, close links exist between colony and metropolis. Most parts of the European colonial territory in Africa and Asia fall into this category and the classical theory of imperialism focuses, therefore, on these relationships. (2) *Settler colonies*, in which the climate favors a permanent settlement of relatively large numbers of Europeans, are distinctly different. More than the relative numbers of Europeans which distinguishes "White settler societies from societies with White settlers,"[25] the relationship to the metropolis is important.

The early independence of the settler colony increases the power of its political institutions, and it is these institutions and not the parent metropolis which guarantees the colony's continued existence. In the conflict between the indigenous majority and the settlers, the metropolis no longer performs any me-

24. See Rene Maurier, *The Sociology of Colonies* (London: Routledge & Kegan Paul, 1949) and Guy Hunter (ed.), *Industrialization and Race Relations* (London: Oxford University Press, 1965), who both suggest this distinction. See also Leo Kuper, "Political Change in White Settler Societies: The Possibility of Peaceful Democratization," in Kuper and Smith, *Pluralism in Africa*, pp. 170–76, for further elaboration.
25. Kuper, "Political Change," on which this description relies heavily.

diating role. The colony of this type is neither exploited in the interests of a foreign power, nor degraded to a market for foreign surplus commodities, but is characterized rather by a domestic colonialism which at certain stages might exceed the metropolitan colonies in degree of exploitation. But it is questionable whether this holds generally true. For as a ruling class, the settlers are also forced to maintain a degree of harmony in the system. They have more at stake than a foreign colonial power: their own survival. Their coexistence in the same social system with strange people whom they cannot integrate is for them a source of permanent frustration but mitigates against direct colonial brutality at the same time.

Arthur Keppel-Jones has pointed to the difference between Afrikaner nationalism and other nationalistic expressions resulting from the intermixed living with outgroup members. In most countries a nation has its own distinctive territory, of which it is in exclusive occupation. The nationalist drive is directed against outsiders and external control. But the Afrikaners have no territory exclusively their own.[26]

The impression of superexploitation by the settlers often derives not from the less exploitative behavior of the metropolitan colonizers, but from wider policy changes in the postcolonial era due to considerations which do not apply for the settlers. The ruling group in the settler state of South Africa has hardly any interests outside the colony apart from its immediate neighborhood and no responsibility toward an empire as a whole to take into account. In practice, its open and racially defined exploitation is a source of increasing embarrassment to the major neocolonial metropolises which have become aligned with her independent offspring in the cold war. In this sense, a real conflict of interests does indeed exist between Britain and Rhodesia as well as between southern Africa and the Western powers as a whole. Marxist interpretations which deny this friction and assert a conspiracy instead,[27] overlook the fact that the settlers are not agents of an imperial power, but a ruling class on its own.

26. Arthur Keppel-Jones, "South Africa: Racialism and Republicanism," *University of Toronto Quarterly* 31 (1961–62).
27. Hans Kistner, "Die Verschwörung im Süden Afrikas," *Deutsche Aussenpolitik* 12 (May 1967):562–77.

This constellation of interests is not altered by the fact that South Africa is considered one of the favored investment countries for Western surplus capital, or, furthermore, that her gold exports still guarantee her an important position in the capitalist monetary system, as does the demand for some rare South African raw materials of key significance. Between 1956 and 1965, investments from the dollar and sterling areas increased by 20 percent, as compared with a 40 percent increase from other West European countries.[28] Direct American investment in South Africa in 1966 figured around 600 million dollars; in 1969 it was estimated at more than 750 million dollars, which constitutes approximately 30 percent of the total American investment in Africa and roughly 1.2 percent of all American investments abroad.[29] However, from 1961 to 1965, Africa took 6.3 percent of fresh American direct investment, compared with 0.9 percent for South Africa.[30] Less than half of the 123 million dollar profits in 1966 has been reinvested in the country.[31] The abundance of a cheap labor supply in South Africa allows a profit rate twice as high as the world average: roughly 15 to 20 percent annually between 1961 and 1965.[32] Other reports state that though American investments in South Africa account for only 1.2 percent of total American foreign investment, they produce 2 percent of United States total overseas earnings.[33]

It is particularly Britain's investments in her former African colonies which ties this part of the world closely in with the

28. Gerard Rissik, "The Growth of South Africa's Economy," *Optima* (June 1967):59.
29. *News/Check*, 24 December 1967, p. 6; *Sunday Times* (Johannesburg) 21 December 1969. According to Rissik, "South Africa's Economy," direct investments from the dollar-area in 1965 constitute only 16.4 percent of the total foreign investment in South Africa, as compared with 70.7 percent from sterling countries and 12.2 percent from Western Europe. It was estimated that the net inflow of capital from abroad during 1968 was about 400 million rand. Total foreign investment in South Africa from all sources, private, governmental, worldwide, is estimated at 5.355 billion dollars. William Frye, *In Whitest Africa* (Englewood Cliffs: Prentice Hall, 1968), p. 126.
30. William A. Hance (ed.), *Southern Africa and the United States* (New York: Columbia University Press, 1968), p. 120.
31. *Die Vaderland*, 8 January 1968.
32. Hance, *Southern Africa*.
33. *Sunday Times*, 21 December 1969.

Western economic network. There are bonds of varying degrees between southern Africa and Britain whose entry into the Common Market is unlikely to lead to a major disengagement between the two countries. Most important for Britain's policy toward the southern African complex is the fact that her investments in the white-controlled South are almost twice those in the North, while the significantly smaller involvement of other countries in Africa (including the United States) have the opposite concentration. The book value of British direct investment in Africa (excluding oil) at the beginning of 1969 was estimated as:[34]

South Africa	£515
Portuguese territories	£120
Rhodesia	£ 89
	£723
Commonwealth Black Africa	£261
Rest of Africa	£112
	£373

The real value of British investment in South Africa and Rhodesia is thought to be about three times the book value. This high British investment rate results partly from the anomaly that South Africa is still a member of the sterling area, although the rand is less connected with sterling than the Canadian dollar, which has been removed from the sterling area. The generous treatment which South Africa enjoys is most obvious in the trade field. Under the Commonwealth Preference System almost all South African goods enter Britain duty-free, two-fifths of them with a preferential margin over mainly developing competitors, averaging 10 percent.[35] Britain's imports from South Africa have, therefore, risen much faster than her exports. In 1965 Britain's exports to South Africa totaled £267 million, as compared with £293 million in 1969. Her imports from South Africa amounted to £200 million in 1965 but £327 million in 1969. On both sides there are large "invisible" exports, earnings in addition to commodities, such as tourism, shipping dues,

34. *The Star*, 22 August 1970.
35. See Barbara Rodgers, Letter to the Editor of *New Statesman*, 31 July 1970.

banking and insurance services. Although the absolute value of
Britain's share in South Africa's trade has gone up, its proportion has decreased between 1964 and 1969. South Africa has increasingly diversified her trade, with substantially increased import figures from West Germany and Japan.[36] This indicates
new competition for the South African market between various
industrial centers. The decision of the British Conservative government under Prime Minister Heath to resume the sale of arms
to South Africa reflects this competition for a wealthy, expanding market, in which the Conservatives openly admit that their
economic interest lies primarily with the white South while the
former Labour government carried out essentially the same
policy only hypocritically disguised by more anti-Apartheid
rhetoric.

Other Western countries, such as West Germany, with a different interest proportion in Africa's two antagonistic blocks
hesitate to make an open commitment in the conflict or, as in
the case of Canada, are outspoken against Britain's policy. This
dilemma is clearly recognized in South Africa and was one of
her reasons for the search for new relations with African states
through a much publicized outward move.

Pretoria realized that it could better maintain Western support if it did not bring its Western allies into a position where
they had to make an open choice between the white South and
the antagonistic North. *Die Burger* comments: "In the principal Western countries there are men in power who do not want
to choose between White and Black Africa. We can help ourselves by helping them that they do not have to do it. In short,

36. At the same time, the direction of South African exports has
changed and indicates diversification with growing exports to other
African and non-European areas such as Australia and Japan. In 1969
the proportions of South African exports were:

Europe		56%
UK	33	
EEC	19	
Other	4	
Africa		15
Other		29
		100%

Source: *News/Check*, 26 June 1970.

our path to better relations with the West lies through Africa."[37]

The interests of both South Africa and Western countries converge in a depolarization of the racial problem and white colonialism. Increasingly more African leaders of independent nations with close ties to their former metropolis advocate a "dialogue" with the white-ruled South—coexistence instead of liberation. Ironically, one of the decisive impacts of South Africa's growing power will be the polarization or fragmentation of African opinion toward the white south. The expectation of continued unanimous African hostility toward the south is likely to be undermined by an increasing split between the so-called militant countries (Tanzania, Zambia) and those favoring the use of South African resources for their own benefit (Malawi, Malagasy, and some West African states). Independent Africa will no longer be able to act as a third power in the East-West competition but will increasingly be drawn into this division with the policy toward the colonial south as the criterion for alliance.

With colonial regimes as allies, the most influential world power and a racialist South Africa do indeed represent different political interests in the overall struggle, regardless of private investments and the high exploitation rate in the settler colonies. In terms of the East-West competition, South Africa as well as Portuguese colonialism constitutes a major blunder for the West in spite of short-term stability in the area through effective minority control. South Africa's ruling group, on the other hand, is increasingly less dependent on foreign capital for economic reasons and, therefore, can be less susceptible to outside pressures for changes of expediency.

The psychological and political consequences of Western investment seem more important now to South Africa as a safety guarantee. Thus, in the words of the former governor of South Africa's central bank, "foreign investment is valuable not only because it provides additional risk capital to speed development, but in that it brings know-how with it and, more generally, provides something of a sheet anchor in troublous times."[38] Prime Minister Vorster declared in 1966: "I have

37. *Die Burger*, 23 June 1970.
38. Rissik, "South Africa's Economy," p. 56.

complete confidence in our future. This is obviously shared by foreign investors, the best barometer for the stability of a country."[39]

How long the Western countries and particularly the United States believe they can afford such psychological support, domestically and internationally, appears to be decisive for future development. If the conflict should come to a head or if the involvement of the Soviet Union or China should increase—for instance, along the pattern of the Middle Eastern conflict—it seems conceivable that the United States would subordinate the private profit interests of some groups to the political interests of the whole.[40] Whether Britain, with roughly 10 percent of its total foreign investment in South Africa, and other West European countries will have to follow such a move immediately is, at present, a matter of speculation.

To conclude: without a perspective applying a truly interdisciplinary approach including economic as well as political insights, an isolated sociological analysis of racialism and colonialism is inadequate. The extreme case of South Africa's continued internal colonialism reveals the shortcomings of a strictly cultural focus instead of a socio-economic one, which alone can come to grips with the decisive contradictions among imperial interests.

39. *Sunday Tribune* (Durban), 16 October 1966, p. 5.
40. All this is speculation of course. It seems highly improbable that either the conflict will come to a head or that the involvement of China or Russia, given their own problems, will increase. With respect to the United States, much will depend on the domestic situation. There is a precedent for suggesting the primacy of domestic electoral considerations: American Middle Eastern policy has been consistently weighted in favor of Israel, despite the economic priority of American-Arab oil investments. Differing policies of the Western countries might result from such considerations and economic competition, as already seen in the arms policy of France toward South Africa and Israel. An interesting speculation about such possibilities is: Robert H. Bates, "A Simulation Study of a Crisis in Southern Africa," *African Studies Review* 13 (September 1970):253–64.

3

Apartheid in Comparison with Other Forms of Domination

Two aspects of domination can be distinguished: the objective one of its function and the subjective one of how it is experienced by the dominated, this relating to the form in which it is expressed. With regard to the objective aspect, a common characteristic of all forms of domination is the exclusion of a group from scarce goods or privileges in favor of a privileged group. In its broadest material form, domination may be defined as the forced renunciation by producers of their right to take full possession of the products they have created.

Such domination can be defined as totalitarian if it suppresses all attempts for change detrimental to the superordinate group. Accordingly, a regime is totalitarian if it excludes alternatives to the established system, if it does not respect boundaries guaranteeing the freedom of political opponents, and if it prosecutes the advocates of structural change and bans their organizations. In this sense, South Africa constitutes a totalitarian state. All efforts which try to bring about changes in the social situation in the country, either wittingly or unwittingly, are defined as "Communist" and, therefore, illegal. The existing liberal white Apartheid opposition has no chance of gaining the support of the exclusively white electorate and is, therefore, permitted to exist but only under permanent supervision and restricted by new forms of censorship and political ostracism.

This relatively broad concept of totalitarianism—as exclusion of alternatives to the established system—offers several advantages over other formulations. It avoids the static, normative distinction between supposedly democratic and supposedly totalitarian states, and focuses instead directly on the operational question of the degree of suppression of opposition. Such a concept implicitly acknowledges the tendency "that the differences between totalitarian and other societies have disappeared in the twentieth century."[1] The discussion of totalitarianism which prevailed during the cold war period of the fifties focused instead on such questions as which phenomena are common to the Fascist and Bolshevist domination, and how far structural characteristics of both systems do exist in other societies. In this line, Carl J. Friedrich and Zbignew K. Brzezinski[2] state six features of a totalitarian dictatorship: an official ideology, a single mass party under a dictatorial leader, terroristic authority of the secret police, a centralized control of the entire economy and a monopoly of arms. Franz Neumann, in contrast to other authors, well aware of the more important differences between Fascism and Stalinism, formulates five essential characteristics of modern dictatorship: police state, concentration of power, monopolistic state party, central social control and the reliance on terror; that is, "the use of non-calculable violence as a permanent threat against the individual."[3] Neumann defines dictatorship as a monopolized power exercised without constraint.

If one presupposes the existence of all these characteristics in the definition of a state as totalitarian or dictatorial, then South Africa cannot be regarded as a totalitarian state, since some of the above mentioned features are either completely missing or exist only in a modified form, this to be discussed in detail later. But this merely descriptive concept of totalitarianism is inadequate in that it does not take into account the historical developments in which these characteristics acquire their significance. As the implicit comparison between Fascist and Com-

1. Barrington Moore, *Zur Geschichte der politischen Gewalt* (Frankfurt: ed. Suhrkamp, 1966), p. 79.
2. Carl J. Friedrich and Zbignew K. Brzezinski, *Totalitarian Dictatorship and Autocracy* (New York: Praeger, 1964), pp. 9–10.
3. Franz Neumann, *The Democratic and the Authoritarian State* (Glencoe: The Free Press, 1957), pp. 244–45.

munist domination indicates, such static-structural thinking overlooks the different historical preconditions and functions of political institutions, often substituting them with arbitrary typologies or abstract analogies. It is essential to abstract not only from the similarities in terror of Fascist and Stalinist domination, but also focus on the qualitatively different utopian goals of the two totalitarian endeavors, which cannot be equated in an undifferentiated form. In this regard the definition of totalitarianism suggested at the beginning—the suppression of all attempts for change detrimental to the superordinate group —seems more useful.

There is another critical reason the prevailing theory of totalitarianism is not applicable in the South African situation. This society is characterized by an extreme cultural, social, and racial pluralism, but the concept of totalitarianism implies the uniform factual and ideological regimentation of component groups. Lewis Coser describes this control of all formerly autonomous spheres: "Totalitarian societies destroy traditional social groups, communities or selfconscious classes and then replace them by new units which are subject to coordination and control by state and Party."[4] The opposite is the case in South Africa. The government attempts to keep the traditional power structure and ideologies alive in order to use them accordingly in the framework of a *divide et impera* policy. Neither the suppression of conflicts between the subgroups nor the total control of relatively autonomous nonpolitical spheres is practiced, but rather the revival of separatist tendencies in language, religion, and ethnocentric tradition. White segregation policy is not based on a mass movement directed at homogeneity; nor do regimentation and coordination characterize the South African scene; but officially segregated and hierarchically ordered racecastes with separate ideologies. It is the specific history and social structure of the country that explains why this sort of manipulation promises to be successful, and why it excludes the mobilization of the population according to totalitarian pattern. Only the constant awareness of the numerical ratios and different levels of consciousness of the various subgroups can

4. Lewis A. Coser (ed.), *Political Sociology* (New York: Harper & Row, 1966), p. 253.

secure the understanding of all the other relevant factors in South Africa. A brief outline of a few sociostatistical characteristics of the race groups and their substructures will illustrate this background.

Each of the four ethnic groups consists of various subgroups, which define themselves according to language, religion, and cultural tradition. Two forces hold this society together in its present form: (1) the common participation in an industrialized economy and, therefore, a certain amount of economic interdependence, and (2) coercion of the state under the control of the white master race.

The most important social distinction between the whites (17.5 percent of the total population) is their language. The Afrikaans-speaking majority still fosters a certain amount of resentment against the English-speaking minority which, for its part, displays noncommitment and dissociation from the ideological course of the Afrikaners. While the political power lies exclusively in the hands of Afrikaners, the English-speaking group controls most of the private part of the economy, especially gold mining. With respect to their attitude toward nonwhite groups, tactical, but no principal differences exist.[5]

The most critical difference within the African group (70 percent of the total population) is the degree of their acculturation to Western habits and values.[6] An increasing number live permanently in the urban areas and have internalized industrial demands. For this group, tribal relationships hardly play any role. The majority of Africans living in the reserves and on the white-owned farms (approximately two-thirds of all Africans), however, have been kept illiterate and rarely speak any lan-

5. On the political structure generally, apart from the already mentioned studies by P. van den Berghe and Gwendolen Carter, see Leo Marquard, *The Peoples and Politics of South Africa* (Cape Town: Oxford University Press, 1960) and L. M. Thompson, *Politics in the Republic of South Africa* (Boston: Little, Brown, 1966).
6. A valuable study of African-European contact among Xhosas is Philip Mayer, *Townsmen and Tribesmen* (Cape Town: Oxford University Press, 1961). On the situation of the urban African middle class, see Leo Kuper, *An African Bourgeoisie: Race, Class, and Politics in South Africa* (New Haven: Yale University Press, 1965) and Monica Wilson and Archie Mafeje, *Langa: A Study of Social Groups in an African Township* (Cape Town: Oxford University Press, 1963).

guage other than the vernacular. Their horizons are limited to the subsistence economy of the tribal hut or periodically to shifting between contract work and traditional life. The resources at their command are scarcely sufficient for bare minimum existence especially in the face of the increasing impact of commodities offered by an industrialized society. Dominant political attitudes also reflect roughly the contrast between the more frustrated but also more intimidated urban proletariat, including many apolitical domestic servants, and frequently more obviously militant rural inhabitants, dependent on the different stature of the chief. Compared with this gap between tribesmen and townsmen, the differences between tribal groupings, emphasized by the government, are of secondary importance.

The Coloureds (9.4 percent of the total population), descendants from miscegenation between the first European settlers and indigenous Hottentots and imported slaves, have completely adopted the white culture. The overwhelming majority living around the Cape Peninsula speak Afrikaans as their home language, and apart from a small group of Muslim Malays, belong to Christian denominations. Although acculturated and in their appearance often hardly distinguishable from whites, their progress toward political and social integration has been reversed in recent years through official race classifications and political exclusion from the common voters' role. Rejected by the whites and divorced from the Africans by culture, status, and certain economic privileges, the Coloureds are in the situation of a typical "marginal group."[7] Political apathy rather than solidarity with the Africans has resulted from this status insecurity.

The Indians (2.9 percent of the total population), descendants of indentured workers in the sugar plantations of Natal in the nineteenth century, have preserved large parts of the subculture of their ancestors.[8] Even within the Indian group, social

7. Hamish F. Dickie-Clark, *The Marginal Situation: A Sociological Study of a Coloured Group* (London: Routledge & Kegan Paul, 1966).
8. On the situation of the Indians, with emphasis on the cultural aspects, see Hilda Kuper, *Indian People in Natal* (Durban: University of Natal Press, 1960). Pierre van den Berghe's *Caneville: The Social Structure of a South African Town* (Middletown: Wesleyan University Press, 1964) offers in the context of a community study an informative

contacts between the economically better off Moslem minority and the Hindu majority are minimal, and marriage is largely endogamous. The various Indian languages, however, are spoken only by the older generation while the youth use English. Mutual support within the extended family has facilitated the efforts of many Indians to make a living in business, particularly as merchants and small dealers. Whites and Africans alike strongly resent this Indian trader class, either as competitors or small scale exploiters. Individual Indians, especially from professional strata, nevertheless, have always played a leading role in the resistance movement, stressing non-white unity.

If one tries to define the political structure of this officially propagated pluralism in terms of a single concept, then the term race-oligarchy would seem most adequate to describe South Africa's system of domination. A comparison with the caste structure is also useful. A racially defined and privileged minority caste rules autocratically over the rest of the caste hierarchy, which, however, does not accept this system unchallenged. This oligarchic domination is neither totalitarian in the usual meaning of the term nor fascist. A detailed analysis of the often claimed common characteristics between fascist, particularly National Socialist dictatorship and Apartheid domination can help to clarify the distinctive features of the latter.

The decisive difference between National Socialism and Apartheid lies in their goals: the former aimed from the outset at aggressive expansion, the latter attempts to defend the status quo. The growing interest of South African capital in other African states of the southern hemisphere does not seem to be a sufficient argument against this definition. Greater South African outside involvement, although creating new markets and resources, essentially constitutes a strategic *defense-move*, aimed

---

description of race relations and living conditions in a small predominantly Indian town in Natal. For more recent studies, see G. G. Maasdorp, *A Natal Indian Community* (Durban: University of Natal, Department of Economics, 1968) and the most informative political and cultural history by sociologist Fatima Meer, *Portrait of Indian South Africans* (Durban: Avon House, 1969). Also see A. L. Muller, *Minority Interests: The Political Economy of the Coloured and Indian Communities in South Africa* (Johannesburg: South Africa Institute of Race Relations, 1968).

at immunizing these territories against "terrorists" through dependency from the white south. It is not a search for new lebensraum with the aim of incorporating these areas in a South African Reich. In fact, more pragmatic Afrikaners, such as sociologist N. J. Rhoodie, propose that Bantustan areas adjoining Lesotho and Swaziland should be formally given away to these states.

The reasons for this difference between aggressive expansion in German fascism and defense of the status quo in South Africa can be traced to the differential power distribution and historical constellation of two structurally distinct societies. Both movements, on the other hand, have similar roots and origins. While the anti-Semitism of the German petty bourgeoisie can be viewed as an unconscious protest against the frustrations and threats of capitalist developments such as monopoly power and economic insecurity, the whites of South Africa reacted against the competitive pressure of their emancipating dependents. They believed that within a supposedly eternally valid estate-like constitution the traditional social order should be preserved and their secured social rank guaranteed, if necessary with massive state interference.

Apartheid dictatorship and fascism resemble each other in the need of the privileged owners to create a strong state machinery without relinquishing it to the democratic control of the population. Psychologically, the fear of the German middle class threatened by the monopolies on the one hand and the socialist workers on the other is in some ways analogous to the reaction of the Afrikaners caught between English imperialism and black nationalism. In both cases it was important to suspend the competition principle and to limit upward mobility to the privileged.

The different authoritarian forms stemmed from the different levels of political development in both countries. In Germany, a dictatorship was faced with the task of abandoning a democracy in which all citizens had at least the franchise; in South Africa, the point was to prevent such a situation from the beginning. Barrington Moore has emphasized "that fascism is inconceivable without democracy or what is sometimes more turgidly called the entrance of masses onto the historical stage.

Fascism was an attempt to make reaction and conservatism popular and plebian."[9] Generally speaking, fascism is aimed at the
abandonment of democracy by a mass movement. In a society in
which democratic conditions—in the sense of legalized pressure
by the ruled on their rulers through the common vote—had
never existed at all, a dictatorship had to cope with somewhat
different problems.

The degree to which such a regime needs the active support
of the masses appears to determine the form and technique of
domination—whether such a government can be satisfied with
passive obedience or whether the active support of the ruled is
required. In the Soviet Union the need for industrialization of
a relatively backward country through collective efforts and the
goal of matching the capitalist competitor economically led to
the Stalinist dictatorship and the mobilization of the masses. In
Nazi Germany the collaboration of the total population was required for the realization of a policy of aggression. Similar conditions and goals do not exist in South Africa. In a hierarchically ordered race society there is no reason for the small master
race to secure its rule through forced and active collaboration of
the populace; such an attempt would in any case have to overcome insurmountable practical and ideological obstacles since
the propaganda focuses on racial differences and not on *Volks-
gemeinschaft* (community). A concept which, unlike liberal democracy, postulates "unity," "harmony," "totality," and abandonment of class struggles and useless party debates is incom-
patible with a racially fixated society. In such a society the race
conflict constitutes by definition the background of all policies.
In this static "persistence-dictatorship" the status quo as the
goal of domination thus determines the role of ideology and
propaganda as well as the extent of coercion. A unifying ideology is of secondary importance here since it would be super-
fluous and unable to mobilize and unify racially separated
masses. With a numerical ratio of one to four between masters
and servants, the South African society as a whole cannot be
aroused by the idea of a "marching column."

In the twentieth century, on the other hand, a paternalistic

9. Barrington Moore, *Social Origins of Dictatorship and Democracy*
(Boston: Beacon Press, 1966), p. 447.

race state of direct domination cannot do without a legitimizing ideology. Domination generally, insofar as it does not perpetuate itself solely through coercion, has to refer to a justifying basis, especially where its character does not allow for rational argument. The theoretical Apartheid program fulfills the ideological function of an apology with the appearance of rationality.[10]

Such a statement, however, can be challenged on various counts. Many critical observers view the Apartheid program only as a cynical rationalization of white rule. Similarly, using the example of National Socialism, T. W. Adorno has pointed out that in such a context the category ideology is inappropriate since even the propagandist did not expect that people would believe in his nonsense or take it seriously.[11] The fascist race ideology, Adorno maintains, comprises no "rational element," no "claim of autonomy and consistency" that reasoning could challenge. Coercion as the threat to the nonbeliever would always be present. In a totalitarian state, "critique of ideology has to be substituted by the analysis of the cui bono."

It does not seem particularly worthwhile to refute again and again the Apartheid program—to compare the reality with the proclaimed Bantustan policy. The discrepancy is evident, and all the critical studies agree that the introduction of the "Ideal Apartheid" would mean a disruption of the economy. However, the present race ideology of South Africa is distinguishable in important aspects from German anti-Semitism and from prior colonialist policies. "Separate development," as the Apartheid program is now euphemistically called, is the theoretical attempt to reduce the irrationalities of former race ideologies. It is aimed at reconciling continued white rule with trends of a waning colonial period. Apartheid policy has long relinquished the former idea of *baasskap*; ideological emphasis no longer focuses on the inferiority of one race compared with another, but on their differences. Encouraged nationalism rather than the

10. One of the most scientifically pretentious Apartheid apologies is N. J. Rhoodie and H. J. Venter, *Apartheid: A Socio-Historical Exposition of the Origin and Development of the Apartheid Idea* (Amsterdam: De Bussy, 1960).
11. T. Adorno and Walter Dirks (eds.), *Soziologische Exkurse* (Frankfurt: Europäische Verlagsanstalt, 1956), p. 169.

master-in-the-house attitude is offered as the ideological solution to preserve white supremacy. In theory, Apartheid aims at the partition of the country so that the various race groups could live peacefully side by side under equable conditions in independent nations. The irrationality of the program lies in the assumption of "natural" instead of sociocultural differences between the race groups which are obviously reinforced by the imposed separation.[12] As a practically fictitious, but theoretically consistent, development program with which a ruling minority intends to secure its dominance, the Apartheid program possesses rational elements. Only if one takes the theoretical plausibility of the Apartheid policy into consideration can the missionary zeal of civil servants committed to paternalistic aid, and the belief in the success and sincerity of their course, be understood. It is within this context that one has to view the role of coercion and terror in the South African system.

The literature on totalitarian states, with National Socialism and Stalinism in mind, describes arbitrary terror as "the very essence,"[13] "the most universal characteristic,"[14] or "the vital nerve of the totalitarian system."[15] This "irrational terror"[16] which has elsewhere culminated in arbitrary mass liquidations and concentration camps did not, however, take this form in South Africa, although this hardly decreases the overall intimidation of the African population. According to a useful distinction by Hannah Ahrendt, "dictatorial terror"—as opposed to "totalitarian terror"—is confined to the authentic opponents of the system. Since all the Africans have to be considered a potential danger, the police can only cope with the authentic opponents, defined as offenders of various laws and petty regulations. By strictly abiding by these restrictions, however, the African can stay out of trouble in contrast to the Jews of German-

---

12. See Leo Kuper, "The Heightening of Racial Tensions," *Race* 2 (November 1960):24–32. Reprinted in van den Berghe (ed.), *Africa*.
13. Hannah Ahrendt, *The Origins of Totalitarianism* (New York: Harcourt, Brace & World, 1951), p. 315.
14. Z. Brzezinski, *The Permanent Purge* (Cambridge: Harvard University Press, 1956), p. 27.
15. Friedrich and Brzezinski, *Totalitarian Dictatorship and Autocracy*, p. 132.
16. Neumann, *Democratic and Authoritarian State*, p. 266.

occupied Europe, for whom no laws existed at all. To stay out of trouble has now become the major overall attitude of most Africans and the political consequences of this way out have to be taken into account.

Other comparisons between National Socialism and the South African race system tend to cloud rather than clarify the specific circumstances. To focus on the differences, therefore, seems more meaningful for an understanding of both systems than to emphasize the similarities.

The white oligarchy hardly displays a glorification of the leader along fascist lines. On the contrary, egalitarian aspects of the settler past have survived. State representatives are considered much more as equals among the Afrikaners than in Western societies; access to them is relatively easy; and although one identifies with the leaders on an emotional basis, their function as proper administrators rather than inspiring mobilizers is dominant. Van den Berghe's term "Herrenvolk-democracy" describes the white political substructure more precisely than a comparison with the Nazi's leader cult or a one-party bureaucracy. South Africa's oligarchy thus has the advantage of greater efficiency compared with the personal dictatorship of fascism. Arbitrary decisions of a single dictator are checked by the consensus of the privileged group, which furthers continuity and dependability. It is highly doubtful that "a dictatorship is. . . . stronger when headed by one dictator rather than a group of dictators."[17] On the contrary, an oligarchic dictatorship corresponds better with bureaucratic domination than a single dictator, often led by irrational, personal motives.

White domination perpetuates itself according to the democratic rules of the game. The takeover by the National Party in 1948 was based on a truly gained victory among the white electorate. Apart from manipulations of constituencies, through which the weight of the Afrikaans-speaking rural districts has been increased, the frequent practices of Latin American dictatorships such as faked election results do not exist in South Africa. For the white voter, there are indeed alternatives to the government. The observer who analyzes the country with ex-

17. Alexander Gerschenkron, "On Dictatorship," *The New York Review of Books* (19 June 1969).

pectations of Fascist or Stalinist prototypes is, at first, surprised by the legal existence of an audible, though weak, Apartheid opposition. (Its more or less conservative program, which coincides with the interests of big business, as well as its function and impact will be analyzed later.) Even though the activity of the very small, radical Apartheid opposition in the South African political climate is hindered by various obstacles, its propagandistic presence in the public opinion would seem to be stronger than opposition programs in some Western states. This situation is allowed to continue partly because of the inefficacy of the racial critique among the white electorate, but chiefly perhaps because of the usefulness of an inefficacious opposition.

A Helen Suzman in parliament—despite the integrity of her conviction and the rationality of her arguments—under South African circumstances serves the system, which she fights with great personal commitment. The undoubted success in her endeavor to make racial repression at least transparent and to ameliorate it on a personal level wherever possible, is balanced by her function as democratic ornamentation for an undemocratically elected parliament. In contrast to its fascist predecessors, the South African system depends on this semblance of democratic legitimacy; the less the actual support of the masses, the more legal restrictions are required to secure white privileges. Since "the law" legalizes white supremacy, whites adhere with fastidious accuracy to its application. With this useful habit, the Afrikaner administration defends its equal status with the English model as well as its standards of civilization compared with the "lawlessness" elsewhere in Africa. This legality also makes it easier to sell totalitarian bureaucratic policy to the electorate as necessary measures in the interest of law and order. Even the unconcealed denial of individual rights to non-whites takes place according to Westminster procedures; all suspensions and restrictions of normal rights refer to proper legislative procedures. Political sentences are imposed by sometimes surprisingly independent judges whose independence, however, becomes increasingly restricted through inhibitive laws. In instances where these laws are nonexistent or in which a general law would be inopportune, parliament itself takes over juridical functions; for example, by a special clause it expanded each year the confinement of the officially sole political prisoner, Robert Sobukwe, whose discharge from Robben Island was due long before 1969, when he finally was released and banned. If accusations that the police torture prisoners gain publicity, the state has been known to even pay compensations, as in the case of Gabriel Mbindi, who was jailed eight months before his acquittal from the charge of terrorist activity.[18] Such legalistic accuracy reconciles the white conscience with the Western norms of democracy while condoning violations of democratic principles that would jeopardize white rule. In spite of the often-emphasized special situation of the country, the air of normality has to be ensured. Only the calculability of domination through accurate law implementation allows the proper, nonarbitrary administration of the subject people within the framework of reliable production.

In contrast to other totalitarian regimes, the relative political stability in the context of white supremacy has so far hardly been disturbed by power struggles among the elite. Permanent purges, infights between various cliques in the party hierarchy, are unknown in South Africa, at least to the extent of the party and military conflicts and the SA and SS battles of Nazi Germany. The numerically superior enemy on the non-white side as well as opposition within the white camp from the English industrialists has thus far prevented such a development. Furthermore, there was no reason for a relatively homogenous rural settler society with common interests to engage in more than ideological quarrels.

This does not mean that there have been no frictions, tensions, and splits among the Afrikaner. These differences, however, were not life or death struggles between rival cliques, as in fascism, but rather arguments about the true ethos of Afrikanerdom, about the influence of *volksvremde* (alien) elements, and the extent of concessions toward a more pragmatic colonial ideology. Never has the principle of continued white rule been at stake; at most, modifications in irrelevant realms of "petty Apartheid" have become issues. What the *verligte* (enlightened) Afrikaners advocate is a more realistic and just

18. *The Star*, 2 November 1968.

implementation of the "separate but equal" ideology which
would result in compromises at the expense of traditions. The
verkrampte (dogmatics), on the other hand, view this as sac-
rilegious. Nevertheless, the *verligte* around Vorster always
proved to be in full control over the party. The electorate has
thus far rejected the extreme right and Albert Hertzog has not
yet lost the stigma of sectarianism or betrayal of Afrikaner
unity. In 1968, Vorster could afford for the first time to use the
security police against the anonymous authors of leaflets from
his own rank. The history of the Afrikaner disproves the con-
tention that the non-white majority is inevitably enforcing total
white unity. During the thirties and forties especially, debates
over German fascism and South Africa's role in the war weakened the white front.

The admiration for Nazi Germany by many leading Afrikaners, including Prime Minister Vorster, is well known.[19] They
rejected South Africa's participation in the war as a British
ally and were active in the pro-Nazi sabotage organization
Ossewa-Brandwag; they were interned by the British in special
camps, the experience of which is still an important informal
bond between various members of the Afrikaner power-elite.
These historic-personal preferences of the present rulers, however, would seem to be insufficient to describe the regime as
fascist, as it has become fashionable in leftist publications. A
perspective that takes solely the former affinity of the present
rulers to Nazism as an indication of fascism could hardly distinguish between ex-Nazi Kiesinger's Germany, for instance,
and South Africa. The limitations of such a personalized
view seem obvious since structural differences do not enter
the picture.

Anti-Semitism as further proof of the Nazi image of the
Afrikaner is doubtful, too, in this generalized form. Even
though anti-Semitic attitudes are latent and widespread among
the Afrikaner, there have been no manifest discriminations
against the Jews. Since its takeover in 1948, the Nationalist
Party has not officially identified itself with anti-Semitic ac-

19. On this aspect and the history of nationalist Afrikaner organizations, see Michael Roberts and A. E. G. Trollip, *The South African
Opposition, 1939–1945* (London: Longmans, Green, 1947).

tivities.[20] It is evident that the white power group cannot afford another split and detrimental criticism abroad, emanating from any manifest anti-Semitism. Furthermore, the emotional connections of the 110,000 South African Jews with Israel—as shown in the highest financial contributions of all Jewish communities abroad to the 1967 war—coincided with foreign interests of the South African government, which allowed substantial capital transactions to Israel.[21]

The undifferentiated comparison between anti-Semitism and South Africa's race discrimination seems also doubtful from a historical point of view. Anti-Semitism and discrimination against Negroes are comparable as psychological syndromes insofar as both complexes of prejudice allow the weak ego a compensation for anxieties and offer an object for the projection of suppressed drives. Beyond this level, however, anti-Jewish and anti-Negro attitudes differ substantially both in their historical function as well as in their appearance.[22] Oliver Cox points out that the potential hate toward the Jews was usually greater, since as a group they were considered equal rivals, while the authoritarian hates the usually dependent Negro only if "he does not know his prescribed place."[23] Virulent intolerance against the Jew, who is portrayed in propaganda as both unassimilable and overadjusted at the same time, has to be distinguished from a race prejudice, which aims essentially

20. E. Feit, "Community in a Quandary: The South African Jewish Community and 'Apartheid'," *Race* (April 1967):395–408. The economic backwardness of the Afrikaner compared with the relatively large numbers of English-speaking Jews in leading business positions plays a role in the ideology as well as the high percentage of Jewish Apartheid opponents sentenced in sabotage trials.
21. At the funeral of Verwoerd, a priest compared the Afrikaner folk with the situation of Israel. Both defied with divine support a powerful hostile environment. Israel's attacks against Arab guerrillas are frequently compared with the restraint of South Africa, while at the same time expressing admiration for the expansive efficiency of Israeli warfare.
22. For an empirical comparison between F-scale items and anti-African attitudes in South Africa as engendered by group conformity, see Thomas F. Pettigrew, "Personality and Socio-cultural Factors in Intergroup Attitudes: A Cross-National Comparison," *Conflict Resolution* 2, no. 1 (March 1958).
23. Oliver C. Cox, *Caste, Class and Race* (New York: Monthly Review Press, 1959), p. 400.

at justifying and rationalizing the continuing exploitation of the Coloured workers and, therefore, goes well together with patronizing benevolence toward the submissive. The Jews could never expect paternalism from their prosecutors, regardless of how they behaved. A similar difference in South Africa is reflected in the intense rejection of the Indians, although the Indian minority constitutes no threat whatsoever to white rule.

In summary: the structural differences between Hitler's Germany and South Africa make a comparison of both societies under the concept of fascism ahistorical and rather useless. The specific new feature of Apartheid, the flexible and pragmatic domination over a racially separated majority, are overlooked. Furthermore, such a comparative attempt does not come to grips with an adequate theory of fascism which has to be more than an analysis of ideology or a personalized description of dictatorial rule. Propagandistic labels cannot replace a thorough sociological analysis of new forms of domination that are far more sophisticated and rational than the dogmatic view is able to detect.

4

Consequences of a
Pragmatic Race Oligarchy

Democratic Police State

WHILE THE CONTENT OF RACIAL BELIEFS IS ALWAYS
irrational, propagated as a justification for existing privileges
or, as in anti-Semitism, adopted as a fictitious explanation for
economic frustrations, this irrationality does not necessarily
characterize the implementation of racial discrimination, which
can be "rational" and efficient with respect to its intended pur-
poses. It is precisely this means-end rationality that seems the
decisive new feature of South Africa's version of racialism. This
pragmatism treats racial and related historical experiences only
with reference to their practical lessons. It overrides the ideological implications of racial beliefs and is oriented solely toward the purpose of the system: the smooth, frictionless, and
tolerable domination over cheap labor and political dependents
as a prerequisite for privileges of the minority.

This domination, which is rationalized by slogans such as
"securance of white survival" or "preservation of Christian-
national identity," however, is secured ultimately by coercion.
Decade-long efforts to achieve some non-white political rights
by peaceful means outside the Apartheid framework have been
rejected with increasingly sterner measures; these also directed
against radical white opponents of the system. In terms of the
questionable distinction between "criminal" and "political"
offenses, approximately 1,300 persons had been imprisoned for

political offenses under the various security laws by the end of the sixties.[1] Almost 1,000 persons (126 whites, 853 non-whites) have been banned since the "Suppression of Communism Act" became law in 1950.[2] Of these banning orders, 355 (50 whites, 305 non-whites) were in force at the end of 1969. While several hundred orders were apparently withdrawn or not renewed after expiry, a number of persons have been banned for a second and even third period. Hundreds have had their passports withdrawn or refused. Many political prosecutees have left the country on exit-permits. This new form of silencing political opponents—applications for exit-permits are usually granted—decreases the domestic political pressure and can be viewed as another new device of pragmatic domination, compared with traditional totalitarian practices elsewhere. The calculated risk which is incurred by allowing opponents to go into exile has so far proved relatively harmless, since the refugees soon lose the vital contact with the local scene and confine themselves to the already existing verbal attacks from outside.

There are various other sophisticated laws, apart from those entailing imprisonment and house arrest, which achieve efficient control of political opponents. The "Suppression of Communism Act" provides for listing of members or supporters of banned organizations. It is an offense for listed persons to change their places of residence or employment without notify-

1. Muriel Horrell, *A Survey of Race Relations, 1968* (Johannesburg: South African Institute of Race Relations), p. 57, mentions 23 whites, 21 Coloureds, and 15 Indians among them. According to figures given by the Minister of Justice, Pelser, in reply to questions from Helen Suzman in Parliament, more than 800 South Africans of all races were serving prison sentences at the beginning of 1970 for contravention of security laws. The vast majority jailed were Africans. There were 332 Africans serving sentences under the sabotage provisions, 51 under the Suppression of Communism Act, 337 under the Unlawful Organizations Act, and 49 under the Terrorism Act. (*The Star*, 19 September 1970.) The daily average prison population in South Africa was 88,000 in 1968/69, in a country with a population of 21 million. This represents an increase of 62,000 over ten years. In comparison, Britain, with a population of 55 million, has an average daily prison population of 25,000. Most of South Africa's prisoners are so-called "statutory criminals," people who were jailed because of pass laws. Nearly 250,000 Africans served sentences of less than one month annually and nearly 150,000 of up to four months.
2. Horrell, *Survey of Race Relations, 1968*, p. 41.

ing the police, or for their utterances or writings to be dissem-
inated or reproduced in any form. Approximately 400 persons
are listed, and may not be quoted in South Africa, in some
instances, even though they are now living abroad. Law professor Ellison Kahn (University of the Witwatersrand) estimated that there are 13,000 prohibited publications, including
those banned by the Censorship Board before the Publications
Control Board was created in 1963.[3]

One of the most striking features of South African cultural
life is the relative intellectual isolation and ignorance about
the changing world of ideas, which whites in particular hardly
seem to notice. While the Boers in the eighteenth and nineteenth centuries were cut off from the ideas of the French
enlightenment by geographical isolation, the ninety-seven definitions of what is "undesirable" in the Publications and En-
tertainments Act achieves largely the same result, in an era
of satellite communication, and this despite the advantage of
the universality of the English language, facilitating access to
the ideas of the Western world. The fear of television as a
liberalizing weapon highlights this situation. It is not surprising then that South African whites display the greatest ignorance about the people with whom they are in closest contact.
The enrichment of creativity and new perspectives through the
experience of cultural diversity exists in theory only. The works
of African writers who have most to say, such as Mphahlele,
Nkosi, and Modisane among others, are banned and even their
names are unknown in South Africa. Deviant whites are still
allowed to deal with African problems and suffering, but
even this tolerance might be more in the interest of white
domination than black liberation, as Nadine Gordimer has
speculated self-critically:

> When it comes to literature, and in particular the literature of
> ideas, there has been precious little tolerance to disguise the re-
> pression. Tolerance has operated in one small area only, and
> provides a curious half-light on the psychology of white suprem-
> acy. Literature by black South Africans has been successfully
> wiped out by censorship and the banning of individuals, at

3. Muriel Horrell, *A Survey of Race Relations, 1969* (Johannesburg:
South African Institute of Race Relations), p. 39.

home and in exile. But white writers have been permitted to deal, within strict limits, with the disabilities, suffering, hopes, dreams, even resentments of black people. Are such writings perhaps tolerated because they have upon them the gloss of proxy—in a strange way, although they may indict white supremacy, they can be claimed by it because they speak for the black man, as white supremacy decides for him how he shall live. . . ?[4]

Under these circumstances the still legal white Apartheid opposition—the English-speaking press, Progressive Party, National Union of South African Students (NUSAS), Black Sash, Institute of Race Relations, and some church circles—serves the function of keeping alternatives in the public opinion alive or, at least, of branding the injustices in the manner of a democracy-conscious enlightenment. Without doubt, such critiques have, on occasion, embarrassed the government, sobered what might be more extreme race laws or ameliorated their implementation. With non-white opposition organizations banned, however, it remains essentially ineffective. Apart from sections of the English-speaking press, which surprises the observer accustomed to totalitarian techniques elsewhere by its outspoken criticism, potential opponents are in general so intimidated that only a small core of dedicated people keep the anti-government organizations alive. The English-speaking press enjoys its restricted freedom, partly because of its ineffectiveness, but also because it receives the backing of business interests.

Some members of the clergy, including the Afrikaans-speaking churches, have distinguished themselves as defendants of racial equality and suffered personal consequences for their stand. The members of the South African Council of Churches have regularly condemned Apartheid, but this critique was mostly confined to the un-Christian consequences of the race policy, assuming that there is a just Apartheid. It was not until September 1968 that this church body denounced racial separation on principle. Whatever the wording of public statements may be, their influence on the church-goer is minimal and the discrepancy between theory and practice continues. As representa-

4. Nadine Gordimer, "Censorship and the Primary Homeland," *Reality* (January 1970):14.

tives of an institution based on the voluntary membership of prejudiced supporters, even a progressive clergyman cannot afford to dissociate himself too radically from his basis. The English-speaking churches in particular need the personnel of foreign missionaries whose visas are dependent on the benevolence of the government, and a substantial number of foreign priests have had to leave the country for political reasons.[5]

Where the domestic institutions dominate, as for instance in the Catholic Church, the vested interest in their continued existence and proper functioning leads to a resigned accommodation to the prescribed conditions. When the Archbishop of Canterbury, Dr. Michael Ramsey, announced his visit to South Africa, a spokesman for the Church explained: "The Anglican Church in South Africa is in a difficult position. It is against Apartheid, but cannot afford to be too outspoken, as the deportation of Bishop Ambrose Reeves showed. If all your Bishops are deported you cannot carry on, can you?"[6] Faced with the choice of institutional continuation or institutional suicide for an uncompromising moral stand, the churches in South Africa have so far preferred the former, similar to the attitude of Pius XII toward Nazi Germany on the question of the extermination of Jews. Increasing verbal militancy, especially on the part of individual clergymen, has been paralleled by practical resignation and declining moral influence over a largely indifferent parish, which reduce the manifestos to well-meaning rhetoric.[7]

It is within this stifling climate of repression that white student opposition has gained particular significance as an articulator of the forgotten. *Die Transvaler* views the National Union of Students (NUSAS) as "a fifth column of the enemies of the Republic and an obstruction in the smooth running of

5. Well known among these is Trevor Huddleston and his account, "Naught For Comfort."
6. *The Star*, 15 November 1969.
7. The situation differs slightly abroad. A consultation on racism, sponsored by the World Council of Churches, held in May 1969 in London, recommended that, if all methods failed, the churches should support resistance movements, including revolutions aimed at the elimination of "political or economic tyranny which makes racism possible." In 1970, the World Council decided to give £83,000 to various guerrilla movements. Almost all clergymen in South Africa criticized this decision as an essentially unchristian support of violence.

healthy race relations in the country."[8] The unpredictable student activity at the white English-speaking universities has developed into a propaganda annoyance for the government. The active members of NUSAS, though a small minority, have succeeded through their imaginative actions in keeping the mood of protest alive. The invitation of Robert Kennedy to South Africa has, thus far, been the most spectacular action, apart from a sit-in at Cape Town University in 1968 against the university's yielding to government demands in academic appointments. Issues which have elsewhere created only internal interest within the university have tended to grow here almost immediately into questions of general political principles. Taking place within the privileged framework, the actions of the white opponents tend to be considered more subversive. On the other hand, the symbolic protest of students who face various personal risks has the same clouding functions as any protest under totalitarian conditions, even though one should not dismiss too easily these isles of liberty. The total boycott of the South African universities as propagated by Apartheid opponents in England is also welcomed by the government in Pretoria, while all admissions of foreign students are carefully screened.

However, it is hardly meaningful to compare the internal South African resistance against Apartheid with political protest movements in Western countries. The specific racial problem has caused political contradictions which lend significance to movements which would elsewhere be classified merely as frictions within a broad right of the center spectrum. In some aspects, particularly with regard to economic planning, the ruling Nationalist Party with its state capitalism might well be regarded as being to the left of the opposition United Party. Some of its supporters and the voters for the small Progressive Party represent a liberal bourgeoisie, which views racial separation as basically detrimental to the economy and unwise with regard to the urban Africans. Similar to the church spokesmen,

8. *Die Transvaler*, 3 February 1970. For an analysis of NUSAS, see Martin Legassick and John Shingler, "South Africa," in Donald K. Emmerson (ed.), *Students and Politics in Developing Nations* (New York: Praeger, 1968), pp. 103–45.

they condemn the inevitable injustices of racial separation without seriously aiming at real equality or equal opportunities for all groups. The Progressive Party advocates a qualified franchise for "educated" Africans, thus substituting an obstructive racial system by a less obnoxious class system.

The Nationalists do indeed score a point when they ridicule Progressive nonracialism as inconsistent and phony in comparison with the homeland-franchise of separate development: "Dr. Jan Steytler . . . cannot seem to see how ludicrously his ardently accepted proposition that 'no person may be denied full political or economic opportunities on grounds of race or colour' contradicts the well-known Progressive policy of a 'qualified' franchise."[9]

Compared with the federation program of the United Party, the theoretical "separate development" of the Nationalists can be considered as radical and democratic. The United Party proposes separate voters' roles in a federal constitution of a centrally controlled state. These separate roles are supposed to provide representation for (1) Coloureds, by six Members of Parliament and two Senators (who may be white or Coloured), (2) for Africans by eight M.P.'s and six Senators who will be whites, and (3) for Indians, by two M.P.'s and one Senator who will be white. "I know" exclaimed the leader of the opposition, de Villiers Graaf, "I shall be told by the idealists that this means that there will not be equality between the race groups. . . . Of course there won't be. Why should there be? The real interests of South Africa as a whole, as well as of the races constituting South Africa, can best be served and advanced by the leadership of the White group. Why should we deny that leadership to the people of South Africa?"[10]

The English language press (with the exception of the *Rand Daily Mail*) applies a similar perspective, which criticizes the government vehemently but agrees with the principle of racial

9. *Die Vaderland*, editorial, 19 January 1970. All quotations from the Afrikaans press are from editorials as translated by the Institute of Race Relations, unless stated otherwise.
10. *News/Check*, 7 February 1969, p. 8. *News/Check* (29 May 1970) commented: "One must ask whether English South Africa, as distinct from the UP, is inherently as conservative as the party that represents it."

separation. The authoritarian method of implementing this policy with its inhumanities and injustices, not the policy itself, is attacked. Occasionally, English journalists even show signs of deference, thanking the government for a gesture of benevolence toward political opponents as if it were a relieving gift, instead of a right to which they are entitled. An illustrative, satirical comment on this topic has been provided by columnist Hogarth Hoogh, of the *Sunday Times,* on the occasion of Sobukwe's release from Robben Island.

> My very warm congratulations to the Minister of Justice, Mr. Pelser, on his decision to release Robert Sobukwe. I will not dwell on the fact that it should have been done long ago. Let us count our blessings and be thankful that this indefensible incarceration is now coming to an end. The Government has feared, of course, that Sobukwe would become a danger to the State if he were released. This is always a possibility, but I doubt whether we really have much to fear (a) because Sobukwe is unlikely to try anything and (b) he won't get very far if he does. The important thing is that a man's liberty is no longer curtailed by arbitrary decree. I always felt a little ashamed when I thought of the way Sobukwe was restricted. Many of us will now be able to hold our heads a little higher as we walk down the street. We thank the Minister.[11]

However, the favorite subject of the English-language press in South Africa is the lack of realism on the part of the Nationalists. Again and again, they are accused of ideological obsessions, which would prevent a tolerant treatment of the non-whites. Neglect of the African's feeling of dignity, it is said, reflects a dangerously unrealistic assessment of economic interdependence. The editor of the largest Sunday paper in the country writes in a debate with his Afrikaner counterpart Dirk Richard: "I quite agree that we would all prefer not to have 'integration.' But that is rather like an Eskimo saying he would prefer not to have ice in Winter. . . . To pretend that the non-Whites are not there, or to persist in futile efforts to remove them is dangerously unrealistic."[12]

Even the irreplaceable Institute of Race Relations whose

11. Hogarth Hoogh (pseudonym) *Sunday Times,* 27 April 1969.
12. *Sunday Times,* 1969.

documentation, research, and objective information is one of the most important sources of internal enlightenment, presents itself as opposing "injustice and unfair discrimination,"[13] which obviously implies the existence of a "fair" discrimination. Its language frequently resembles official announcements, often more or less identifying with a South African nationalism against the liberation movements in other African countries. The Fortieth Annual Report 1968/1969, for example, states, without qualifying the terms used: "Terrorism will continue to be a potential threat. Despite internal problems, other African territories must continue to arraign South Africa and will continue to agitate against South Africa's membership of international organizations." One can anticipate the time when "the emergence of a sense of 'Black Power' in undemonstrative assertions of purpose," which the same report mentions, will dismiss the Institute's well-intentioned striving for a nonracial society as the irrelevant and futile efforts of guilt-ridden dogooders.

Since the Rivonia arrests, active opponents inside the country have learned to assess realistically the power of the state machinery. The system of police informers in all potential opposition groups has been improved to such an extent that this surveillance alone guarantees an effective check on all opponents inside and outside the country. Wide powers, without interference of the courts, together with effective methods of interrogation, give the political police virtually unlimited authority. Solitary confinement and permanent interrogations replace direct physical torture.[14]

Police brutality is present in South Africa as it is in various other countries; but on the whole it has become the exception

13. See "The Nature and Aims of the South African Institute of Race Relations," last page of each annual survey.
14. For an extensive legal analysis of the 90- and 180-day detention laws including their psychological implications, see A. S. Mathews and R. C. Albino, "The Permanence of the Temporary: An Examination of the 90- and 180-day Detention Laws," *South African Law Journal* (February 1966):16–43. Various personal reports of jail experiences have been published. The most well known is Ruth First, *117 Days: An Account of Confinement and Interrogation under the South African Ninety-Day Detention Law* (London: Penguin, 1965).

rather than the rule since psychological torture makes physical assaults unnecessary. Officially, police brutality is not encouraged; confrontations such as the Sharpeville massacre have become extremely embarrassing for the government, since it demonstrates that the system does not, in fact, function as smoothly as propagandized.[15] Apart from individual sadism and the institutionalized violence of repressive laws, the direct brutality of traditional master-servant relations, however, remains an ever-present threat, in spite of official admonitions to avoid embarrassing incidents. Sharpevilles on a smaller scale still occur as a matter of routine, and are hardly noticed as exceptions, since they have become part of the accepted body of sanctions against deviations from role expectations. Three times during one week in February 1970 the police opened fire on African crowds on different occasions.[16]

The report of a clash on a Transvaal farm characterizes the typical mentality of the police when confronted with a threatening situation involving Africans who are ready to challenge police interference. "According to Brig. E. de W. Brandt, Divisional Commissioner of Police for the Western Transvaal, a strong force of police (35 White and African men) was sent to the farm of Mr. Faan Bekker after a complaint had been received. The police parked their vehicles some distance from where the group of about 150 Africans were screaming and holding war dances. The Africans all work on near-by mines.

15. There are still reports of police torture, even in prominent trials. In a well-published case in which 22 Africans, including Winnie Mandela, the wife of Nelson Mandela, were facing charges under the Suppression of Communism Act at the beginning of 1970, an urgent application for an order protecting the accused from assault and torture by Security Police was brought to the Pretoria Supreme Court by relatives of the detainees. In the written statements it was said that they were made to stand on two bricks for hours on end holding bricks above their heads. One of the statements by Rita Anita Ndzanga alleges that a white policeman stood on a chair, picked her up by the hair and let her fall onto a gas pipe. During her interrogation, she states, she was beaten in a room. When she screamed, the windows were covered with thick planks and police worked on shifts, questioning her day and night. (*The Star*, 21 February 1970, p. 2.) According to Helen Suzman there have been 578 reported cases of assault by policemen of all races in two years. (*The Star*, 19 September 1970.)
16. *The Star*, 28 February 1970, p. 10.

Brigadier Brandt said the mob taunted the police and refused to disperse despite repeated warnings. When the mob started throwing stones, the police opened fire. According to Brigadier Brandt, the crowd scattered in all directions after the first burst of fire. Police arrested 22 during mopping-up operations and found four wounded Africans."[17]

More indicative than the actions of the police is the reaction of the white public toward such reports. The Afrikaner press, if at all, reports such incidents in the same manner as road accidents—regrettable, but hardly altogether avoidable. The English opposition press similarly reveals the basic consensus about white authority enforcement, only modified through a more humane implementation. In this vein, *The Star* comments: "There ought to be a great deal of understanding for the police when duty requires them to face a mob that has got out of hand. Their position is often dangerous. In the last resort there may be no alternative to firearms, but are there not other steps that could be taken before this drastic order is given? For instance, tear gas."[18]

On the other hand, the guilt feeling of whites, when confronted with obvious injustice, is an important factor of the South African political scene. The *baasskap* attitude, even in its bureaucratized form, disturbs the conscience-easing tranquility of many whites whose professional ethics are closely linked to universal values of equality and justice. The more South Africa deviates from world trends and the *total* subordination of her colonized population becomes a necessary fact of Apartheid life, the more pragmatic domination has to insist on its proper legitimation in terms of otherwise acceptable values. The guilty white frequently articulates this gap, however, without being aware that his own group policies lie at the root of his uneasiness. He hopes to reconcile the unreconcilable; his moral indignation remains confined to the realm of self-assuring protest without impact; if there are consequences of his protest over secondary injustices it lies in a further streamlining of the system of primary differentiation. The following letter by an attorney to the editor of a Johannesburg paper represents a typi-

17. Ibid., p. 9.
18. Ibid., p. 10.

cal illustration of this system-immanent protest of the perturbed white mind. The writer at the same time documents well the complex situation of race relations in the country by portraying all the main typical attitudes of interracial contacts in a single incident.

SIR,—We are sometimes inclined to regard any criticism of our social and political system in South Africa as biased and vicious. Yet do we ever stop and think for a moment whether our hands are really so clean?

I want to relate the happenings in a magistrate's court in which I appeared for an African client today. My client was charged with trespass and the State alleged that he was found on private property (a farm) without the owner's or lawful occupier's consent. The State's case disclosed the following facts:

Late one evening my client, at the request of his sister, went to this particular farm by motor-car to repair her car which had been involved in an accident on a public road on the same farm and left at the dwelling of an African man who lives on complainant's farm.

The man at whose house the car was, told my client that before he could grant permission for him to see the damaged car, he must first get permission from his "Baas." He then sent one of his children to the White farmer's homestead two miles away and requested my client to wait. After a while the farmer arrived in an aggressive mood. He asked my client who gave him the right to trespass on his ground and told him to leave immediately. My client explained the reason for his mission but the farmer produced a revolver and my client drove off. The farmer took down the registration number of my client's car and reported the matter to the police, and my client was charged with trespass. All these facts were given to the court and I explained that my client had no other way to get to the damaged car. He did not know the name of the White farmer who owned the ground. The only person on earth that he could approach was the African man who lives at the spot.

My client was found guilty of trespass and fined R15 or 30 days imprisonment. My client earns about R40 a month and therefore the fine is the equivalent of a fine of R150 to a man earning R400 a month.

The tragedy of it all is that this is not an isolated case. This sort of justice is meted out every day. I have been practising law for 18 years and I have seen the changing attitude in our courts.

I want to be clear on the point that I do not blame the Government. I am a supporter of the Government's policies. At the same time I am perturbed at the harshness of some of the sentences imposed in our lower courts for seemingly minor offences.

The Supreme Court does not have the manpower to review the thousands of cases that come before our lower courts. The chief magistrates of medium-sized towns report 12,000 to 15,000 criminal cases annually.

People are simply herded to court on dozens of statutory charges. Some are detained, await trial for a few days in jail and then are fined for the most trivial offences.

The attorney is regarded as a troublesome timewaster. Are we really honest when we say that we are striving for sound human relationships between the races of this country?[19]

In spite of such experiences, the South African system of internal colonialism has largely managed to convey the impression that the colonized are no longer entirely the victims of their masters. Courageous verdicts from some members of an independent judiciary have contributed to an awareness of injustice as much as the public discussion about it. It is still possible for example, for twenty-one Africans, held in prison for seventeen months and charged with Poqo membership, to be finally acquitted after the judge found that the key witness of the Secret Police had lied.[20] The insistence of white domination on properly legalized repression, to a certain extent clouds the content, and the power of the state seems impartial, merely abused by individual transgressions. Fatima Meer emphasizes the political significance of this legalistic attitude. She argues that South Africa preserves its "structure through a highly sophisticated administrative technique which carefully mixes personal benevolence with the impersonal and hence 'impartial' mystique of the law, which transcends mere human considerations. The non-White victim is beginning to believe that he has the sympathy and support of minor and senior officials, including the Prime Minister, and that both Blacks and Whites are equally victims of South African customs and the laws of Apartheid. This myth has the probable effect of improving race relations while retaining the deprived status of the non-White."[21]

19. Ibid., p. 11.
20. Ibid., 11 October 1969, p. 11.
21. Fatima Meer, "African Nationalism—Some Inhibiting Factors," in Heribert Adam (ed.), *South Africa: Sociological Perspectives* (London: Oxford University Press, 1971).

The arbitrary powers of government officials are also counterbalanced to a certain extent by the relative "integrity" of Afrikaner bureaucracy. Compared with the widespread corruption in Latin America and many other states, the Afrikaner civil servant adheres to a Calvinist-inspired work ethos which is more oriented toward the benefits of his group than toward individual advantages. Laws are created and bent to fit this collective goal of group protection and not to further the advancement of officials in power or lobbyists connected with them. Although the typical rank-and-file public servant is known to represent one of the staunchest supporters of the National Party, he has hitherto been debarred from formally belonging to political parties because of his image of objectivity. When the government counters criticism with the assurance that the sweeping powers of its executives will not be misused, it can, for the most part, rely on this ingroup integrity which has proved to be a considerable source of strength and efficiency in the implementation of extralegal control.

The freedom of helpless protest the few dissident whites enjoy also contributes to the overall strength of the system rather than its downfall. If the much misused formula of "repressive tolerance" has any meaning, it applies in South Africa. For example, with a kind of masochistic satisfaction, cabinet ministers undergo the experience of being heckled by white nonbelievers, thus demonstrating their democratic tolerance toward a powerless opposition.

The press reported a meeting between 2000 Witwatersrand University students and a cheerful Minister of Mines: "The last question put to Dr. de Wet concerned the deaths of political detainees. In reply he said there was a procedure by which magistrates could visit political detainees, adding the question was an attack on the integrity of the Bench, not the Government. At the conclusion of the meeting nearly half the students stood up and, after lifting their hands in the Nazi salute, chanted 'Sieg Heil, Sieg Heil' for a good 30 seconds."[22] While such expressions of dissent would hardly be tolerated in totalitarian regimes of the Fascist or Stalinist version, the South African rulers

22. *The Star*, 4 April 1970.

can afford such marginal deviation among their restricted constituency.

What really matters is the successful check on the non-white opposition. As long as this potential threat can be arrested, and the organization of the fragmented and atomized subordinates can be prevented, no real danger for white rule exists. With all the non-white leaders of the Apartheid opposition either in jail, in exile, or under house arrest, and with their organizations banned, the active mass resistance within South Africa is paralyzed.[23] It is wishful thinking to state from a position of safety abroad: "But the tendency for new men to take the place of those imprisoned or on trial shows no sign of halting or of being intimidated by countermeasures."[24]

Nevertheless, it is not only the development of the country into a democratic police state that secures the white supremacy. Given the numerical ratio, increased terror by the white minority would have enhanced the likelihood of a revolutionary upheaval. The key to an explanation of the present situation lies in two other factors: (1) the partial successes of the program of "separate development," and (2) the consequences of an unexpected economic boom, neutralizing dissatisfaction by channeling it into other goals.

Apartheid as Utopia and Reality

Promise of Independence Instead of "Petty Apartheid"

Any analysis which focuses only on the repressive aspects of the South African race system overlooks the new elements of the pragmatic oligarchy. These are most clearly embodied in the

23. For a detailed discussion of the failure of African resistance, see later. An outline of the history is Mary Benson, *South Africa: The Struggle for a Birthright* (London: Penguin, 1966). A valuable critical analysis of the organizational weakness of the ANC is Edward Feit, *African Opposition in South Africa: The Failure of Passive Resistance* (Stanford: Hoover Institution on War, Revolution and Peace, 1967). Important self-presentations of African leaders are Albert Luthuli, *Let My People Go: An Autobiography* (New York: McGraw-Hill, 1962) and Nelson Mandela, *No Easy Walk to Freedom* (London: Heinemann, 1965).
24. J. E. Spence, *Republic Under Pressure: A Study of South African Foreign Policy* (London: Oxford University Press, 1965), p. 125.

utopian aspects of Apartheid, from which the traditional race separation can be distinguished.[1] This traditional Apartheid represents no invention of the National Party, but has always been part of the South African way of life, whether in English-speaking Durban or in Afrikaans-speaking Pretoria. These special relationships of contact, or rather distance, between the race groups, were simply legalized by the laws of petty Apartheid, and only in a few instances newly introduced. Pierre van den Berghe has called this sphere micro-Apartheid as distinguished from meso- and macro-Apartheid.[2] Meso-Apartheid aims at the geographical separation of residential zones in the urban areas, while macro-Apartheid is directed toward the future coexistence of ethnically homogenous nations. It is this third aspect of Apartheid, occasionally referred to as "ideal" or "theoretical" Apartheid, that dominates the contemporary discussion compared with the two other forms of separation. This partly reflects the fact that micro- and meso-Apartheid have largely been realized. There is hardly any sphere which has not yet been separated. In addition, the emphasis on Utopian Apartheid can be understood as an attempt to overcome the repressive features of this traditional pattern, and in face of this endeavor, the significance of petty Apartheid is steadily decreasing. It is with the dominance of Utopian Apartheid as compared with administrative-repressive Apartheid in mind that the new forms of racial oligarchy can best be analyzed.

Afrikaner domestic neocolonialism, at least the Verwoerd and Vorster version, is much more enlightened than the traditional colonial methods of an Ian Smith in Rhodesia or of Portugal in Mozambique and Angola, both of whom manage without formal racial separation. Under the pressure of world opinion and a growing urbanized African proletariat, as well as a small non-white professional elite with a fifty-year-long strug-

1. See Douglas Brown, *Against the World: A Study of White South African Attitudes* (London: Collins, 1966), p. 54, who makes a similar distinction between administrative-repressive and declamatory aspects of Apartheid.
2. Pierre van den Berghe, "Racial Segregation in South Africa: Degrees and Kinds," *Cahiers d'Etudes Africaines* 6 (1966):408–18.

gle for emancipation behind them, Verwoerd realized that he had to create a political outlet for African nationalism. The Bantustan policy is supposed to fulfill this function. It deflects political aspirations to areas where they are no danger to white rule. It meets the worldwide demand for African political rights in a fading colonial period by granting them the vote in remote areas, but not in their living and working places where they are merely given the status of rightless "guest workers."

Furthermore, the Bantustan policy conceals continued white control over development under the guise of convincing examples of African pseudo-independence. This device has already proved useful in the case of the other independent neighboring states of Lesotho, Botswana, and Swaziland. The status of "satellite" applies to the independent neighbors of South Africa at least as much as in some Latin and Middle American countries, where the economic dependence on the United States had led to a situation "in which sovereignty of a country becomes a mere fiction in many spheres."[3] The planned Bantustans will constitute a new model in this respect. Numerous studies point convincingly to the illusory aspects of the program, and the increasing gap between promise and reality is regretted even among Afrikaner intellectuals.

After a thorough survey of the Transkei, American political scientists Gwendolen Carter, Thomas Karis, and Newell Stultz reach the conclusion:

> The almost total dependence on the South African economy for even the livelihood of those in the territory, the lack of attractiveness of rural life to Africans brought up in urban areas, and the relatively small numbers affected in relation to the total African population of South Africa would all seem to make independence for the Transkei relatively unimportant in the total context. Even if the South African government should decide to pour massive funds into the Transkei and other African areas for which it plans comparable development, it can hardly be expected that either the Africans themselves or the outside world would feel that what was virtually a unilateral settlement by Whites for a small, impoverished area could compare with the

3. B. Gustavson, "Versuch über den Kolonialismus," *Kursbuch* 6 (July 1966):117.

progressive extension of political, social, and economic rights for
Africans within the present boundaries of South Africa.[4]

Nevertheless, the program of separate development has been
partially successful, not through a real redistribution of power,
but through psychological impact. This is true mainly for two
aspects: (1) the compensation for absence of real political rights
by so-called local self-governing bodies and (2) the increase of
non-white fragmentation through the separation of the population groups.

Less important political decisions and bureaucratic functions
are delegated to various non-white local and regional self-governing bodies, whose members work under white supervision.
Apart from the propaganda effect, these institutions prove useful for the central authority in at least three respects: first, up-
wardly mobile and politically ambitious individuals are ab-
sorbed into this administration; second, immediate discontent
of non-whites is directed toward members of their own groups,
since they represent the overall system; and third, the real authorities are freed from burdensome and tedious spade work
and thus can confine themselves to "advisory" functions without losing factual control. As Barrington Moore writes: "Totalitarianism represents, in part, an attempt to allocate functions
without granting control over the resources that the function
requires, in order to prevent the growth of independent bases
of power in the hands of subordinates."[5]

Under these circumstances the pragmatic Afrikaner no longer
insists on *baasskap* but practices an enlightened coexistence. For
the first time in their history, they shake hands and organize
civil receptions for foreign African dignitaries; as Nationalists
of similar status they are allowed entry into the best white hotels
while in daily life, black and white are not even allowed in the
same elevator. In contrast to Portuguese and Rhodesian politicians, the enlightened sector of the Afrikaners have long realized that the era of traditional colonialism is definitely over.

4. Gwendolen M. Carter, Thomas Karis, and Newell M. Stultz, *South
African's Transkei: The Politics of Domestic Colonialism* (Evanston:
Northwestern University Press, 1967), pp. 180–81.
5. Barrington Moore, *Political Power and Social Theory* (Cambridge:
Harvard University Press, 1958), p. 22.

The editors of two Afrikaner papers P. Cillie and S. Pienaar have expressed this attitude frankly: "Old-time colonialist *baasskap* has not only become impractical in the modern world; nor does it only make our coexistence with other peoples impossible; we can no longer live with ourselves under such an order ... we cannot and may not become the last fortress of a wrong order in the fighting against which the Afrikaner people were formed in a large degree."[6]

From the awareness of this necessity stemmed at first the practice of racially defined discrimination without, however, justifying it with the classical ideology. According to a frequently used distinction, the South African system is characterized by "racialism," but no longer by "racism." Pointing to the biological inferiority of the blacks and the natural superiority of the whites—a central feature of Social Darwinist race theories—is officially regarded as outdated, though latently still assumed; the underprivileged are no longer held to be inferior but solely different. Furthermore, from this perspective, the underprivileged are depicted as desiring to be different. The tendency toward greater rationality in the implementation of domination has been preceded in the ideology by a focus on social and cultural traditions instead of on dubious biological assertions. The inherited inferiority was a matter of mere belief, fictitious and constantly refuted by experience to the contrary; but the reference to cultural pluralism has indeed a real basis, especially since it is promoted by the forced separation of an ethnocentric policy. This policy no longer requires traditional ideological rationalization: its justification is demonstrated by its very existence.

Apartheid reinforces the existing group differences. It need not create them altogether but can build on the traditional syncretic structure and thus prevent non-white unity. Nothing seems further from reality than to assume a conscious homogeneity of non-white interests as opposed to their rulers. In Marx's categories, they constitute most certainly a class "in itself" but they are further away than the European proletariat ever has been from a consciousness with which they form a class

6. Quoted in E. S. Munger, *Afrikaner and African Nationalism* (London: Oxford University Press, 1967), p. 81.

"for itself." So far as subjective intensity is concerned, the conflicts among and between the non-white groups at many levels exceed the frictions between white and non-white. Fostered by this situation, the government was able to propagandize a policy that effectively blocked the politicizing attempts for non-white solidarity. Anthropologist Ellen Hellmann states that tribalism was until recently a waning force in South Africa. "Under the spur of the present Government's policies and in the absence of any alternative, Bantu tribalism is growing in strength in this country. The signs of this abound."[7] It is, however, not the disunity among the subordinate groups that accounts for the present stalemate, but rather the strength of the ruling group.

The ethnocentric nationalism provided by Apartheid is thus distinct from cultural imperialism, particularly of the French version, which aimed at the extinction of any memory and pride of the colonized toward their own history and dignity in favor of complete adoption of colonial culture. In a way, the Apartheid ideology has anticipated what Frantz Fanon describes as the central feature of the "Wretched of the Earth" and what concepts such as "Negritude" and similar ideologies of black nationalism attempt to revive. Theoretically, Apartheid promises the abolition of cultural and finally material discrimination. The defensive Afrikaner nationalism does not glorify its own superiority toward other nations as it was the rule among the aggressive European nations of the nineteenth century. Whether the Afrikaner past with its former progressive nationalism is projected onto the other groups, or whether Apartheid is merely a witting device of *divide et impera*, is hardly significant compared with the fact that obviously a widespread ethnic narcissism in all groups responds to such offers. That for which

7. Ellen Hellmann, in a reply to N. J. Rhoodie, *Sunday Times*, 4 January 1970, p. 13. Of course the "revival of traditional structures" represents more wishful government's dreams than an actual reality in the historical sense. A historical analysis would reveal that many of the "traditional" patterns have a rather short history and are more rooted in the offices of government bureaucrats than in indigenous preconquest culture. Whatever the case, their function as instruments of colonial rule and their imposition upon Africans ("detribalized" through the same conquest) makes them as much part of cultural imperialism as any assimilationist move could be.

minorities in other parts of the world struggle—the right to keep their cultural identity—is granted readily in South Africa. While in other countries the quest for autonomy on the part of minorities has a progressive function in furthering their partial liberation from the majority's domination, the same process under South African conditions means that the existing domination thereby secures its continuity and refuses political autonomy to the majority.

Control Through Self-Government

In this endeavor, the South African whites are, however, confronted with a dilemma that makes the effective use of indirect rule, as successfully practiced by colonial predecessors, difficult if not impossible. Indirect government through the chiefs and headmen presupposes respectful acceptance by their subjects: it was successful because of the unchallenged loyalty of the illiterates in the wisdom of their leaders. However, today the traditional rulers often represent the backward part of the population and often are illiterate themselves, and thus for a growing number of tribal people their legitimacy derives solely from their white mandators, by whom they are paid and controlled.[8] This does not necessarily decrease their actual power. Although the prestige of the collaborating bureaucrats within their group might be questionable, even their most outspoken enemy is forced to yield to the channels which they provide if he expects any chance of obtaining any gratification from the system. The increased bureaucratization and regimentation of life chances of the non-white population has thus strengthened the power of these secondary rulers, despite their waning traditional legitimacy. Whereas under the former "pure" colonial conditions, the white bosses were satisfied if the chiefs kept their followers

8. As a striking impression from talks with Africans in Bantustans, the author remembers the contempt with which many talked about the chiefs and headmen as drunken illiterates. The same, of course, holds true much more for the urban African. According to a survey of a market research institute, the freedom from the control of the chiefs ranks second among the reasons why Soweto dwellers prefer the restricted urban life to the rural situation. (*The Star*, 2 November 1968.) In the meantime, a special institution has been set up in which the sons of chiefs are trained for their future tasks.

"in their place" and provided the imposed services and taxes, they now have to insist that the politicized subjugates are in fact ruled, administered, and controlled.

This task, however, seems to be beyond the capacity of the traditional chiefs under Apartheid conditions. In their public statements, especially in their speeches to their own group members, many avoid identifying themselves too much with the government's race policy. If they intend to be not merely policemen who implement the duties delegated to them by a foreign dictate, then they must demonstrate their independence and usefulness in order to counteract the charge of being collaborators and traitors. This is especially so for the Coloured and Indian representatives who lack traditional legitimacy and are thus faced with an even greater ambivalence. The following speech delivered by the Chairman of the "South African Indian Council" at its constitution is characteristic of the way the Council members reconcile their dependent role with the fact that they hold their position due to their readiness to cooperate and not on the basis of an electoral mandate. In a similar way the African speakers defend their cause by emphasizing that they, for the first time, are allowed political influence:

> Under the Chairmanship of Mr. van der Maree, during the last four years, members enjoyed complete freedom of speech, a privilege that will be maintained in all our future deliberations. In this regard, I wish to recall the words of Mr. Maree, when he said that he did not want stooges, neither did he want members to regard themselves as a rubber stamp for the actions of the government.[9]

While one is easily inclined to dismiss such statements as rhetorical declamation, they, nevertheless, reflect an important aspect of rational oligarchy. System theorists have stressed the negative correlation between the information a government has about a specific situation and its use of force.[10] Under South African circumstances, the government is indeed interested in the

9. Hajee Joosub, speech as reported in the Indian weekly, *The Graphic*, 27 September 1968.
10. David E. Apter, *The Politics of Modernization* (Chicago: University of Chicago Press, 1965), p. 40.

disagreement and not the conditionless agreement of the controlled voice of its dependents. In the absence of other representative channels for complaints and demands, "constructive criticism" in the framework of the prescribed responsibility serves to illuminate early dangerous areas within the system. The recognition of dissatisfaction among the ruled becomes in itself an important instrument of enlightened neocolonial domination.[11] Potential conflicts are no longer merely suppressed, with the risk of their becoming explosive as in former authoritarian regimes, but are disarmed and mastered by controlling dissatisfaction within the framework of the system.

> Mr. Maree invited members to express their disagreement whenever they were so inclined, or to differ with actions and decisions. However, if the Council found it necessary to express any disagreements, he appealed that they do so in a sensible, constructive and reasonable manner as might well be expected of a responsible Council.[12]

On the other hand, the granting of codetermination and political rights, though minimal, does contain the nucleus of future conflicts that inevitably will change the carefully established system in its old form. The dialectic of oppression and necessary concessions to the oppressed leads to an increase in opposition demands which in their turn either sharpen the conflicts or have to be countered by steadily greater concessions, for which, however, shifting limits exist in the system of totalitarian domination. Suppression is either absolute and total or it develops an inner dynamic toward its own abolition. In this sense, the promise of independence for the Bantustans and similar self-governing bodies for the other groups indicates not only strength but also the retreat of formerly undisputed domination.[13]

---

11. So far the most pretentious research undertaking in the history of the social sciences centered precisely around this political goal: to localize scientifically potential revolutions in order to counteract the threat by political and not military means. See I. L. Horowitz, *The Rise and Fall of Project Camelot* (Cambridge: Massachusetts Institute of Technology Press, 1967).
12. Joosub, *The Graphic*, Ibid.
13. Pierre van den Berghe mentions this aspect of Apartheid in his "Racial Segregation."

A closer look at non-white elections, at the program of non-white parties, and at the behavior of their representatives under Apartheid conditions can illustrate this dialectic inherent in the concession of self-administration.

An ill-founded assumption widely held within white government circles is that the so-called pro-Apartheid groups do indeed support the white policy. However, in the first Coloured election in September 1969, all three pro-government parties defended only "the positive aspects of separate development" (expanded educational institutions, for example) and were strongly opposed to petty Apartheid and some of the ways the Group Areas Act is being implemented. The rival Labour Party which won a clear majority of elected seats in the Council rejects any form of Apartheid whatsoever, and is in principle and spirit a multiracial party.

It is possible to classify the political activity of non-whites in South Africa into three main groups, according to program and tactics:

1. Groups that reject the discriminatory aspects of Apartheid, but work legally within the prescribed limits to improve their racially defined situation. In all important questions they collaborate with the central government (Federal Party of the Coloureds, Transkei National Independence Party under Kaiser Mantanzima).

2. Groups that use permissible political activity to combat Apartheid as a principle, and secondly to oppose ethnocentrism within their own group members (Labour Party of the Coloureds, Democratic Party in the Transkei under Knowledge Guzana).

3. Groups that consider any legal political activity in the prescribed Apartheid framework meaningless, and, therefore, recommend passivity and the boycott of elections.

It is impossible to draw definite conclusions about the strength of the three groups simply from election results. The voting system of single constituencies and also the form of participation leave scope for contradicting explanations. For example, between 75 and 80 percent of the Transkeian voters (men and women over 21) are illiterate: at the polling station they communicated their vote verbally to the officials who marked the required "X" for them. In the Coloured elections, the total percentage poll was 48.7 percent, the highest participation in the rural constituencies and the lowest in the urban areas of the Cape, only 16.4 percent in one Cape Town seat.

In the Coloured elections the Labour Party (group 2) won a majority of seats but not the majority of votes. In the second election in the Transkei the Democratic Party (group 2) won 16 of 45 elected seats, a loss of 13 compared with the previous election, and there was no coercion.

However, to ensure that the institutions of separation are not used against government's intention, one-third of the members of the Coloured Representative Council are appointed by the government; for the most part, candidates have been appointed who were in fact defeated in the elections. The appointed chairman of the Executive of the Council Tom Swartz, for example, ran third in his constituency in the election. The blatant action of the government, which did not even attempt to conceal its motives by appointing seemingly "neutral" candidates, was aimed at silencing its right-wing critics. Among the subordinates it dispelled any illusions that the elections could in practice be anything more than a symbolic demonstration.

Nevertheless, there is a discernible trend among the politically conscious non-white elite in South Africa to move away from protest through passivity and boycott, and to use the limited possibilities for practical political action. In the face of total subordination, political behavior becomes redefined as a technique of maximum survival. No longer can victory be expected or even sought. The choice they have to make is between political suicide or accommodation. Realizing this alternative, many opted for pragmatic survival. "One has to be practical in one's approach. Here in South Africa we are faced with a situation that is not of our making. We have learnt from previous experience that total opposition does not help us in any way. So what do we do? I know that we on the Council are often called Government men. This is absolute nonsense. We serve on the Council only because we feel that we might be in a position to obtain opportunities for our people that were denied in the past."[14] If this view is correct in expecting opportunities to improve the fate of the governed, then it must coincide with the rulers' readiness to make concessions.

The interest of the rulers in the smooth functioning of the subordinates' self-administration is based mainly on political and propagandistic considerations. But, in addition, the expansion of Apartheid administration using only white manpower would be economically impractical. One out of every nine white South Africans is already employed in government service (central, provincial, local agencies, and railways). This high ratio of state employment as compared with other Western countries such as Britain or the United States results partly from the increased bureaucratization required for the implementation of Apartheid laws, but above all from the exclusion of non-whites from state administration in the past. Given the white manpower shortage, the "self-policing" of the colonized on the payroll and under the control of the colonizer becomes a desirable if not necessary goal.

The following table illustrates the well-known fact that Public Service employs a higher percentage of white workers than does the private manufacturing industry.[15]

	Whites	Coloureds	Indians	Africans
Public Service	40.2	10.0	2.2	47.6
Provincial Administration	50.1	6.8	1.2	41.9
Private Manufacturing	25.3	16.2	5.9	52.6

If this employment pattern is to change, the middle and upper stratum of non-white administration will have to be staffed by the non-whites themselves. This would mean creating entire civil services including a formal top of the hierarchy for each racial group. After stating that only one in every thirty Bantu is employed in government service, *Current Affairs*, the outspoken daily political commentary of the South African Broadcasting Corporation, elaborates: "This means that the White

14. A. M. Rajab, member of the Executive Committee of the Indian Council, *The Graphic*, 23 January 1970.
15. Muriel Horrell, *South Africa's Workers* (Johannesburg: South African Institute of Race Relations, 1969), p. 119. Figures at the end of 1968. Private manufacturing 1967. Public Service excludes the Railways administration.

population is carrying a grossly disproportionate burden in the management of the country and people as a whole. There is only one effective solution here: it is to enable and encourage more Bantu—and Coloureds and Indians—to participate in the running of their own affairs. Only when the various groups have civil services of their own will the imbalance be corrected—and this is a major objective of the policy of separate development."[16]

"Running their own affairs," however, is an issue where white and non-white interests will inevitably conflict over the extent and meaning of autonomy and participation in power. The limitations presently set on self-control will affect political consciousness among the men in a new ethnic political context. The more clearly the non-white administrators become aware of their pseudo-control, the more their resentment increases. To be sure, there are for the first time channels within the system through which complaints may be launched and limited changes obtained, but these possibilities prove insufficient, if for no other reason than the continued economic dependence. Although criticism has now become legal, this does not necessarily render it less dangerous; for the former clearcut fronts between the system's enemies and its supporters have now been obscured.

Subversion within the scope of permitted political activity could become difficult to control. As long as such activity used the logic and the jargon of the government, it remains relatively safe for its advocates. Informed observers point to some of the chiefs in the Transkei who cleverly use Apartheid to fight the Apartheid inventors with their own arms.[17] Although such chiefs share governmental interests in the maintenance of the traditional tribal structure, the latent potential of conflict between these uneasy allies could develop into a major political factor. Similarly, the pressure emanating from the voters, merely administered on behalf of the real power, increases. Granting the franchise for all Xhosas of the Transkei inevitably raises the question for the voter as to what his vote really means and de-

<hr />

16. *Current Affairs (South African Broadcasting Corporation)*, 22 February 1968.
17. Govan Mbeki, *South Africa: The Peasants' Revolt* (Baltimore: Penguin, 1964), p. 137, interprets the motives of Kaiser Mantanzima this way. Evidence of this trend among rural politicians increases.

cides. Politicized for the first time by fictitious alternatives, they will probably feel more frustrated in the long run than before, by having formal political rights and yet remaining basically rightless subjects.

In the short run, however, the extreme racial structure in South Africa might well support the temporary "satraps"; that there are fellow non-whites with certain minor privileges has a powerful appeal for those who are used to nothing but subjugation. The historical degradation of the South African non-whites is so absolute and uniform that any role of authority feeds the desire to identify and participate, if only symbolically, in the control of their own lives.

Having launched the program of self-government for ethnic minorities, however, its initiators cannot now reverse the process even if it should backfire on them. A return to the former *baasskap* policy is no longer possible. Were the government to withhold the realization of these heightened expectations, greater dissatisfaction and subsequently more direct oppression would be the inevitable consequence. The rulers too are subject to the dialectical forces inherent in the conditions of modified rule. For instance, the government has had to withdraw police measures on several occasions, after protests from Transkei politicians, and to reluctantly concede contrary decisions on the part of the new self-government. The reintroduction of English as the language medium instead of the mother tongue in Transkeian schools is one such example. The more the Transkei population, for whatever reason, applauds the Apartheid cooperation of their tribal leaders, the greater the pressure on the government to discharge the promise of independence. What seems advantageous for propagandistic reasons and of limited significance in view of the continued economic dependence of the territory does, however, include a military risk. In contrast to the geographically isolated former British territories, the maritime Transkei could import armaments by sea. It would seem, therefore, that the white state cannot afford to relinquish its direct or indirect control of the territory, which could in the long run become politically explosive.[18]

18. The final point of Mbeki's study is "The Transkei, showplace of the Bantustan scheme, could well be the first battlefield on which

Stabilization Through New Role Relations

The utopian Apartheid program has resulted in developments often unnoticed outside the country. Compared with the
baasskap era, race relations appear to have assumed the form of
a relatively smoothly functioning, correct business relationship
despite increased institutionalized separation. Non-white cus-
tomers assert they are now served more politely in the shops due
to their growing purchasing power. The civil servant has officially been told to avoid blatant discriminatory treatment, and
direct confrontation in an arrest or a police raid is largely carried out by black constables. It would appear that the African
in Pretoria, at present, has a greater chance of being correctly
treated by the police than the black in Chicago. These superficial changes in race relations do not indicate a greater tolerance of the South African system, but rather the complete absence of alternatives for the ruled. The control of the state
machinery is so absolute, and the certainty of this total dependence so universal, that no individual dares to claim what ought
to be his rights. The state official, therefore, can afford to demonstrate a generous benevolence.

On the other hand, the rulers for the first time make conscious efforts to dampen potentially explosive situations. The
commander of the Johannesburg police declared that policemen treating Africans not as human beings would be regarded
as "saboteurs."[19] Piet Koornhof, the Deputy Minister of Bantu
Administration and Education, emphasized that government
officials who had to deal with Africans were taught early in their
careers that the African was "a human being just like the
Whites" and that he merited his own place in the sun.[20] The
Bantu Affairs Commissioners were proud of the fact that the
African rightly looked on them as "fathers." "We do not believe
in fraternization—but we do believe in honesty and sincerity.
We do not want to create false illusions and we want the Bantu

---

Apartheid will be defeated" (p. 148). This theory of peasant-based
revolt leaves, however, serious questions which will be discussed later.
19. *The Star*, 14 December 1968.
20. Piet Koornhof in an address to the Johannesburg Sakekamer, as
reported in *The Star*, 23 August 1969.

to know exactly where he stands and what our intentions are with him." To a large extent this intimidating bluntness would seem responsible for the overtly smooth race relations. The Afrikaner does not allow any doubts that he would use his powers. This clear role definition allows him to behave according to collective dictates and to avoid, as far as possible, individual deviations. Other emotions which always characterized and "humanized" even the most brutal master-servant relationship are ideally excluded in this definition. Master and servant ought to be reduced completely to their prescribed role. The surprise effect of individual reactions precludes calculation and, therefore, has to be avoided.

The former racialists have realized pragmatically that the future of white South Africa depends on the extent to which it can gain the acquiescence of the African masses. When the army goes into maneuver to exercise guerrilla warfare it is accompanied by ethnologists and other experts to make sure the native population is not offended by white ignorance of local customs, and that they understand their intended part in the armed struggle. An editorial of the *Die Burger* states: "Today we realize better than before that the stirring up of race tensions is preparatory to revolutionary war, which cannot be carried out without the enemy winning friends within our internal life. And to counteract these race tensions is not just a military task in the narrow sense. It calls for effort at all levels under the leadership of our chosen political High Command. It is time for all South Africans to see the connection between the Government's political plans for the non-White people of the country and our military security."[21]

Even though the practice of such insights in daily routine is often still more an exception rather than the rule, and though paternalistic master-servant relationships dominate in the working sphere, an African is no longer only an object of personal white arbitrariness. Awareness among non-whites of at least their formal rights when confronted with individual discrimination has contributed in some measure to the belief in the justice of Apartheid order. Frequently the subordinate prefers this

21. *Die Burger*, 11 December 1967.

openly announced and admitted dictate to the facade of equality presented by many of the English-speaking whites. All empirical surveys revealing the attitudes of Africans toward the openly racialist Afrikaners and the less outspoken English-speaking whites showed greater suspicion and aversion toward the latter.[22] The guiding theme of many responses is that the Afrikaner could be taken seriously, in contrast to the Englishman who was too hypocritical to admit his prejudice. This reaction suggests that the group discrimination by the confessed racialist is experienced as less offensive than the mere rhetorical advocacy of equality. The awareness of belonging to a group of equally oppressed provides collective psychological protection; while in the case of individual discrimination, disappointed expectations are frequently explained as personal failure.

White Resistance Against Race Utopia

A decisive obstacle for the implementation of theoretical Apartheid is that it is accorded only rhetorical rather than factual support among the white electorate. The majority are openly unwilling to support a government that would take such a program seriously. The gap between the Apartheid ideologists in the government or press and the reactions of the majority of white citizens is openly admitted and regretted in many editorials. In a commentary on the Transkei elections, *Die Beeld* writes:

> The Transkei must—and not some day in dreamland but acceptably soon—develop in such a way that it will become a vital Southern African state, capable not only of maintaining its own people but also of attracting its best sons and daughters back from across its borders, where they are liable to become permanently estranged from it. It is doubtful if the South African general public, too, has any conception of what such a task embraces, and it is, therefore, doubtful if the South African public is in a position to view the result in its proper perspective.[23]

22. Pierre van den Berghe, "Race Attitudes in Durban, South Africa," *Journal of Social Psychology* 57:55–72; Kurt Danziger, "Self Interpretations of Group Differences in Values," *Journal of Social Psychology* 47 (1958):317–35; Kurt Danziger, "Value Differences among South African Students," *Journal of Abnormal and Social Psychology* 57 (1958):339–46.
23. *Die Beeld*, 3 November 1968

Here only abstract economic and political sacrifices are demanded, but the real attitude of the white South African becomes evident in matters that affect his immediate comfort. Nearly all white households employ African servants; the early morning coffee or tea served at the bed of the *baass* belongs as much to the sacred colonial relic as the freedom of women from tedious housework and supervision of children. The purists in other spheres have no objection to their children being bathed, dressed, and sometimes tutored in their school work by African servants. Some women, reports a paper with disgust, even ask their servants to curl their hair and permitted African men "to make beds and handle nightwear."[24] When, during the resistance campaigns, the number of Africans being housed in white backyards reached a supposedly dangerous limit, a law was passed that allowed only one servant per household to stay overnight. All further attempts "to keep the cities white" at night encountered fierce rejection by housewives and other affected parties.

> Householders can allow only one servant to sleep in without a permit. But experience shows that the local authorities are not sparing in the issue of permits, for after all, fewer Bantu in White back yards imply a greater demand for accommodation in municipal locations and the White ratepayer is not prepared to supply it.[25]

The following selection from editorials of Afrikaans papers during a single week in November 1968 gives a further insight into the reality of separate development from the perspective of its most active interpreters. It documents at the same time the thinking of leading government circles.

> People who call aloud for a solution of the race question continue to keep a small army of non-Whites in their homes or on their farms. They even shut their eyes to the fact that Bantu stay overnight on their property. It simply does not enter their heads to investigate who is sleeping on their property. Early in the morning, it is not only Lyttleton that looks like a "black antheap." Let every Johannesburger, for example, take the trouble

24. *Sunday Times*, 9 December 1968, quoting *Dagbreek en Landstem*.
25. *Dagbreek en Landstem*, 3 November 1968.

to stroll through the streets of his suburb between five and six in the morning. He will then see how potential thieves, thugs, robbers and so forth are exuded in their dozens from the backyards.[26]

In contrast to such statements it looks like a magic incantation when the same paper writes six days later:

> The Nationalist Afrikaners are like other people, selfish, as Mr. Gerdener says; unthinking, as Professor Rhoodie avers. But one thing is certain about them: they are prepared to make separate development a vital, practical reality in South Africa and when the sacrifices for doing so are required of them, they will be ready for them.[27]

The contrary view seems more realistic despite the fact that it generously overlooks the government's inability to do much against the interests of its electorate:

> It is very clear that there can hardly be any question of voluntary cooperation. The Government will simply have to see that its laws are carried out, for to an increasing extent, Nationalist governments will be required to give an account of the way in which their "white cities" policy is being implemented—even though the big critics will also be the big offenders. The excuse that the public will not cooperate will in course of time become an indictment.[28]

Ominously realistic, another Afrikaans paper close to the government warns:

> Should things one day collapse here in the Republic the Whites will only have themselves to blame. There have been enough warnings to make everyone appreciate the race problem properly, but too many Whites choose not to take notice.[29]

An Afrikaner psychology professor seems to represent the mood of many similar statements of his peers when he ends an article on the topic, "The Afrikaner Intellectual and Apartheid" with the conclusion:

26. *Die Vaderland*, 21 November 1968.
27. Ibid.
28. *Dagbreek en Landstem*, 24 November 1968.
29. *Die Transvaler*, 26 November 1968

The acceptance of ethical equality means that those of us who believe in the positive aspects of Apartheid can be satisfied with nothing less than the implementation of policies aimed at the eventual complete independence and viable nationhood of those peoples with whom we do not wish to integrate and who are at present under our control. If we fail to achieve this, I see a dark future for my people, whose need for apartness may lead them in the event of a catastrophe to a wandering existence such as befell the Jews, who also saw themselves as a chosen people.[30]

This extensive documentation of the self-understanding of Afrikaner intellectuals seems to indicate a schizophrenia that, on the one hand, realistically assesses its own situation and sees the hopelessness of continued rule in its traditional form, but, on the other hand, adheres to fictions that prevent a realistic policy. Karl Mannheim has described such a consciousness as the "utopian mentality" which tends to burst the bonds of the existing order. "A state of mind," Mannheim defines, "is utopian when it is incongruous with the state of reality within which it occurs. This incongruence is always evident in the fact that such a state of mind in experience, in thought, and in practice is oriented towards objects which do not exist in the actual situation."[31] For this state of mind, Apartheid functions as a magic formula with which the status quo is conjured and transformed into a past utopia at the same time. The more the fiction becomes obvious, the more its reality has to be averred. In an editorial on the practicability of Apartheid, the author states: "If there is one thing we must guard against it is the spreading of doubts."[32]

It is useful to illustrate further this gap between the promised equality of the subordinates and the entrenched racial obsessions of their rulers in an entirely "unpolitical" sphere. The much-discussed realm of interracial sport contacts highlights the issues of where and when whites, both officially and unofficially, are prepared to have equal status contact with their fellow countrymen. A closer look at this aspect of racial separation also sheds light on the intra-white differences regarding the feasibil-

30. T. M. D. Kruger, *New Nation* (October 1968).
31. Karl Mannheim, *Ideology and Utopia* (New York: Harcourt, Brace & World, 1936), p. 192.
32. *Dagbreek en Landstem*, 29 December 1968.

ity and extent of contact avoidance and the psychology of racialism in general.

It is indicative of South Africa racialism that even in the somewhat unreal world of sport a white cannot allow himself to be defeated by a non-white, for this would place traditional role-expectations in jeopardy. In an immobile race society more than anywhere else, competitive nonsegregated sport would be political insofar as it provided a symbolic arena for asserting equality of ruler and ruled. The image of the master cannot risk the damage of defeat by the servant, though only symbolically. With the collective narcissism attached to sports victories in a tense, emotionally laden atmosphere, failure in the arena means the first step in abdicating political superiority. This is more or less realized by the majority of South African whites who reject mixed sport in public opinion polls.

QUESTION: Are you for or against white and non-white competitive participation in all forms of sport in South Africa?[33]

	Total	Afrikaans-speaking	English-speaking
For	18.3%	4.3%	37.7%
Against	64.7	84.3	37.6
Neither	8.6	4.7	14.0
Uncertain	5.8	3.7	8.7
No answer	2.6	3.0	2.0
	100.0%	100.0%	100.0%

This attitude is held in spite of the sanctioning of South Africa by International Sport bodies because of her racial discrimination. When it comes to a decision between the desirability of international recognition on the one hand and internal ideological security on the other, the majority clearly prefer the latter. In the Assembly on April 21, 1969, Prime Minister Vorster stated: "If any other country, or the representatives of any sport, want to put it to us as a condition that they will only maintain sports relations with us provided we allow mixed sport here in

33. Quoted in *STATS*, 8 (February 1970):1096. "Gallup Poll type survey of the South African political scene," as commissioned by *Dagbreek*, and carried out by Mark-en Meningsphame without stating the size of the sample. An 84% return of completed questionnaires is mentioned in *STATS*.

South Africa among our own people, then these sports relations will immediately be broken off." The extent to which the collective self-image is, nevertheless, hurt by such sanctions is revealed in the staging of local substitute Olympic Games for whites and non-whites separately. All white games were organized in Bloemfontein in April 1969 imitating the Olympic ritual and even temporarily lifting the ban for non-white spectators who are traditionally debarred from watching white sporting events in arenas under municipal control in this town. (This does not apply elsewhere in South Africa.)

In this respect South African racialism clearly differs from similar attitudes in the United States. Here, white racialism has attributed to blacks the image of physical strength and animal-like superiority. Condescending paternalism grants blacks their "natural" talents and, therefore, is easily able to reconcile black sport victories with the traditional notions of black and white roles. White American nationalism gratefully attributes black Olympic medals to the power of a great nation from which ego-weakness can borrow strength through fanatic identification regardless of skin color.

This attitude is not possible for South African whites. They can hardly expect to identify with their potential enemies, of whom they are afraid. It is doubtful whether Leo Kuper's suggestion holds true that white South Africans would "take pride in the prowess of their non-White countrymen, thus forging another link with non-racialism."[34] Even if the whites were to identify with their subordinate group, given an opportunity, it certainly does not apply the other way around under present conditions. Africans are not proud of the sports victories of their masters, but rather enjoy their defeat. There are many reports of non-whites cheering for non-South African teams that come to the country. A report about a British–white South African rugby games states: "Africans are permitted to sit at one end of the De Beers Stadium at Kimberley. Many thousands more stood in the distance, out of sight of the game, cheering when they understood from the White crowd's silence that their

34. Kuper, *An African Bourgeoisie: Race, Class, and Politics in South Africa* (New Haven: Yale University Press, 1965). p. 363.

bosses were being beaten."[35] If many white clubs were not dependent on non-white spectator fees, all non-whites would probably be debarred from attending white sports performances. Such a decision in Pietermaritzburg has been reversed after a controversy about the financial consequences for the soccer league involved.

White racialism in sport, however, does not exclude making concessions toward single non-white players by including them in a Springbok team. The government was prepared to pay this price for South Africa's admittance to the Olympic Games in 1968. It promised the following five compromises with the hope of being admitted to the 1968 Olympics: (1) a white and non-white team to represent the country, (2) the team would travel together, (3) they would stay together, dress alike, and march under the flag as a group, (4) the whites and non-whites could compete against each other at the Olympics, and (5) a black and white Committee (under a chairman) would select the participants according to merit. Since the training opportunities for non-whites are limited and the entrenched social role differentials can hardly be overcome on the sports ground, it would not have mattered anyway whether South Africa's representation abroad had included some token non-white sportsmen.

The majority of whites are also quite willing to forego obsessions with racial purity by admitting *foreign* non-whites to compete against whites inside the country.

QUESTION: Are you for or against admission of players with Maori blood possibly being included in a team which will be visiting South Africa in the near future?[36]

	All respondents	Afrikaans-speaking	English-speaking
For	59.6%	46.3%	77.9%
Against	19.8	30.8	4.7
Neither	14.1	14.3	13.9
Uncertain	5.2	7.1	2.5
No answer	1.3	1.5	1.0
	100.0%	100.0%	100.0%

35. John Morgan, "The British Lion's Tour of South Africa," *The Listener* 79 (8 August 1968).
36. Quoted in *STATS*, Ibid.

What became a major issue of the ultra-right in the white national elections in April 1970—whether to allow Maori players to have contact with Afrikaner girls, and if so how many, and how much contact—was indeed only an indication of an increasingly less irrational and more pragmatic outlook among urban Afrikaners. What matters to the whites of all shades is not the occasional black *visitor* with whom they have to have contact in the interest of their own survival, but the symbolic defeat by the *local* challenger, even if it takes place outside the South African border.

The prominent Johannesburg white soccer team, Highland Park, arranged to play a match against the (African) Orlando Pirates team in Swaziland at the end of August 1969, but the Minister of the Interior announced that the government would prevent this by refusing or withdrawing passports. Several boxing tournaments have been held in Swaziland including both white and non-white competitors from the Republic; but in August 1969 the Minister of Sport and Recreation announced that, if promoters persisted in arranging mixed tournaments, in contravention of the government's policy, travel documents would be refused.

A similar trend applies in the much published case of Arthur Ashe, the black American tennis player who was to play in the South African Open Championships in April 1970. In spite of pressure put on the South African government by the American State Department and local Sports Associations to grant Ashe a visa, the government flatly refused on the grounds of Ashe's outspoken hostility toward Apartheid. Had it granted the visa, the ultra-right would have had an additional campaign issue and this may have been the main reason for the tactically stupid refusal since nobody would expect an American black to favor Apartheid anyway. However, it is interesting to note that Sports Minister Waring elaborated that Ashe, as a member of the American Davis Cup team, would be admitted if the team were scheduled to play in South Africa. As a team member, Ashe's potential victory would not have been a defeat of whites by blacks, but of South Africa by another national team.

What South Africa's minority is most worried about is the possibility that a Coloured cricket player, a black tennis star, or an Indian golfer might function as a political spark igniting the suppressed hopes of equality. The times when the non-white sections in the stadium cheered the foreign team instead of the local whites gave an indication of the true feelings of the subordinates. South African whites prefer to suffer the humiliation of exclusion from the world's sport scene rather than accommodate an even symbolic abandonment of their color privileges and master role. This reveals the liberating potential of equal sports competition in an unequal social environment and the limitations of symbolic liberation alike.

Political Intentions and Demographic Trends

The belief in the possibility of implementing Apartheid goals with regard to the geographical separation of the racial groups, and the return of Africans into developed "homelands," is refuted above all by simple demographic and economic data. The success of the policy is no longer measured against the initially proclaimed goals, but against the speculation of what would have happened without influx control. Some more realistic politicians of the opposition suggest that the African townships in the urban areas be declared part of the "homelands." Other officials of the white bureaucracy think that urban Africans could best be induced to settle in the Bantustans by increasing their insecurity in towns and restricting their recreational and educational facilities.

Press reports that the Department of Bantu Administration had circulated an order to local authorities that non-white doctors and other professional men should not be granted consulting rooms and offices in urban African townships because such communities were in white areas, were later denied by the Minister M. C. Botha. He declared that established African doctors would be allowed to continue practicing in the townships, but would, however, "be encouraged to offer their services in the homelands." New African doctors who applied for facilities in the townships in the white areas for the first time would, therefore, "not be granted these facilities lightly."[37]

The very existence of Africans in the townships has become increasingly dependent on labor needs and centralized govern-

37. *The Star*, 23 August 1969.

ment decisions. If the government should implement the "Bantu Administration Boards Bill" then the last guarantees and securities of Section 10 of "Bantu (Urban Areas) Consolidation Act, 1945" will have been abolished. This means that even those Africans who were born in the cities or have continuously worked there for ten or fifteen years will have no guaranteed right to live there any longer. In 1969 the Minister for Bantu Administration stated: "As far as I am concerned, the ideal condition would be if we could succeed in due course in having all Bantu in the White areas on a basis of migratory labour only."[38] This legislation alone makes clear that the Apartheid ideal can only be achieved by coercion and force, against the will of the people concerned. Assuming for a moment that the Bantustans were indeed to be developed or the government were to succeed in reducing the number of Africans in the cities, it would never be considered a "success" in the view of the Africans.

Dozens of competent observers have pointed to the demographic and economic factors that make the utopian Apartheid program illusionary. Some of the facts, familiar to the most superficial analyst of the South African political scene, are: the influx of Africans into the urban areas is continuing, despite increased control and rigorous enforcement of existing restrictions. Although according to official statistics the African population of the "homelands" increased from 37.5 percent in 1960 to 46.5 percent in 1970 (from 4.1 million to 7.0 million), nearly 8 million Africans now live in white areas, compared with 6.8 million in 1960. While the proportion of Africans in white areas has fallen from 62.5 percent in 1960 to 53.5 percent in 1970, the black/white ratio has not changed.[39] All these figures, however, are arbitrary, based, for example, on the registration of migrant workers in the "homelands," although most of their time is actually spent living and working in the white cities on which they are so totally dependent. On the basis of the conservative estimate of the Tomlinsson Commission that in the year 2000, 10 million Africans could live in the industrialized reserves, including 2 million migrant workers, the majority of the then

38. Quoted in Ellen Hellmann, "Urban Bantu Legislation," *New Nation* (September 1969):7.
39. *News/Check*, 2 October 1970, p. 10.

living Africans will still have to live outside their prescribed "homelands." C. J. Jooste, director of the government-aligned South African Bureau of Racial Affairs (SABRA), estimates the expected African population in the year 2000 at 30,591,000 of whom 22,838,000 (at present less than 5,000,000) will be in the urban areas.[40] The development of the reserves, however, has hardly progressed during the sixties. Consolidation of the over 200 separate territories remains a catchword in spite of limited state purchase of land for this purpose.

The military budget alone is six times the amount of expenses incurred for the reserves: only about 6 percent of all investments for public projects are flowing into the Bantustans. Within the Transkei, the most progressed Bantustan, only 42,401 Africans were in paid employment in 1969. The Bantu Investment Corporation through which all investments are channeled has, during its existence since 1959, only succeeded in establishing some small enterprises which employ no more than 2,000 people. In the Transkei, where 285 of the 600-odd trading stations have been taken over by the Xhosa Development Corporation, a mere thirty-five have been sold to African owners.[41] The reserves, altogether 13 percent of the South African total territory and approximately 25 percent of the country's fertile soil, are already hopelessly overcrowded, hundred ten persons per square mile compared with thirty-four in the other parts. Although in many respects capable of developing, the rural Bantustans are dependent on additional food imports due to soil erosion, unprofitable farming methods resulting from lack of capital for mechanization, and disproportional livestock. The white agricultural officers and other civil servants work with undoubted dedication to produce a higher maize yield or better bull breeds in the reserves. They blame failure on the resilience of tribal attitudes and the human potential of their black clients,[42] but fail to take into account the political

40. *Die Transvaler*, 30 April 1969.
41. *News/Check*, 5 September 1969, p. 7. By the end of March 1969 the Xhosa Development Corporation reported that it had granted loans of R1,700,000 to more than 300 Africans during the past two years.
42. Many studies emphasize the idealistic and paternalistic dedication of South Africa's domestic colonial officers, devoted to the unsolvable

aspects of their role and African reactions toward it. Official predictions that with the development of the reserves the influx of Africans in the urban areas will be reversed by 1978 are pure illusion in the face of the above data. In the country as a whole, as well as in the urban centers, the percentage of whites decreases in spite of a net gain of approximately 35,000 immigrants annually.[43] However, it can be expected that the incentives to immigrants will be increased substantially.

Increased mechanization and the general trend toward more qualified work in highly industrialized societies could diminish the demand for unskilled African labor. As yet, however, the abundance of cheap labor has prevented increased mechanization, even though the migratory labor system keeps the individual productivity extremely low. Furthermore, any intensive mechanization and automation would presuppose a mass market with high purchasing power, which as yet does not exist in Africa.

The program of developing border industries on white land close to African reserves, with which the government hopes to counteract the influx to the cities, has to be considered as essentially political self-delusion, regardless of the increasing success of this decentralization scheme as such. In its initial stages the border industries program appealed almost entirely to labor-intensive industries such as textiles. Border industries have been established in close proximity to an already existing urban in-

---

task of "preparing the natives for self-government fifty years too late." Douglas Brown states: "Their professionalism does not exclude a certain idealism, of a kind seldom encountered elsewhere in South Africa. In the white man's paradise they have accepted the task of dealing with the serpent. The community has shifted onto their shoulders the most essential responsibility of all. They discharge it faithfully, even humanely, like game wardens who are fond of animals." *Against the World: A Study of White South African Attitudes* (London: Collins, 1966), p. 115.

43. The estimated increase in the African population is 2.2 percent per year, less than that of the Asian community (2.3 percent per year) and of the Coloured community (3 percent per year). The white population growth of 2.1 percent per year includes the net inflow from abroad and reflects a low natural rate of increase. Between 1960 and 1970, the proportion of the whites in the total population decreased from 19.3 to 17.5 percent; the percentage of the African population increased from 68.3 to 70.2 percent.

frastructure, favorable for future development. Since 1969, however, more and more companies operating in capital-intensive industries have announced plans to expand to, if not actually move to, border areas. There are several reasons for this new trend: (1) The government has encouraged this development by compensating investors for the loss of advantages in the urban areas. These compensations include tax concessions and other financial assistance as well as the provision of basic services and technical aid. (2) While new growth points in remote areas were actively encouraged, expansion on the Witwatersrand has been drastically restricted. But so much hinges on the mobilization of African labor resources that industrialists had to follow the political restrictions. (3) New state sponsored developments in rural areas[44] have also created new growth centers closer to African reserves.

However, even an increased border industry development does not solve the issues of white-African contact and competition in urban areas; it even multiplies or at most decentralizes them. Although the individual African worker enjoys greater freedom from restrictions with regard to his family life and the right to own land, he still encounters the disadvantage of lower wages and the low ceiling of job reservation. With regard to wider questions of economic growth, the Stellenbosch sociologist S. P. Cilliers suggests that border industrial development, although "admirably suited to the policies and needs of South Africa" will be insufficient to provide a continued high growth rate for the economy of the country as a whole. "Development in and around the existing industrial complexes will, at the same time, have to be maintained at a steady rate, and although it may be expected that the intake, especially of Bantu labour, into this growth will be slowed down and supplemented by immigration and by the use especially of indigenous Coloured and Asiatic labour, no great exodus of Bantu from these areas can at this stage be foreseen."[45]

44. For example, Richards Bay and Newcastle where the South African Iron and Steel Development Corporation is setting up its third steel producing plant which will employ 4,000 whites and 20,000 non-whites.
45. S. P. Cilliers, "Border Industries," *Optima* (September 1969): 164–73.

Discussion about theoretical Apartheid among the whites has become more or less an abstract matter of definitions and classifications, untouched by the suffering of those concerned, so long as white dominance is not jeopardized. The pompous debates over the proper use of the labor commodity become cynical rationalizations of a reality in which the non-whites, the white electorate, and the audience abroad are fed utopias that, because of only minimal political concessions, prove to be guarantees of continued white rule. It seems possible only post facto to indicate how this device for the perpetuation of white rule has on the contrary fostered its decline.

Implications of Economic Integration

South African society, with its repressive oligarchy and its deep group antagonisms, is above all cemented by a common economy. Although the various racial groups realize differential rewards from this economy, they are, nevertheless, dependent on each other. Leo Kuper has frequently emphasized this mutual interdependence in thus far preventing the breakdown of the racial order, but argues that it does not necessarily exclude a sudden explosion.[1] At present, however, the integrative forces of a rising economic growth rate dominate. Both antagonists are interested in its continuance.

As in no other capitalist society, the producers here are reduced solely to their role in production—elements in an exchange process, cheap raw material in the calculation of costs. A Nationalist member of parliament summarized this situation with the statement: the Bantu "only came here to supply labour. They are only supplying a commodity, the commodity of labour. . . . As soon as the opposition understands this principle that it is labour we are importing and not labourers as individuals, the question of numbers will not worry them either."[2]

This view, however, avoids the omissions of its European predecessors. Forewarned by the events that characterized European industrialization, and alert to the potentially explosive racial situation, the South African hegemony introduced, at an

1. Leo Kuper, *White Settler Societies.*
2. Quoted in Horwitz, *Political Economy*, p. 412.

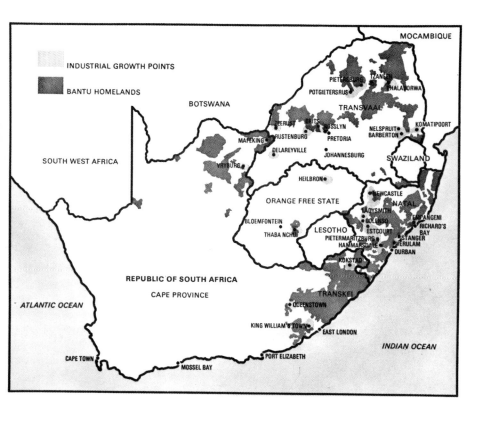

INDUSTRIAL GROWTH POINTS

BANTU HOMELANDS

MOCAMBIQUE

BOTSWANA

SOUTH WEST AFRICA

PIETERSBURG · TZANEEN
POTGIETERSRUS · PHALABORWA

TRANSVAAL

ZEERUST · BRITS · ROSSLYN
MAFEKING · RUSTENBURG · PRETORIA
DELAREYVILLE · JOHANNESBURG

NELSPRUIT · KOMATIPOORT
BARBERTON

SWAZILAND

VRYBURG

HEILBRON

ORANGE FREE STATE

NEWCASTLE
LADYSMITH · NATAL
COLENSO · ESANGENI
ESTCOURT · RICHARD'S BAY
STANGER
VERULAM
DURBAN

BLOEMFONTEIN
THABA NCHU

LESOTHO
PIETERMARITZBURG
HAMMARSDALE

KOKSTAD

REPUBLIC OF SOUTH AFRICA
CAPE PROVINCE

TRANSKEI

QUEENSTOWN

ATLANTIC OCEAN

KING WILLIAM'S TOWN
EAST LONDON

INDIAN OCEAN

CAPE TOWN

MOSSEL BAY

PORT ELIZABETH

early stage, a social policy designed to prevent extreme and dangerous poverty. The typical African industrial worker has been moved from self-built shacks into tolerable housing schemes. Compared with the fifties or the conditions of his tribal fellow brothers elsewhere he now has easier access to medical care, his children can attend better equipped schools, and he himself can enjoy more of the comforts of a westernized consumption culture, according to his financial limitations. All sections of the African population have increasingly become part of the money economy. The number of wage earners (economically active persons) has increased from 5,692,000 in 1960 to 6,744,000 in 1968, and 68 percent of these were Africans. Wages increased at a considerably faster rate than did the cost of living index. In spite of recent wage increases for all groups, the gap between white and black wages has widened, as it has, for example, in mining from 17.6:1 in 1968 to 19.9:1 in 1970. Economists point to the increased food consumption as "perhaps the most striking quantitative illustration of the gain achieved in real living standards —but also of the tremendous income disparities which exist."[3] While urban whites spend only 19 percent on food consumption, the underprivileged majority has still to devote around 40 percent on food.

Even though half of Soweto's 500,000 Africans still live below the poverty line,[4] the relative improvement of their economic situation takes the sting out of their deprivation. After the widespread slums of the fifties were cleared, for strategic reasons

3. Merton Dagut, "The South African Economy through the Sixties," *Optima* (September 1969):119.
4. Sheila Suttner, *Cost of Living in Soweto* (Johannesburg: South African Institute of Race Relations, 1966) and several other studies. Dagut, "South African Economy," mentions that: "A study of Pretoria showed that, after having grown at an average annual rate of 5.1 percent for five years, the median African household income in the city in 1965 was R 52.93 per month. Household heads consumed slightly less than 65 percent of this amount. A study of Port Elizabeth for the same period reported that in that town Africans (the poverty datum line for whom was calculated to be R 63.89) had an average household income of R 59.16 per month. In 1967 some 68 percent of African families in Soweto, Johannesburg, had monthly incomes below the austere minimum requirement of R 53.32, even though, as the City Council had discovered, average wages had risen by approximately 14 percent between 1962 and 1967."

TABLE 1

EMPLOYMENT AND WAGES IN THE
MAJOR SECTORS OF INDUSTRY

	1958		1968	
	Non-white	White	Non-white	White
Mining and Quarrying:				
Employment	499,000	65,000	550,000	61,000
Proportion of total	88.5%	11.5%	90.1%	9.9%
Compound average rate of increase			1.1% p.a.	-0.65% p.a.
Average wages per year	R145.6	R2,079	R372.5	R3,389
Compound average rate of increase			9.8% p.a.	5.0% p.a.
Manufacturing:				
Employment	462,000	163,000	772,000	259,000
Proportion of total	74.0%	26.0%	74.9%	25.1%
Compound average rate of increase			5.2% p.a.	4.7% p.a.
Average wages per year	R371.9	R1,816.4	R627.0	R2,998.6
Compound average rate of increase			5.3% p.a.	5.1% p.a.
Construction:				
Employment	93,000	28,000	212,000	50,000
Proportion of total	76.9%	23.1%	80.9%	19.1%
Compound average rate of increase			8.4% p.a.	5.9% p.a.
Average wages per year	R332.8	R1,485.3	R680.3	R3,158.7
Compound average rate of increase			7.4% p.a.	7.8% p.a.

SOURCE: Merton Dagut, "The South African Economy Through the Sixties," *Optima*, 9, No. 3, September 1969, p. 119.

among others, their dwellers, though reluctantly at first, settled down in the prepared standard homes; the experience of a more hygenic civilization here has soon made the white patterns of consumption a dominating desire. In 1968, 31 percent of the urban Africans had electricity in their homes and 66 percent had water. Over a period of two years (1966–1968) radio ownership among the urban Africans increased from 26 percent to 48 percent.[5] The number of private cars owned by Africans doubled within five years and stood at 7.8 percent of all registered

5. All figures from *STATS* (February 1969)901–6.

TABLE 2

ESTIMATED PER CAPITA INCOME BY RACIAL GROUP

	1962	1967
Whites	R 782	R 1141
Coloureds	120	165
Indians	139	233
Africans	62	82
All races	207	298

SOURCE: W. Langschmidt, Managing Director of Market Research Africa, derived from National Readership Survey 1967/68 as reported in *STATS*, February 1969, p. 906.

The differential wages between the race groups are more evident in cases in which the persons have equal qualifications. Thus for instance, male teachers with Standard 12 start with the following annual salaries: Africans—R 660, Coloureds and Indians—R 1320, whites—R 1920. (*The Star*, October 10, 1969). The provincial government of Natal declined in 1967 to adjust the 50 percent income of the non-white doctors to the level of their white colleagues at the same hospital in Durban. The reason given was that the non-whites in South Africa traditionally have a lower living standard and, therefore, need no pay raise. The average African servant earned R17.40 ($24.50) monthly in 1968 plus housing and food for a working day which often exceeds 12 hours.

private cars in South Africa in 1968 (whites 85.4 percent). Firms that aim at African buying power in the townships advertise increasingly with African models and African themes.

Although the white builder earns more in two hours than his "boy," who does most of the actual work, during the whole day, this inequity has been clouded by gradually rising wages. Due to the continuing boom, the average African worker receives more than he could otherwise realistically expect. Such experiences and hopes encourage him to scratch along. In material terms the South African black proletariat is without doubt far better off than most of the workers in the neighboring industrially underdeveloped African states, for whom migratory work in the African mines is often the only opportunity for cash income.

With regard to educational opportunities, the five non-white universities have on the whole been successful in terms of the Apartheid programs, despite the limitations placed on them as separate institutions under paternalistic Afrikaner guidance.

TABLE 3

COMPARATIVE ENROLLMENT IN SOUTH AFRICAN UNIVERSITIES

	1958				1970			
	White	Coloured	Asian	African	White	Coloured	Asian	African
Orange Free State	1,709				4,222			
Potchefstroom	1,474				4,212			
Pretoria	6,324				12,500			
Stellenbosch	3,694				7,827			
Port Elizabeth*	—				1,144			
Cape Town	4,408	388	127	37	7,528	291	148	2
Natal	2,530	31	373	188	5,706	43	331	163
Witwatersrand	4,756	22	158	73	9,041	29	293	5
Rhodes	1,098				1,803		40	
South Africa**	6,144	204	601	1,179	17,899	584	1,006	2,397
Rand Afrikaans*					1,322			
Fort Hare				320				610
The North								810
Zululand								591
Durban-Westville							1,654	
Western Cape		59	59			936		
	32,137	704	1,318	1,797	73,204	1,883	3,472	4,578

* A new university founded in 1967.
**Bilingual correspondence university.
SOURCE: Horrell, M., *A Survey of Race Relations in South Africa, 1959–1960*, p. 227. Ibid., 1970, p. 243.
The percentage of pupils in secondary schools per group is:
Whites—38.1; Coloureds—11.1; Indians—23.9; Africans—4.2.

Their facilities are frequently better and the teacher-student ratio much lower than in the white universities, now as well as previously when they were "open." This limited advancement in non-white higher education has been allowed partly for propaganda reasons and to meet economic needs.

An equally important consideration, however, was that this expansive provision of separate institutions proved to be the most expedient way for the government to retain control of facilities for non-white education.[6] At the same time it opened new avenues for an ambitious non-white middle class for whom other channels of upward mobility were blocked.

There are contrary opinions in the studies on South Africa regarding how revolutionary consciousness may be influenced by a rising standard of living.[7] Leo Kuper, obviously with the bourgeois revolutions in mind, comments: "The greater the advance, the greater the impatience with arbitrary restraint."[8] Other authors surmise on the contrary, "If a revolution is to have a chance to succeed in South Africa, the economic situation will have to grow worse instead of better."[9] Both opinions are able to point to strong arguments and historical experiences in other circumstances. Nevertheless, both seem insufficient in this generalized form for the South African circumstances since they fail to take specific aspirations into account. Only where concrete expectations are disappointed and where a general politicization emphasizes the gap between claim and reality, can revolutionary action be expected. Dire poverty alone has hardly ever led to political initiatives. In South Africa, an expanding economy has made it possible so far to meet the rising material

6. See Kogila Adam, "Dialectic of Higher Education for the Colonized: The Case of the Non-White Universities," in H. Adam, *South Africa*. She notes in addition that the non-white universities proved a welcomed avenue for the entrance of Afrikaner civil servants into "academia," even though in remote areas. The majority of faculty, teaching at the "tribal colleges" is still white, and almost entirely with Afrikaner background.

7. Edward Feit, "Conflict and Cohesion in South Africa: A Theoretical Analysis of 'Separate Development' and Its Implications," in *Economic Development and Cultural Change* (Chicago) (July 1966): 484–96.

8. Kuper, *African Bourgeoisie*.

9. I. Th. M. Snellen, "Apartheid: Checks and Changes," *International Affairs* (London) (April 1967):303.

expectations and not to heighten the discrepancy between ideology and reality.

While relatively unthreatened by an economically motivated
rebellion, however, most observers suggest that the status quo is
particularly vulnerable to the political aspects of race relations.
Frequent arrests and charges with respect to the pass laws or
other noncriminal offenses, it is argued, create an explosive potential of hate and threaten the dissolution of a social order
based on compliance with laws. However, the restrictions imposed on the mobility and freedom of the urban worker have
as yet had no visible political effects since the final prohibition
of African political organizations in 1961. The necessity for migratory workers to live alone and leave their families behind in
the reserves has had more severe consequences for the rural
families than for the urban dweller who soon finds substitutes.
One effect of such repressions is that the crime rate in the urban
locations has risen dramatically to a level that is possibly the
highest in the world. The frustration generated by this imposed
coercion is increasingly released through aggression against
other ingroup members, since they are the most vulnerable persons. In only one out of every ten cases of known assault and
robbery committed by a non-white is the victim white.

TABLE 4

CONVICTIONS FOR VIOLENCE BY RACIAL GROUPS

Crime	Race of victim	Convicted Persons			
		Whites	Coloureds	Asians	Africans
Murder	White	20	15	3	59
	Non-white	10	151	14	1,381
Rape and	White	57	93	4	29
attempted rape	Non-white	24	362	19	2,290
Culpable	White	21	8	—	15
homicide	Non-white	23	264	3	1,533
Totals 1966/67		155	893	43	5,307
Totals 1965/66		134	748	33	4,516

SOURCE: M. Horrell, *Survey of Race Relations in South Africa*, 1969, p. 50.

Reports describing the hazards of life in the townships are typical in South African papers:

The Russian Gang—the dreaded township mobsters—was active in Naledi Township, Soweto, at the weekend. Armed with iron bars, kieries and sjambocks and chanting Sotho tribal songs, they roamed the streets, molesting and terrorizing residents. And not far from the sports field in Naledi, they pounced upon a man who was walking past them in the street. The man, not known in the vicinity and thus unidentified, was beaten to death. Terrified residents, including children, simply stood in their yards watching as the mobsters killed their victim. They dared not intervene.[10]

The statement by an unknown African in Johannesburg has become famous: "A lot of people die in Soweto and not all of them were sick." Observers reckon there are a thousand and more murder cases annually in Soweto alone. In a letter to a newspaper an African housewife describes "Zola and Emdeni, where the knife is used in the worst form of assault and children seem to be used to seeing corpses lying around as if that was just one of the day's happenings."[11] Such immediate fears of survival affect political consciousness and revolutionary potential. Among the various anxieties of an urban African, the fear of being robbed after being paid on a Friday evening perhaps ranks first. The growing number of criminals in the townships—plus the young *tsotsis* who have developed a specific subculture of violence to compensate for the omissions and frustrations of the system, comprise a considerable reservoir of brutality.[12] While the displacement of hostility away from political goals and the whites functions for the time being to support the status quo, it, nevertheless, represents a continuing menace. The perpetuation of frustration and hostility always leaves open the possibility of its being mobilized and directed

10. *The Star*, 10 January 1970, p. 9.

11. *The Star*, 2 November 1968.

12. This situation exists in spite of rigorous laws and police measures. South Africa imposes the death sentence more frequently than any other country in the world; 47 percent of the world's executions fall to South Africa (*Sunday Times*, 3 November 1968). The daily prison population increased from 38,380 in 1955 to 88,079 in 1969. Ninety-four percent of all prisoners are non-whites (*News/Check*, 11 August 1967). The daily average number in custody, per thousand of the population, would work out to 0.87 for whites, 1.76 for Coloureds, 0.19 for Asians, and 1.13 for Africans. Horrell, *Survey of Race Relations, 1969*, p. 49.

toward political ends. For an African, being political is becoming increasingly synonymous with being anti-white, making a transition from unpolitical criminal behavior to politicization. In fact, one reason for the failure of the ANC campaign was the indifference of these *tsotsi* groups toward an organization that relied on the support of the "decent" Africans. On the other hand, under these circumstances, the government encounters no difficulties in recruiting African policemen. As remarked by Alan Paton, as long as the police force continues to be able to recruit African policemen, a strata that would be the first object of hate from the general population, there can be no hope of revolution.

Similarly motivated, though more masochistically exhibited substitute reactions are the Sunday rituals of the growing Zionist sects. Recent estimates suggest there are 5,000 independent church sects scattered throughout the thirty-four African countries, more than half of them in South Africa. While in 1946 approximately 10 percent of the African population in South Africa belonged to these organizations, their numbers had increased to 21.2 percent by 1960. The original close association between the sectarian ideology and the anticolonial, political resistance movement cannot explain their growth, which continued after the achievement of independence and even survived prosecutions of the new governments, as in the case of the Lumpa-sect in Zambia. Sundkler states in the second edition of his book *Bantu-Prophets* that the politically conscious and activists in South Africa, insofar as they belong to Christian denominations at all, are not among the nativist separatists.[13] An explanation of the sectarian appeal must take into account the cultural discrepancy between the traditional African way of life and the norms preached by the Christian churches as well as the simple continuation of material frustrations for the mass of the population. In South Africa particularly, rational behavior cannot be expected where irrational conditions officially

13. Bengt G. M. Sundkler, *Bantu Prophets in South Africa* (New York: Oxford University Press, 1961), p. 305. Compare also David Barret, *Schism and Renewal in Africa* (London: Oxford University Press, 1968); V. Laternari, *The Religions of the Oppressed: A Study in Modern Messianic Cults* (New York: Knopf, Mentor Books, 1963).

dominate and the frustrations reach a particularly depressing level.

A person who expects to spend his whole life in dependency, with no way out, tends to reduce his needs and aspirations to the prescribed measure. He finally learns and internalizes how to react in due form to the expectations, sanctions, and rewards of his masters since this attitude alone secures his survival under the existing circumstances. In the psychological state of mind of South Africa's subject people the same process seems to occur that integrated the former proletariat into a petty bourgeoisie in countries of earlier industrialization. The dependency of the dependents consists no longer only of coercive circumstances but of internalized coercion. In terms of psychoanalytic theory the response known as "identification with the aggressor," tends to be revealed collectively in South Africa. The subjugated group takes over the explanations of its rulers and identifies with their strength. The oppressed rationalize their suffering with the very ideology of their oppressors, since this is the only way out under conditions of overwhelming, one-sided power. The government and many of its strongest critics agree in this evaluation. Thus Laurence Gandar, one of the most astute opponents of Apartheid, writes: "For so cowed are these sections (non-Whites), so subservient are their leaders, and so preoccupied are the non-Whites generally with the basic requirement of making a living and keeping out of trouble that they now appear as anything but menacing to even the most faint-hearted of White people."[14]

While the majority of politicized and educated Africans are forced into obedience by the awareness of the overwhelming state power, many peasant workers on the white farms lack the consciousness of alternatives although they experience daily the different life of their masters. The ability to project the possibility of such a life for themselves is impaired by their very existence in the system as well as a view of the Apartheid order as an imposed and inevitable system. To experience Apartheid as unjust presupposes the idea of a society of equals. Even though the African living conditions are so much lower, this

14. L. Gandar, "Economic Wind of Change," *Rand Daily Mail* (Johannesburg), 26 August 1967, p. 11.

objective difference does not automatically lead to questioning of the system. This fact is clearly recognized by the government, which is suspicious of "agitators" who incite the "otherwise happy natives." The frequent banning of "undesirable" books, films, and the much debated prohibition of television not only reflects an attempt to preserve an isolationist puritan Afrikaner way of life in the cultural sense, but to maintain the lag in political information on which its domination largely rests.

One of the most powerful tools of social control over the urban African, apart from legal impositions, has proved to be the use of the mass media, some specifically devised to cater for the non-white audience. Radio Bantu, established in the early sixties, now broadcasts in seven African languages for a daily audience totaling more than 3 million. A network of 65 completed FM stations at the beginning of the seventies, 2 short-wave and 12 medium wave AM stations ensures that 95 percent of the South African population can tune in. In 1970 the South African Broadcasting Corporation proudly announced that daily services to remote groups such as the Ovambos (in both Kuanyama and Ndonga), the Hereros and the Nama/Damaras in South West Africa have been added to the program. A number of African broadcasters enjoy popularity, similar to disc jockeys in Western countries. Radio Bantu receives letters at the rate of 5 million a year. It considers hundreds of original plays, legends, or songs for Radio Bantu prizes. A famous Zulu drama was broadcast in the original vernacular by several stations in Europe. The few political programs aim at interesting the urban African in the events of his "homeland," such as the Xhosa feature "Today in the Transkeian Parliament." Sometimes appropriate world news is given prominence, especially when they demonstrate "the might of the White man," as in space flights and moon landings. Not less important appears to be the special school program of Radio Bantu which regularly reaches 13,000 teachers and 600,000 pupils according to the SABC. FM sets for this purpose are supplied by the Department of Bantu Education and booklets are distributed to supplement the programs. The National Readership Survey of 1967/68 showed that over a period of two years radio ownership among the urban Bantu had increased from 26 percent to 48 percent.

The conspicuous display of a transistor is no longer a status symbol in the townships.

Compared with the radio, the press has relatively minor influence among the 70 percent urban Africans who are able to read. Virtually no Afrikaans newspapers are read among this group. Thirteen percent read a daily paper in English. The "Bantu weeklies" and magazines which are mostly white-financed apolitical products, focusing on crime, sport, and other sensationalism, have the highest readership. Table 5 indicates the percentage and number of urban Africans reached by the various media.

TABLE 5
USE OF MEDIA BY URBAN AFRICANS

		Percentage	1,000s
Dailies	English daily	13.0	378
	Afrikaans daily	0.7	20
	African daily	11.7	340
Weeklies	English Sunday	15.2	442
	Afrikaans Sunday	2.1	61
	African Sunday	28.0	814
Magazines	English magazines	12.8	372
	Afrikaans magazines	5.4	157
	African magazines	23.8	692
Radio	Radio Bantu	36.0	1,047
	Springbok	2.5	73
	Laurenco Marques Radio	3.1	90
Cinema		7.9	230

Source: National Readership Survey 1967/68 as quoted in STATS (February 1969): 905. Radio use: "yesterday"; cinema attendance: "last month."

The big, and as yet unanswered, question is what political impact the eventual introduction of television will have on the rigidly stratified and segmented society. While few Africans could, at present, afford the cost of a television set, communal sets will undoubtedly prove popular entertainment for low-paid workers whose bleak environment predisposes them for projection through the television screen. However, they will have to watch a program made for whites. A separate Bantu television seems difficult when the task of creating a home-made or dubbed Afrikaans program is already considered a costly enterprise. Vistas opened by features from other societies

will undoubtedly undermine the isolationist tenets of Apartheid. The programs do not openly need to stimulate black
aspirations in order to create appetites, difficult to satisfy for
the rulers. In this sense, the warning by extremist Albert Hertzog that "television means the end of the White man in Africa"
could prove more correct than the confidence of the censors in
their ability to restrict and confine television-initiated black
expectations. On the other hand, there seems good reason not
to overestimate the short-term political impacts of television in
South Africa. A medium which has in other societies on the
whole integrated masses into the existing status quo, rather than
enlightened them toward changing it, seems unlikely to suddenly lend itself to a revolutionary change, especially when
carefully controlled to achieve the contrary.

From an African perspective, furthermore, the "superiority"
of a white is not a mere myth. Their "advancement" is not only
due to their advantageous environment and better educational
conditions. The self-assurance ensuing from membership in a
group that enjoys structural supremacy in itself reinforces personal capacities and, hence, encourages achievement. The objects of this authority, meanwhile, blame themselves for their
"inferiority," which is in fact caused by the vicious structural
circle of crude domination.

The idea of equal chances obviously encounters serious obstacles when transformed from its historical origin in French
enlightenment to different circumstances. For many of the South
African subject people the idea of equality and dignity for all
human beings still remains abstract. Since the various race
groups obviously differ on the surface and are not equal, and
since the formal dignity now is somewhat respected, there is for
many little reason to complain about the unequal though improved living conditions. They continue living passively with
God-given poverty and the apathetic dependency they have
known from childhood, with any small improvement appearing
as progress. Even if they experience obvious injustice—when,
for instance, the Group Areas Act drives them out of their
family home into a strange suburb—under the peculiarity of
South African circumstances they are forced to rationalize their
predicament instead of fighting the cause. The talk of the

awakened masses of the developing countries is based on what has yet to germinate under the influence of education, a higher horizon of expectations, and above all, a higher standard of living, which are the prerequisites of sophisticated political awareness.

Under present circumstances manifest frictions and latent tensions among the subordinate groups occur more frequently than between them and the ruling race. Factors that are irrelevant when compared with the dominant power structure, such as differential economic advantages, differences in the tribal origins, religions and shades of skin, serve as criteria for distinction among the subordinates, and function as substitutes for the enemy. The assumption that the three non-white groups are equally pressed into a united front by the indiscriminate Apartheid restrictions is open to question. In contrast to this position, van den Berghe writes: "Political consciousness militates against ethnic particularism."[15] Yet in fact there is hardly any realm in which the "success" of racial separation has shown itself more clearly than in the increased significance of a racially defined ethnocentrism. Apart from a few intellectuals in the three non-white groups, Coloureds and Indians are less afraid of whites than of Africans. The latter, on the other hand, find a substitute for their aggressions in the profiteering Indian trader or the Coloured boss workers. In response to their marginal situation, the majority of Coloureds have always favored stronger affinities to the whites. The Indians, on the other hand, tend to isolate themselves from other groups by pointing to their distinctive cultural tradition and their relatively higher living standards.[16] Were the Indians faced with the choice of a non-racial state under African leadership, or the continuation of the present situation, it is probable that a sizable majority would opt for white rule. The same applies for Coloureds, affiliated more strongly with the whites through heritage and cultural tradition than with Africans. Since most Africans in the

15. van den Berghe, *South Africa*, p. 68.
16. For example, among the Indians there is a widespread tendency to compensate for the denial of political equality by stressing ethnocentrism in nonpolitical areas, and by the creation of reversed culture-hierarchies, which grants them the fictitious satisfaction of superiority in spheres in which it remains without consequence.

Cape Province live there without their families, the sexual contacts between both groups have increased, but, at the same time, the sexual resentment of the Coloureds against this Africanization has also grown.

The enforced ethnocentric structure and indoctrination of South African neotraditionalism—separate living areas, schools, and finally ethnic universities—pays off for white rule. The policy designed chiefly with the goal of *divide et impera*, but also partly a simple projection of the Afrikaner's own nationalist ideologies onto other groups, is beginning to bear the expected fruit of increased group prejudices, despite the universality of Apartheid repression.

In summary, it is suggested that the economic boom and resulting upward mobility has mitigated the effects of ethnic disprivilege. This does not mean the material aspirations of the Africans are satisfied, but rather that the average African is not sufficiently dissatisfied to involve himself in risky efforts to break down the system. They tend to estimate the future in terms of their present experiences and, hence, do not expect riches, but only a somewhat better standard of living plus a potential upward social mobility. The feeling of being better off than can reasonably be expected is reinforced by the large influx of immigrant workers from the underdeveloped neighboring countries, for whom low South African wages are still far higher than they could earn in their home countries where there are often no employment opportunities at all. A psychological mechanism Herbert Marcuse applies to advanced industrial societies can also be applied to a certain extent in the racially segmented South Africa: "Under the conditions of a rising standard of living, non-conformity with the system itself appears to be socially useless and the more so when it entails economic and political disadvantages and threatens the smooth operation of the whole." Economic advance thus tends to reduce political tensions to a manageable point. On this basis the government is able increasingly to replace coercion with built-in self-policing, self-regulating, and self-perpetuating psychological and institutional controls, by steadily increasing the numbers of non-whites with a vested interest in the maintenance of the system. Many of those who have been through the fallacy of false accommodation have had to retreat in resignation in the face of stronger antagonists and the failure of their past endeavors.

Resigned adjustment to the inevitable seems at present the dominating tendency among the politically aware non-whites inside the country. This alone is the success of Apartheid in moral terms, but this is all the white rulers needed to achieve in terms of political control.

The Failure of the Internal Resistance

The three major factors outlined in the previous chapters— effective police control, symbolic alternatives in the form of the Apartheid-Utopia, and the implications of economic integration—illustrate the strong obstacles the internal resistance movements faced until their final prohibition in 1961. In a detailed analysis of the African opposition, Edward Feit has stressed that the government was incalculably stronger in physical resources, while the African National Congress had immense symbolic appeal to the Africans. In this conflict the government merely called for passivity and acquiescence, while the ANC asked for active participation in a nonviolent, though violently menaced, campaign to disregard the race laws. In 1952 the country experienced the first height in passive resistance when 8,000 Africans and Indians packed the jails for civil disobedience. However, means that effectively hastened independence in India, where the colonial administration was more dependent on local cooperation, were bound to fail in South Africa, where the rulers as a local group were not only stronger in numbers but also remained unimpressed by the moral principles implicit in passive resistance. Passive resistance promises success only where there is at least a minimal concensus over basic moral principles between rulers and ruled. The *satyagraha* mobilized on the assumption of this common ground, which they aimed to bring dramatically into the open. Passive resistance presupposes a functional public opinion whose influence cannot be ignored by the ruling power. In South Africa the leaders of the various protest campaigns in the fifties overestimated the power of their boycott as a political force as well as their own organizational power to mobilize support in the face of the white reprisals. Despite some impressive local successes, their calls for general strikes on national issues failed, largely because the political reasons for these strikes remained abstract for many Africans. There were several other factors. For instance, breaches of working contracts and strike participation by Africans were usually treated as criminal offenses. Furthermore, they caused the loss of the right to live in urban areas. It is not surprising, therefore, that African unions, though not formally outlawed, have never gotten off the ground. In addition, union organizers have never had access to the compounds of the mines.

Hence, it was the predictable consequences for the individual, rather than an underdeveloped political consciousness, that made solidarity impossible. When Africans have been asked to walk miles daily to boycott increases in bus fares, they followed readily; living near the poverty line, they could not afford, however, to jeopardize their families' entire existence in a long strike.[1]

Feit points to a "lack of realism" on the part of the Congress leadership, "which, given the intelligence of many Congress leaders, is all the more remarkable."[2] In analyzing possible reasons for this incorrect ANC assessment, one factor that played an important role in shaping African resistance can be singled out. The Christian-liberal outlook and the bourgeois values of

---

1. Compared with the poverty and police coercion, the cultural reason which several studies use to explain the relatively peaceful black/white labor relations seems questionable. In contrast to a white worker, it is maintained, the job is never the subjective center of an African's life. His work is not the basis of his status and object for identification. A migratory laborer, for instance, would not include his employer in his system of loyalties since work is only considered as a necessary means to lead a "real life," either in the kraal or during one's free time in the townships. This cultural argumentation seems questionable on the basis that the unskilled work to which an African is legally confined hardly allows any identification and status. Refer on these points to Sheila van der Horst. "The Effects of Industrialization on Race Relations in South Africa," in G. Hunter (ed.), *Industrialization and Race Relations* (London: Oxford University Press, 1965), p. 130; D. H. Reader, *The Black Man's Portion* (London: Oxford University Press, 1961), p. 86; S. Biesheuvel, *Work and Its Effect on Personality Development* (Durban: Social Science Research Conference, 1962).
2. Feit, *African Opposition*, p. 192.

many African leaders, who received their education in missionary schools, hindered an early change of tactics even when their failure became obvious.[3] The records of several hundred speeches collected by police informers and used as evidence in the treason trials[4] reflect in the majority, contrary to the prosecuter's charge, the conviction that the government ought to be impressed by sacrifices and nonviolent solidarity. They hardly challenge the legitimacy of the government, but rather advocate changes through the "proper" channels and within the existing legal framework. Many of the speeches were concerned with answering the rhetoric of the government and, hence, were limited to this rhetoric. In their endeavor not to step outside the bounds of legality, African spokesmen viewed themselves more as a pressure group than as a revolutionary movement. Again and again it was emphasized that the Africans were ready to die without counting the cost. The sacrifices were conceived of as a moral lesson for the whites, based on the bourgeois conviction that history embodies the inevitable unfolding of freedom. From this optimistic view of history stemmed an underestimation of the rulers. The latter gained their ends by a systematic increase of the risks so that ultimately the punishment became greater than the majority of the participants in the unequal struggle were prepared to suffer.

Passive resistance as a political tool to force an unbroken domination to compromise seems highly unrealistic. In a totalitarian state the "shock-therapy of suffering," with the goal of unnerving the oppressors as Theodor Ebert suggests,[5] expects sacrifices from the oppressed out of all proportion to their foreseeable success.

In addition, the opposition is weakened by its open activity under such circumstances. In its efforts to remain legal it can easily be kept under surveillance. In most cases the opposition is reduced to the role of primarily reacting to government measures, at the expense of initiating action itself. Furthermore,

3. I am grateful to Fatima Meer and E. Tuemp for various clarifications of the ANC policy.
4. *Regina versus Adams*, 3 vols. (Pretoria: Government Printer).
5. Theodor Ebert, *Gewaltfreier Aufstand: Alternative zum Bürgerkrieg* (Freiburg, Rombach, 1968), p. 399.

the tactic of remaining legal prevents the more radical potential of the movement from being sufficiently motivated to join. For South Africa, Feit states: "Espousing non-violence—however ethically attractive—plus the appeals to allies from other ethnic groups represented essentially bourgeois values not held by the more radical Africanists in Congress."[6]

The radical Africanists, who referred to themselves as "Pan-africanists," finally left the ANC in 1959, the main issue being whether the ANC was dominated by Indian and white Communists in the background. When the ANC finally went underground and founded the sabotage organization *Umkonto we Sizwe* (Spear of the Nation), the government had already established effective machinery for control of the movement, through emergency laws, the repeated arrests of its leaders, and the infiltration of police informers. With "a record of generosity, of almost foolhardy decency," as Mary Benson comments,[7] the ANC was not prepared in terms of personnel or organization, for existence underground. "Poqo" the militant wing of the PAC, withered away in indiscriminate, uncoordinated acts of terror of doubtful political significance.

Furthermore, a racially structured society such as South Africa discourages the creation of any active unity among the oppressed that could potentially threaten the rulers: the mechanism of racial identification is much more effective with regard to the privileged, who are able to cement their solid front institutionally. Hence, decisive intermediate positions diminish. Apart from the case of an outside war against South Africa, it is difficult to conceive how a revolutionary movement within the country could be successful without the backing of a large number of white persons ready to transform the military and bureaucratic apparatus—before, during, and after the revolution—into a new social infrastructure. As long as the clearly defined ruling race group shows no signs of deterioration or schism, and as long as there is no necessity for interracial coalitions or pragmatic concessions, a downfall of the existing power structure in such a society is hardly conceivable. It seems

6. Feit, *African Opposition*, p. 192.
7. Mary Benson, *South Africa: The Struggle for a Birthright* (London: Penguin, 1966), p. 283.

illusory to assume that this overthrow will occur in the form of a brief explosion in which the oppressed masses suddenly liberate themselves. The days in which 40,000 Africans in spontaneous organization could march on the Parliament in Cape Town are unlikely to return in view of laws that now define the obstruction of traffic as sabotage. Considering only the internal factors, the subjective starting point for a change of the fossilized structures seems, therefore, to lie more in developments and contradictions within the ruling group than in initiatives of the subordinates, even though the dialectic of both factors cannot be overlooked.

In the meantime, however, the faction fights from the time of the ANC–PAC rivalry continue to divide active Apartheid opponents abroad. The PAC especially has gone through repeated struggles for leadership and expulsions of former members. Both organizations, however, emphasize their nonracial stand and have members from all ethnic groups.[8]

The accuracy of their statements regarding the extent to which both organizations maintain a widespread underground network cannot be checked. According to all available evidence, this seems, at present, to consist, except for occasional individual actions, of inactive sympathizers rather than of systematic resistance. Revolutionary rhetoric frequently misinterprets the symbolic and inconsequent actions of less than a dozen brave militants as the determination of the masses to seize power at any moment.[9]

In light of the abstract revolutionary rhetoric so widespread among self-styled revolutionaries outside the real struggle, Leo Kuper's question seems well justified: "What grounds are there for declaring that they prefer death to oppression, the finality of annihilation to the indeterminacy of existence?"[10] All evidence indicates that, even at the height of African militancy in the early sixties, *Umkonto we Sizwe*, whose members were

8. Concerning the alleged racialism of the PAC, see the sharp exchange between Matthew Nkoana and Pierre van den Berghe in *The New African* 53 (November 1969):41–2 and 44–5.
9. *Sechaba* 4 (March 1970), p. 3.
10. Leo Kuper, "Nonviolence Revisited," in Robert I. Rotberg and Ali A. Mazrui, *Protest and Power in Black Africa* (New York: Oxford University Press, 1970), p. 797.

Madelakufe (those who despise death), never did get off the ground as envisaged by the leadership, mainly because of the fear of white reprisal. Operation *Mayebuye* ("Come Back"), which aimed at frightening whites into making concessions, instead resulted in a strengthening of the repressive machinery and a general discouragement of African militancy closer to general resignative despair than determination to actively resist white domination.[11] In spite of the structural violence embodied in South African society, individual violent reactions against this situation have been remarkedly limited.

On the other hand, there is still a widespread tradition of equally apolitical moral rigorism which functions as a substitute for the frustrating art of achieving only the possible under the given circumstances. As it has frequently been pointed out, mere rage transfers a political problem with moral aspects into a moral problem with political aspects. Consequently, politics is not viewed as a means for the social implementation of the moral, but as its counterpart and source of immorality.

Without the backing of a social force which would transfer protest into political action, it tends to become an end in itself, not primarily interested in its success. In an editorial on the occasion of Gandhi's birth centenary, the editorial writer of a South African liberal journal states: "The important thing is not whether we succeed, though that would be highly acceptable, and should never be thought to be impossible. The important thing is that life and truth and light should persist in us."[12] In a similar way, the leading spokesman of South African liberalism Alan Paton represents a vast body of articulate opinion when he asks half heroically, half resignatively: "There are those who ask, what good has it done? It has done a lot of good. It enables us to say, South Africa is a land of fear, but it is a land of courage also. Yet nevertheless, whatever evil, whatever good, has come of this, we are here to make our protest against this act of tyranny and inhumanity."[13]

11. For an informative description of the difficulties which Umkonto faced, see: Edward Feit, "Urban Revolt in South Africa: A Case Study," *The Journal of Modern African Studies* 8 (1970):pp. 55–72.
12. *Reality: A Journal of Liberal Opinion* 1 (November 1969):3.
13. *Reality* 1 (September 1969):12.

The inhumanity, of course, is unlikely to be changed by the roused conscience of its few brave or guilt-ridden opponents. However important the individual moral commitment may be as a prerequisite for political enlightenment, it remains apolitical as long as it is cut off from social forces which have the power to implement enlightened policy.[14]

If the latent potential for an alternative system is to be mobilized, then more is demanded than outworn clichés and stale oratory, which the critics of white South Africa have so far profusely displayed. Compared with the ineffective threats of sanctions or resolutions against discrimination, the progressive alternative to Apartheid remains surprisingly vague. Even the much quoted "Freedom Charter" constitutes a declamation rather than a concrete political program with an indication of how to implement it. What doubtlessly derives its final form from a changing practice and what cannot be anticipated in detail beforehand, however, comprises in itself a potential for change, the more concretely it is anticipated and compared with the existing situation.

It is characteristic of the failure of the nonracial Apartheid opposition that even the most astute analysts of white oppression are pessimistic about the outcome of an eventual change. Many non-Africans (including Indians and Coloureds) fear a reversal of the racial order and are ambivalent about the risk of supplanting a white dictatorship with a black one. In the event of a revolutionary change, Leo Kuper expects "racial

14. On the occasion of a controversy about Russia's occupation of Czechoslovakia, Hans J. Morgenthau reiterated the futility of moral indignation from a political perspective: "Political analysis of a very elementary kind tells me that the weak are always at the mercy of the strong. The strong may have no 'right', whatever that may mean, to abuse the weak, but they will do it anyhow when they deem it in their interest to do so, and it will avail the weak nothing if they and benevolent bystanders express their moral indignation. The weak will be saved from abuse by the strong only by becoming strong themselves or by being protected by one who is strong. That is what all history teaches us and what Machiavelli and Marx have formulated in philosophic terms. It was Marx in particular who demonstrated the futility of moral indignation in view of the capitalist exploitation of the proletariat and the need for the proletariat to develop power sufficient to break its chains." (*The New York Review of Books*) 26 March 1970, p. 46.

radicalism rather than economic radicalism,"[15] especially in light of the fact that common race but not common class would be the denominator for joint action of the African proletariat and the African bourgeoisie. Pierre van den Berghe has probably most clearly expressed this growing and now widespread pessimism about an initial African government: "The end of White supremacy must come in South Africa, and it will come through revolution and violence. But the end of White supremacy will not mean the end of racism. I have little doubt that the first African government of South Africa will be better than the present government. It could scarcely be any worse. Unfortunately, I am not convinced that it will be enough for an improvement to want to fight for it."[16]

But only when the real and imagined risks of the alternative society are gradually demolished in the perception of non-Africans in the country can their greater susceptibility for and nonresistance to change be expected. This does not place a naïve hope in the change of heart by South African whites, but stresses that their fear of revenge is a major political factor which blocks African advancement. Some analysis of the efforts to overthrow the Apartheid regime from outside has, therefore, to supplement the picture of the internal power relations.

15. Leo Kuper, "Stratification in Plural Societies: Focus on White Settler Societies in Africa," in Leonard Plotnicov and Arthur Tuden (eds.), *Essays in Comparative Social Stratification* (Pittsburgh: University of Pittsburgh Press, 1970), p. 92.
16. Pierre L. van den Berghe, "A Reply to Matthew Nkoana," *The New African*, 53 (November 1969):42.

5

Chances of Change
from Outside

Guerrilla Warfare and Sanctions

STRUCTURAL CHANGE IN SOUTH AFRICA, IT SEEMS, CAN
only be brought about through outside intervention or interference. The historian Keppel-Jones writes: "Whatever changes,
it will not be the forces within South Africa."[1] The studies on
South Africa, predicting changes from outside, seem, however, to have mostly been proved incorrect. Most authors seem
to accept implicitly, and at times state explicitly, "that one can
safely predict that *external pressure* will steadily increase and
eventually help in bringing about radical change in South
Africa."[2] This prediction, made in 1965 by one of the most
cogent analysts, has not materialized. As an explanation one
hears that "in Africa history catches up with prophecy at a dis-
concerting speed."[3] The reasons for such frequent errors would
seem to lie in a sociological method that, due to the partition of
science, disregards the approach of classical political economy
and conceives itself as pure sociology or political science. It
seems worthwhile to investigate this point a bit further in relation to South Africa since illusive hopes instead of realistic

1. A. Keppel-Jones in *The Canadian Journal of African Studies* 2
(Spring 1968):108.
2. Pierre L. van den Berghe, *South Africa: A Study in Conflict* (Middletown: Wesleyan University Press, 1965), p. 247.
3. Keppel-Jones, *The Canadian Journal of African Studies* 2 (Spring
1968):108.

analyzes are not a surprising consequence for an approach that relies mainly on verbal statements without distinguishing the underlying power structures from the ideological battles. Without a notion of the interdependence of the mighty interests in the South African economy, an isolated study of the colonial revolution is misleading.

Some of the shortcomings of such studies can be demonstrated by a consideration of Pierre van den Berghe's *South Africa: A Study in Conflict*, the most thorough overall study of South Africa published in the sixties and an analysis relying less than others on a single social science. Van den Berghe bases a single chapter on "External Pressures" on no fewer than eight fallacious predictions and assumptions that cannot all be dismissed as historical accidents. A review of these errors can illustrate at the same time how much the African situation has changed since 1965.

(1) "Basutoland and Bechuanaland will most probably adopt a hostile policy towards White South Africa" (248). After the independence of the British protectorates "the collapse of White supremacy will be imminent" (262). Due to their economic dependence, both countries, however, have proved themselves as obedient satellites of South Africa.

(2) On the issue of South West Africa before the International Court of Justice in The Hague "the final judgment is unlikely to be favourable to South Africa" (252). Though hardly predictable, the Court failed to rule against South Africa. The controversy about South West Africa, which was supposed to be the legal lever for a more farreaching challenge, exhausted itself in mere rhetoric in the United Nations.

(3) "African States are quickly intensifying their manoeuvres to bring about South Africa's expulsion from the world body, and these pressures are likely to be successful in the near future" (251). On the contrary, some African states now consider the UN membership of their main enemy to be in their interest and South Africa herself has considered withdrawal.

(4) "The most obvious impact of world condemnation on South Africa has been to force the latter to retreat into increasing diplomatic and military isolation" (225). "All African States are unanimous . . . in their readiness to combat it (Apartheid)

by all available means" (253). Instead, by 1970 South Africa had formal diplomatic relations with four independent African states, and trade relations with several others. It is likely that this trend will continue with the increasing gap between the industrialized South and the underdeveloped North. Even though these countries, like Malawi, do not approve of Apartheid, under economic pressure they settle for peaceful co-existence with the colonial South.

(5) "Afro-Asian solidarity on the South African issue, by neutralizing the threat of Soviet intervention, thus deprives the South African government of its last trump card *vis-à-vis* the West, namely that it is anti-Communist and strategically important in the Cold War" (258). The Vietnam War and the closure of the Suez Canal have instead increased the strategic significance of South Africa for the West. The protection of the Cape route and the Soviet threat in the Indian Ocean have become South Africa's most inflated argument for Western supply of arms.

(6) "South Africa cannot count on any foreign aid against internal or external hostility" (255). Although several countries adhere to the arms boycott, the country receives all necessary arms from France and, since 1971, from Britain.

(7) South Africa "will be highly vulnerable to foreign based terrorist organizations" (255). As it will be analyzed in more detail later, South Africa is far superior from a military point of view. She has already sent regular troops for the defense of Rhodesia. Furthermore, within the southern hemisphere of the continent, South Africa seems increasingly to play a role similar to the United States in Latin America. It is most likely that South Africa might intervene directly should the conservative governments of Lesotho or Malawi be jeopardized internally. Help for the defense of the Portuguese colonies has already been given.

(8) The "alliance between racialist South Africa and the supposedly 'nonracial' Portugal involves ideological strains and international embarrassment" for Portugal (255). The days of her presence in Africa "are definitely counted" (259). In actual fact both governments cooperate increasingly, particularly in military matters, and Portugal openly welcomes South Africa's

assistance in joint projects such as Cabora Bassa and its wider implications.

A discussion of South Africa's external relations has to begin with a comparative analysis of the military situation inside as well as outside the country. Against the optimistic prognosis of guerrilla theorists, it must first be pointed out that the anticipated general triumph of the partisans as "the result of inevitable historical, economic and political circumstances"[4] adheres not only to a false determinism, but is in itself ahistorical since it does not take the different circumstances into account. It still remains to be proven whether Guevera's Cuban success would be possible along the same lines in countries such as Bolivia or Venezuela, which are in fact much more important for the United States.[5]

The doubt about a generalized theory of revolution for the Third World applies not only in Latin America, but much more in southern Africa. Geographical, historical, military, and sociological reasons can be cited for this argument.

In all revolutions so far, the strength, equipment, training, and above all the loyalty of the government forces has still proved to be decisive. To be sure, primitively armed guerrilla fighters can in fact maintain their stand against the most sophisticated army if the latter has to limit its destructive power. Against the will of this armed technocracy, however, even in Vietnam, the guerrillas cannot hold a town. Hence, the reliability and the use of this army decides in the last analysis the form of the government.

This applies all the more since most threatened governments have reacted to the guerrilla tactics by adopting these very methods for their own strategy. In 1961 South African police and army officers visited Algeria to become acquainted with the

---

4. E. Guevara, *Der Partisanenkrieg - eine Methode* (Köln: 1966), p. 30.
5. The particular characteristics of Cuba (monoculture, island, extreme dictatorship of Batista, and above all, commitment of the USSR) make a successful repetition of the Cuban example along the same pattern highly doubtful. Shortly afterwards, the United States did not hesitate, in spite of propagandistic disadvantages, to send troops to the small Santo Domingo. Since Cuba most governments have greatly strengthened their counter-revolutionary forces.

French methods of combating partisans. Since the widespread unrest of the early sixties, white rule is efficiently prepared for internal conflicts. The design and location of the African townships has been planned on the basis of strategic considerations. Within a short time such a location could be cordoned off, and in its open streets any resistance could be easily smashed. In spite of numerical superiority of the Africans, an extended race war is not conceivable in South Africa. Franz Neumann emphasized that today any halfway totalitarian state in full control of the common means of power can cope without difficulties with its internal opposition.[6] If the irrational fascist domination in Europe could achieve this, it applies all the more to a flexible oligarchy that calculates its chances of survival pragmatically and uses its means accordingly.

Since in South Africa the monopoly of arms is exclusively in the hands of the whites it can never be expected that even a small part of the white army or police would join a cause the goal of which would be the abolition of its own privileges.[7] In South Africa, what the resistance movement lacks is the decisive opportunity to prepare an upheaval within the State bureaucracy. What was an important incentive for the conservative opposition of 20 July, 1944, in Germany—the realistic hope of being able to overthrow the National Socialist system from within—does not exist for the non-white opposition in South Africa. It can only operate from outside and cannot rely on the support of secret conspirators from within. However, as Neumann states: "In the modern period of conscious precedence of politics, revolution can be successful only within the ruling class and only with the help of the political machinery itself."[8]

Certainly, in comparison with Leninist theory which is pred-

6. Franz Neumann, "Notes on the Theory of Dictatorship," in *The Democratic and the Authoritarian State* (Glencoe: The Free Press, 1957), p. 267.
7. As amply proved by the example of the Rhodesian and Portuguese colonial army, whose members consist of more than 50 percent Africans, the arming of trained and led native force can even strengthen white rule. Given the history of South Africa, such a step seems highly unlikely there.
8. Neumann, "Notes on the Theory of Dictatorship," p. 267.

icated upon the *seizure* and destruction of the state apparatus by agents from without, it would seem a rather pessimistic theory of revolution that is predicated on support from within the state apparatus. Many do not want to have to sit and wait for it. Nevertheless, it could be argued that both the Cuban and Russian revolutions were initiated by forces that were internal to the state apparatus, although they responded to external pressures. However, there are limitations to generalizations drawn from historically and structurally vastly different situations. Unique constellations call for fresh analysis and frequently turn out to be very different from those based on dogmatic perspectives. A structural change, not only a transfer of power, in a developed industrial economy, if at all possible, will certainly be qualitatively different from a political change in a relatively underdeveloped society, with no necessity for conflicting groups to collaborate in a sophisticated technological structure.

In the case of larger military conflict it can be expected that the whites of South Africa will fight with the same determination as the Israelis demonstrate against the Arabs. In the ongoing small-scale guerrilla war at the northern borders, the South African army has, at present, several advantages apart from better technology. Crossing the Zambezi, the trained guerrilla is, at present, already endangered in his contact with the local population. Dependent on powerful chiefs, who are in turn paid and protected by the government, the backward tribesmen threaten the "freedom-fighters" as much as the army and police, frequently through fear of informers from within their own ranks.[9] The South African Army, specially trained and

9. It was reported that African tribesmen in Rhodesia who helped to capture guerrillas were also given cash rewards. About the somewhat different situation in South West Africa, in speeches made during October 1968, the Deputy Minister of Police said that the guerrillas were using new tactics. In the past, men had crossed the border heavily armed, using their weapons to terrorize the local inhabitants. Now they were coming unarmed, avoiding clashes with the police, and attempting to influence chiefs and others to cooperate with them. A fact that aggravated the situation, the Minister continued, was that most of the Africans in the area were poor, illiterate, and not at all well disposed toward the whites. The Caprivi African National Union, which had a strong following, was anti-white in sentiment. It was stated by the Commissioner of Police that the police had a network

equipped for guerrilla warfare, and coordinated with Rhodesia and Portugal, is, at present, superior in power to all other African armies south of the Sahara together.

In spite of the arms boycott, South Africa is equipped with the most modern armory. Its own airplane production industry is being built. The production of an atomic bomb from her own resources and partly imported know-how seems not impossible. In the deserts of South West Africa or in the underground mines ample test possibilities exist. It can be assumed that the preparation for atomic and chemical warfare has progressed more than is usually known. Defense Minister Botha mentioned repeatedly the existence of a "secret weapon." In Fall 1968, South Africa launched her first guided missile. The Cactus surface-to-air missile, a highly sophisticated weapon against low-flying aircraft, was sold to Lebanon in 1970.[10] Total defense expenses have risen steadily and rapidly from R 40,000,000 in 1959 to seven times that amount in the official budget for 1969/70.[11] According to the Defense Minister this expenditure would represent 2.5 percent of the total national product.[12] The strength of South Africa's military force under training at any one time is given at 13,200 men in the regular and 26,500 in the citizen force. If men who have completed their citizen force training are included, South Africa's total armed forces when fully mobilized would total 85,500. There are an additional 58,000 commandos, described as part-time rural militia.[13]

Five special "anti-terrorist" training camps have been strategically established for training in camouflage and disguise, the establishment of bases, tracking, field shooting, convoy, and ambush drill. The Defense Minister told Parliament that the men were kept informed of countermeasures against the latest terrorist tactics throughout the world. The Air Force had been reorganized for greater mobility and is being integrated with the

---

of trained informers scattered in the strategic areas; it was unlikely that many men had slipped through the security screen. Muriel Horrell. *A Survey of Race Relations, 1968* (Johannesburg: South African Institute of Race Relations, 1968), p. 64.
10. *News/Check*, 23 January 1970, p. 8.
11. Muriel Horrell, *A Survey of Race Relations, 1969*, p. 31.
12. *Hansard* 13, col. 5289, 5 May 1969.
13. Horrell, *Survey of Race Relations, 1969*, p. 31.

antiguerrilla combat forces. An underground air defense radar station has been constructed at Devon in the eastern Transvaal as the nerve center of the northern area's early warning system. Information is fed into computers from radar heads above ground and from various remote satellite stations. Three thousand miles of South Africa's northern borders are reported being patrolled night and day by 800 white and 300 non-white policemen at any one time. An underground radio communications center is being built at Westlake near Cape Town. Its computer produces on demand a map of the shipping in any selected portion of the ocean.

In addition to the technological strengths of the whites, geographical conditions in the Transvaal with vast open areas offer hardly any cover for guerrillas; the neighboring black satellites are no basis for retreat. Any warfare along the Vietnamese, Algerian, or Latin American lines, which always presupposes the opportunity for retreat, is difficult to conceive of in South Africa.

South Africa's military situation will depend in the future to a large part on how successful the liberation movements in Rhodesia, Mozambique, and Angola will be. More than a dozen offices of guerrilla organizations existed in Dar es Salaam and Lusaka in 1969. Neither the Organization for African Unity (OAU) nor the pressure of the host countries' governments succeeded in stopping the various rivalries and infights between the groups. The OAU resolved in September 1967 to allocate more than half of its annual budget to the support of freedom-fighters' movements in southern Africa. In mid-1968, it decided to withdraw assistance to three organizations it considered ineffectual (PAC, SWANU, UPA); 1971 ZAPU followed suit.

Apart from ANC and PAC, there exist SWAPO (South West African People's Organization) and SWANU (South West African National Union) for South West Africa. Members of ZAPU (Zimbabwe African People's Union) and the rivalling ZANU (Zimbabwe African National Union) were together with ANC members for the first time active in northern Rhodesia in 1967. In turn, South Africa officially sent police units to support the Rhodesian forces. Three organizations operate in different parts of Angola: GRAE (Angolan Exiled Revolutionary Government) under Holden Roberto, which does not appear to have been active in recent years; UNITA (National Union for the Complete Independence of Angola), of which Joseph Savimbi is the leader; and finally MPLA (People's Movement for the Liberation of Angola), led by Agostino Neto. MPLA is the most effective organization. It controls large semiliberated areas and has mounted continuous offensives in South East Angola.[14]

The hitherto most successful African liberation organization is PAIGC (African Party for Independence for Guinea and Cabo Verde) led by Amilcar Cabral and holding much of Portuguese Guinea.[15] Like Cabral, FREMILO tries to establish an effective administration and school system in the two northern provinces of Mozambique.[16] In contrast to South Africa, the success of the guerrillas in Portuguese controlled territo-

---

14. For more comprehensive information about the Angolan situation prior to 1962, see John A. Marcum, *The Angolan Revolution, Vol. 1: The Anatomy of an Explosion, 1950–1962* (Cambridge: Massachusetts Institute of Technology Press, 1968). Marcum stresses that in Angola, one of the greatest obstacles for the revolutionary movements has been the failure to coordinate the efforts between urban-oriented intelligentsia and rural leaders represented by MPLA and GRAE respectively. In the meantime, however, MPLA has considerably extended its grass-roots support among peasants while GRAE has become inactive and discredited by Western support. For later developments, especially with respect to MPLA, see D. L. Barnett, "Report from Hanoi II," *Ramparts* (April 1969):49–54; and D. L. Barnett, *MPLA and Documents from the Guerrilla War*, forthcoming. For a view sympathetic to Portugal, see A. J. Venter, *The Terror Fighters* (Cape Town: Purnell, 1969).

15. For a commited account of Cabral's movement, see Basil Davidson, *The Liberation of Guinea* (Baltimore: Penguin African Library, 1969).

16. On FRELIMO, see Eduardo Mondlane, *The Struggle for Mozambique* (Penguin African Library, 1969). Also, Glen Hughes, "FRELIMO and the Mozambique War of Liberation," *Monthly Review* 20 (December 1968):7–18. The situation in Rhodesia is outlined optimistically by Davis M'gaba, "The Beginning of Guerrilla Warfare," *Monthly Review* 20 (March 1969):39–47. For an actual report of the guerrilla activity in 1968, see *The Times* (London) (11 and 12 March 1968). This survey of a reporting team has been published in book form under the title *The Black Man in Search of Power* (London: Nelson, 1968). For a critical review, see John Woolgar, *Venture* September 1968, pp. 4–9. An interesting analysis of the ideological and tactical differences between the Liberation Movements is given in Matthew Nkoana, "Southern Africa: International Problems of the New Phase," *The New African* 52:12–17.

ries, due to brutal Portuguese reprisals, is frequently actively supported by the population. The main strategic goal of FRELIMO and the smaller organization, COREMO (Mozambique Revolutionary Committee) is the Cabora Bassa project. This dam, after Aswan the biggest in Africa, is not only aimed at the supply of electricity to the Rand, but is also expected to develop a new white settlement area of important strategic significance in northern Mozambique. A decisive question for future development is whether, with the military aid of South Africa, a white border can be stabilized at the Zambezi and in Angola, so that South Africa is not directly threatened. While the white colonial powers increase their preparations to this end, thus rendering Portugal and South Africa all the more dependent on each other, the guerrilla organizations receive increasing logistic support from Eastern powers, including China. A "Liberation Committee" in Dar es Salaam set up by the OAU, coordinates and administers such aid, which since 1970 even comes from such reputed bodies as the World Council of Churches.

It can hardly be predicted how long Portugal, with the backing of South Africa, will be able to support the military commitment on all her fronts. Despite the burden of the disproportionately high military budget on the Portuguese economy, a voluntary retreat seems unlikely at present, especially since the rewards of the colonial area compensate for the underdevelopment of the homeland. On the other hand, the enthusiasm to continue fighting colonial wars is considerably lower in Portugal itself than in the colonies. Judging from the French involvement in Algeria and the American war in Vietnam, events in the metropolitan country are more decisive for the fate of the colonies than developments in the colonies themselves. With increased strain on the home economy in the post-Salazar era, the perpetuation of Portugal's policy will depend on the continued financial and military backing of her NATO allies. The nature of this alliance, as well as the strength of the opposition (both in the military and on the left in Lisbon), will in all likelihood determine whether the current stalemate in the colonies will drag on or be resolved through a withdrawal of Portugal from Africa. In such a case, however, the behavior of the Portuguese settlers has to be taken into account. Having vested interests in the colonies and, therefore, being much more committed than the Portuguese leaders in the home country, their declaration of independence along the lines of the Rhodesian example is possible. Since Portugal's declared nonracial policy encounters much less aversion in the Western world than Apartheid, such a UDI (Unilateral Declaration of Independence), linked with formal African participation, could well become a serious alternative to a neocolonial solution.

There is also always the possibility that South Africa would step for security reasons into the vacuum created by Portuguese withdrawal. Such an expansion of South African colonialism, however, would have to overcome an ideological and a military obstacle. There is a certain resentment among the average Afrikaner to associate fully with Portuguese who do not belong to the proper racial and religious group. The close collaboration between the higher echelons of the Portuguese and South African political and military leadership for strategic reasons has so far no emotional equivalent among the rank and file Afrikaner. Attempts to establish friendship committees in South Africa, which would give moral support to the fighting Portuguese soldiers, were met on the whole with far less response than similar campaigns earlier for Rhodesia. The ambivalence of the South African attitude is most clearly reflected in the discriminatory immigration policy. When attacked for the heavy inflow of Catholic immigrants from southern Europe, Piet Koornhof, the minister in charge, explained: "As a result of economic pressure and circumstances that prevailed in a certain period, it was necessary for us to bring people into the country on occasion who perhaps did not always quite meet the requirements." He reiterated the government's policy not to admit people who could not be "easily assimilated with our White nation."[17] It is not only the ultra-right that views Portuguese immigrants in Hertzog's description as "White people with Black hearts." The editor of *Dagbreek*, after a visit to Luanda, concludes: "The average South African would only have to glance at most Portuguese immigrants to say with a shake of

17. *Sunday Times,* 29 July 1969.

his head, 'No, they are not our people. How on earth did they get into the country?' "[18] These sentiments would seem to indicate the limited enthusiasm of the average Afrikaner soldier for fighting side by side with them against "terrorists" in the interest of people whom he despises. It would also make at present improbable any resettlement of large numbers of Portuguese from Angola and Mozambique in South Africa. But these attitudes could change rapidly in a white crisis situation.

More decisive obstacles to a wholehearted South African-Portuguese collaboration in southern Africa are the manpower limitations of the settlers' expansion. Without an African army, it is in the long run impossible for South Africa, in terms of sheer numbers, to substitute for the frequently demoralized Portuguese soldier on all fronts. This situation is realistically appraised in Pretoria as the following editorial indicates, recognizing, however, that the central aim is to mobilize the readers:

> It is essential that every White person in South Africa should understand how great the threatening danger is. We would be living in a fool's paradise if we imagined that the dangers are over or that they are not great. It should be realized that the days of the knobkierie and the bow and arrow are over. The approximately 300 million Africans are being rapidly provided with modern weapons. Every year there are more thousands of Blacks who are being equipped with weapons and who are receiving better training in warfare. The sporadic attacks on our borders are changing their pattern. The methods now being used show clearly that their training is improving and that attacks are being carried out more systematically and more ingeniously. While we still have the time, South Africa must consolidate her position especially as an influential country in Southern Africa. The Communists and other Leftist and subversive organizations within the borders of South Africa are today no immediate threat. It would, however, be fatal to believe that they are entirely wiped out.[19]

There is some evidence that offensive actions along the Israeli example are also being considered. Already in 1967 Vorster

---

18. Ibid. The author, however, made a characteristic distinction between "Madeira gardeners, who do not represent the best of Portugal" and people from northern Portugal, who are "as white as you and I—possibly even whiter," because "the higher the standard of living, the greater the difference."

19. *Die Transvaler*, 12 June 1968.

threatened "to hit Zambia so hard that she would never forget it," if the country continued harboring guerrillas. Later in 1970, while offering nonaggression pacts to African countries Vorster stressed in the same speech that "if terrorists attacked South Africa from countries which allowed them to do this, she would fight them and pursue them right into the countries from which they come." A modern airfield in the northern corner of the country (Mpacha in the Caprivi strip) could serve as a basis for such operations and helicopter flights into Angola.

However, only if the military preparations are backed by economic expansion, and, hence, further buffer zones come into indirect South African dependency, can a long term continuation of the present situation be expected. In the instance of the former British protectorates, this dependency is guaranteed by the necessity for large parts of the male population to work in the South African mines; and, furthermore, by a common customs and currency system, and the complete dependency on South African imports. In other areas, particularly Rhodesia and Malawi, reliance on South African capital and expert advice has been firmly established; overtures with Madagascar are likely to be successful. In 1968, for the first time, a mission of the *Afrikaanse Handelsinstituut* visited Angola, reflecting its new-found importance due to recent oil discoveries. Such perspectives are linked with special Afrikaner hopes, as *Die Transvaler* comments:

> It is possible that the Afrikaner may attain his rightful place all the sooner if he takes the lead in the formation of an economic block extending to the North of the Zambesi and Kuene. It is no secret that such an objective is in line with what the Government has in view. With an eye to the security of the Republic and its economic welfare such a block is of the utmost importance.[20]

Whether South Africa is successful in her attempt to establish a broader buffer zone will depend to a great extent on the attitude of landlocked Zambia toward her white neighbors.[21] Zambia's internal divisions together with her sizable expatriate

20. Ibid., 18 June 1968.
21. For a well-informed analysis, see Richard Hall, *The High Price of Principles: Kaunda and the White South* (London: Hodder & Stoughton, 1969).

population and dependency on imports as well as vulnerable outlets could well work in favor of South Africa in the post-Kaunda era. Some dissatisfied tribal leaders from the Barotse region are reported to have already made contacts with the white South.[22] The key role of Zambia is well recognized in South Africa as the following editorial illustrates: "Zambia still remains a danger point by continuing her futile enmity against the White South. Because of her strategic position as far as the terrorists are concerned it is, however, necessary that Zambia should also eventually be persuaded to accept our hand of friendship. A minister with the authority of Mr. Ben Schoeman last week again indicated that we have by no means written off Zambia as a country with which friendly relations can never be established."[23]

While the largest part of the South African trade (mainly gold and raw materials) is still conducted with industrial states, mostly Britain, export to other African territories is increasing rapidly and already comprises 15 percent of the total South African exports. In November 1967 Prime Minister Vorster declared: "We are of Africa, we understand Africa . . . and nothing is going to prevent us from becoming the leaders of Africa in every field."[24] Thus, the more South Africa seizes her "natural market,"[25] the more difficult it will become for political opponents of Apartheid to achieve more than a verbal condemnation.

This becomes particularly evident in the discussion of economic sanctions against South Africa. The existing sanctions now mainly serve to protect the African states against South Africa's expansionist drive rather than to harm her economy. Martin Legassick comments: "A flood of South African goods and capital moving northwards would retard the growth of indigenous African enterprise, further stunt the African economies, and arouse the serious danger of an export of South

22. Gerald L. Caplan, "Zambia, Barotseland and the Liberation of Southern Africa," *Africa Today* 15 (August/September 1969):13–17.
23. *Dagbreek en Landstem*, 12 April 1970.
24. *The Star*, 9 November 1968. See J. Barrat, "South Africa's Outward Movement," *Modern Age* 14; A. Vandenbosch, *South Africa and the World* (Lexington: University Press of Kentucky, 1970).
25. *Die Transvaler*, 23 November 1967.

African racial attitudes."[26] Nevertheless, sanctions are still the focus of hopes for a nonviolent abolition of Apartheid. Leo Kuper ends his study with the statement: "And it is in effective sanctions by international agencies against the violence of racial domination, and in effective support for the principles of non-racialism, that there may be some hope of nonviolent resolution of the conflict."[27] Long debates in the United Nations, resolutions, and expert meetings[28] are devoted to the topic of boycott. A dominant characteristic of these debates is good faith, which believes in the influence of moral principles, but neglects economic power relations. Notwithstanding her strong economic outside ties, South Africa is largely self-sufficient. Only in the imports of crude oil is she dependent on outside sources. But even in the hypothetical case of a total blockade of the southern continent, the country could carry on for at least two years with her present oil supplies. This time is sufficient to increase considerably the synthetic production of oil from coal, already covering almost 20 percent of the country's needs.

The weakness of sanctions has been demonstrated in the much more favorable Rhodesian experiment. The imposed sanctions against Rhodesia remained ineffective on the whole and boosted the resistance of the whites instead of forcing them to compromise.

It could be argued that the backing of an industrial state of the kind received by Rhodesia from her southern neighbor would be nonexistent in case of sanctions against South Africa. This, however, would imply a total blockade of the whole southern continent, including the Portuguese territories.[29] Only if the United Nations, with the support of the United States and

26. Martin Legassick, "The Southern African Bloc: Integration for Defense or Expansion," *Africa Today* (October/November 1968): 9–12.

27. Leo Kuper, *An African Bourgeoisie: Race, Class, and Politics in South Africa* (New Haven: Yale University Press, 1965), p. 410.

28. R. Segal (ed.), *Sanctions Against South Africa* (Baltimore: Penguin, 1964).

29. For a concrete evaluation of the needs and costs of such an undertaking in the framework of a UN intervention, see A. C. Leiss (ed.), *Apartheid and United Nations Collective Measures* (New York: Carnegie Foundation, 1965).

the Soviet Union, were prepared to engage in armed conflict would the imposition of economic sanctions be an effective first step.

According to Leo Kuper, a "world ethics of racial equality" and the tensions "between doctrines of universal human rights and the systematic negation of these rights"[30] could, among other factors, be viewed as a lever for restructuring race relations in South Africa. While one might hope for such benign influence, it would seem more realistic to expect change from the gradually changing interest constellations within South Africa or on war from without. The ongoing war in the Portuguese territories and Rhodesia, to which South Africa has committed herself, is unlikely to exceed the local success of guerillas in the foreseeable future. Hence, the dynamics of the internal political and economic scene remains a primary consideration, especially since the whites continue to aim for a universally acceptable legitimation of their policy and the avoidance of reliance on brute force.

In summary, it may be concluded that the rhetoric of economic sanctions against southern Africa not only has little chance of being implemented, but even if it were, it would remain inefficient in the light of the self-sufficiency of the blockaded countries. Fierce international trading competition and complex international interdependencies prevent an effective blockade. The domestic economies of the old metropolises, particularly British, are still so strongly interwoven with the former colonial areas that a total trade boycott would collide with powerful interests in the metropolis. This would cause a backlash which the British government believes it cannot afford. Thus sanctions test the strength and patience of their initiators rather than the survival power of the sanctioned. There is a decisive difference between the aim to weaken and reform an enemy and the aim to destroy its internal political structure and bring about its total capitulation. A boycotted ruling class will turn first to its subordinates who thus become the main sufferers from the sanctions. It is not at all certain whether this

30. Leo Kuper, "The Political Situation of Non-Whites in South Africa," in William Hance (ed.), *Southern Africa and the United States* (New York: Columbia University Press, 1968), p. 104.

pressure drives the subordinates toward their outside allies or to the side of their local oppressor.

In the case of southern Africa, it must be added that the dependency of landlocked African states on the transportation lines and power resources in the surrounding colonial areas also hits the enemies of Apartheid. Generally it can, therefore, be concluded that economic sanctions as a kind of limited warfare can only be successful if their initiators are also prepared to intervene militarily sooner or later. Only then could they continue to influence their nonmilitary actions within a mutually tolerable time limit. In the absence of readiness and ability to intervene militarily, the demand for sanctions remains the militant decoration of actual passivity.

There are "non-justifiable" disputes, because "state refusal to entrust such conflicts . . . to third party determination, is another hard fact of international life."[31] A possibility for an intervention by a Third Party does not exist unless at least two of three main conditions prevail: (1) the internal conflict must polarize to such an extent that major violence and other irrevertable acts by either party demonstrate the need and give a justification for outside interference, (2) the Third Party must have sufficient interests at stake which are jeopardized by the polarized conflict, and (3) the intervening power must realistically expect relatively high gains (not just moral rewards) from such an enterprise. Neither of these conditions are fulfilled for any major world power which would have to back United Nations' intervention in South Africa. On the other hand, the white settler regimes consciously undertake efforts to prevent an extreme polarization, which would justify Third Party interference. South Africa's geographical isolation from the primary centers of world conflict in Asia and the Middle East, aids her perseverance as much as international reactions to the other conflicts, such as the no-more-Vietnam syndrome in the United States.

In the absence of any likelihood of Third Party interference in South Africa, the illusionary striving for such action can be as apolitical as the sole belief in the use of force by the oppressed as the only possible way to change their situation. Leo Kuper

31. Julius Stone, "Reflections on Apartheid after the South West Africa Cases," *Washington Law Review*, June 1967, pp. 1069–82.

has correctly stressed that the failure of certain forms of non-violence in South Africa does not logically imply that only the opposite will succeed. Furthermore, if the Mao slogan is true, that all power comes out of the barrel of a gun, then this would apply to both sides, revolutionaries as well as their opponents. Given the differential military power of the antagonists and the likely widening of this gap in the future, the reliance on this solution of the South African problem has depoliticizing effects insofar as it fails to do what might be possible to mitigate the existing stalemate. It tends to abandon the people who have to live under such conditions instead of realistically aiming at their gradual advancement through slow improvements in their standard of living, education, employment, and organizing capacity within the contradictions of oppression. "What such a view finally leads to, is really rather tough thinking in which idealism is disciplined and attuned to work in the environment which it cannot in any case escape and can only slowly mould."[32] It does not imply giving up the full demands for abolition of racial domination but on the contrary brings this goal nearer by actively combating the otherwise growing despair, resignation, and ignorance on which so much of the system's stability rests.

The African Dilemma

The weakness of the independent African states is the strength of white South Africa. Developments in other parts of the continent, no less than internal political factors, have determined the political situation in the South. As Stalinism discredited the idea of socialism outside of the Eastern block, events in the Congo or Nigeria have militated against a change in the south. In addition, in terms of relative power, the African states have lost rather than gained since independence. A more detailed analysis of these aspects must, therefore, supplement the description of South African developments.

Any discussion of general tendencies in Africa south of the Sahara inevitably overgeneralizes and discounts substantial differences among over thirty independent African states. The 11

32. Ibid.

percent growth rate of the Ivory Coast can hardly be compared with the stagnation in poorer Somali, Chad, or the Central African Republic. Relatively stable political conditions in some East African states contrast with extreme disintegration or changing military dictatorships in many western states. Socialist undertakings in Guinea, Mali, or Tanzania differ from a neo-colonial policy favoring the old European and new local bourgeoisie in nearly all the other states.

However, notwithstanding these important differences, certain general characteristics of the current African situation can be discerned. All African countries suffer from the long-range consequences of colonial exploitation and subjugation. This colonial impact has become more evident than at the time of independence. The omissions and neglect of the long era of foreign domination will affect for a long time the character of the new states. These common scars of underdevelopment exceed the differences in their subsequent development as well as differences in the cultural impact of the metropolis.[1]

In strictly economic terms the trends in Africa, as compared with other parts of the world, are hardly encouraging. Indicators for four areas of the so-called Third World—Latin America, East Asia, Middle East, South Asia, and Africa (excluding Egypt and South Africa)—show that Africa ranks lowest in nearly all spheres.[2] It is hindmost in total GNP, annual growth of GNP, electric power per capita, life expectancy, people per physician, pupils as percentage of the population. Only in acres of agricultural land per capita does Africa rank relatively high.

While the population increases at an estimated rate of 2.3 percent annually, food is not produced at the same pace. Birth

1. This analysis summarizes relevant aspects noted by several Africanists, especially Stanislav Andreski, *The African Predicament* (London: Michael Joseph, 1968) and Aristide R. Zolberg, "The Structure of Political Conflict in the New States of Africa," *American Political Science Review*, March 1968, pp. 70–87. My short outline relies heavily on these two sources and I am aware of the shortcomings of "tribal" explanations for African affairs. Tribe is used in the sense of traditional group loyalties as opposed to identifications with a political center, which aim at national solidarities.
2. Agency for International Development, "Selected Economic Data for the Less Developed Countries," quoted in *Venture* 20 (November 1968):6.

control, possibly the most urgent single prerequisite for material progress, hardly exists and is frequently rejected by the
political leadership.

This material underdevelopment is not without political-
social consequences, and, of course, on the other hand, political
disintegration reciprocally hampers economic progress. African
states can be compared with usual state structures only in a legalistic sense. The mere existence of sovereign states does not
necessarily mean their governments exercise authority over the
whole territory—that is, that they can enforce their orders
against the will of the population. Their borders were mapped
out according to the interests of the colonial power, often without consideration of the traditional loyalties of the native population, and as a result many of the newly independent African
states have inherited a heterogeneous ethnic structure. In the
self-conception of the inhabitants, the new nation hardly forms
a salient reference point; instead identification with the clan
and the tribe persists. The tribes themselves differ in their organization and value system often even within an ethnic group.
Andreski emphasizes that such disparities exceed the variety of
ethnicities in the old Habsburg Reich. This syncretic structure
is heightened where some tribes within the new states have had
more contact with missionaries who provided westernized
school opportunities, or where a tribe's geographical position
has made it more urbanized or richer than the other more backward parts of the country. Thus, the seeds for conflict had been
planted. These collective disparities between ethnic groups
within a common border have served to reinforce and confirm
traditional affiliations rather than creating new cross-cutting
ties between equally educated or rich members of different
tribes. Even the group of relatively "detribalized" urban Africans does not simply move from an old order into a new one but
maintains extensive traditional solidarities, if primarily for the
sake of material security. Even in the nations where the traditional institutions and norms have formally been abolished,
they retain substantial significance and have survived the colonial change.

In the absence of national instead of tribal identifications, the
leaders of the political center are isolated, or are viewed only as

an extended tribal authority. The anticolonial liberation movements did not change much in this respect. They constituted temporary alliances against the colonial rulers rather than a permanent base for national unity. Furthermore, these weak unifying links withered away with the disappearance of European rulers, the fading of the heroic myth of the first liberation leaders, and the realization that the new government was more or less a black continuation of the old one with hardly any real changes in the life of the people. The whites in the south are too remote to form a substitute for the old colonial enemy as a focus for collective mobilization. They serve at most as an ideological clamp between the divergent states in the Organization for African Unity, or as an excuse for failure. I. L. Horwitz summarizes the maxims of this policy: "Only when nations like Angola and South Africa are liberated from White domination will it be possible or desirable to focus attention on internal imbalances between social sectors within the continent."[3]

This approach, however, overlooks the fact that African policy and African strength must first create the prerequisites for a change in the south. As long as African unity is a dream without economic and social reality, the highly equipped industrialized state of the south will not be threatened. On the other hand, the forthcoming long struggle with the racial system of South Africa and the Portuguese colonial policy may contain a future unifying potential if the conflict heightens and extends the present guerrilla stage. The relatively voluntary departure of the colonial powers in most countries of Africa—partly because the investment profits in the advanced metropolitan areas gradually exceeded the gains in the colonies—removed the necessity for developing a politicized "unity feeling" comparable to the European nationalism in the war-stricken nineteenth century. In Europe a mobilizing nationalism preceded the final industrialization, while the modernization of Africa can still hardly rely on a collective ideology of service to the state.

In this situation in which neither consensus nor loyalty to the central institutions counterbalances the disintegrative tribal

3. I. L. Horowitz, *Three Worlds of Development: The Theory and Practice of International Stratification* (New York: Oxford University Press, 1966), p. 241.

tendencies, the state's existence is frequently based on the suppression of the weaker part or, at best, on a truce. Constitutions, carefully designed according to European models, prove to be empty formulas without reality. Party democracy with all its implications was the expression of specific interests in the European setup—of the rising bourgeoisie against the ruling aristocracy and later of the labor movement against the bourgeois polity. Where these interests do not exist, democratic rules of the game along the Westminster pattern hardly make sense. In the meantime, the military coup has become the customary way to change a government; indeed, there is no African state so far where the ruling group, which gained power through independence, has changed constitutionally. As the ousting of Nkrumah in February 1966 has shown, even supposedly stable one-party dictatorships with a mass basis and pronounced ideology are not immune to toppling. The same applies to other countries like Nigeria which have possessed the material preconditions of a progressive development. The tribal loyalties and general underdevelopment seem to engender still other consequences that jeopardize the functioning of a state along European lines. Four decisive national power groups in the African states and their complex interdependence merit special attention: (1) the armed forces, (2) the politicians and their active supporters, (3) the civil servants, (4) neocolonial economic and political interest groups, and (5) trade unions.

It is not surprising that armies in Africa mirror the contradictions of their nations. Whether the soldiers obey their officers and whether the latter follow the orders of the civilian government can frequently be decided only in the specific case and not generally. In countries where the army has been led and trained by expatriates, a relatively greater discipline has been the norm, but there are also examples of mutinies against the colonial officers. In most of the former French territories, small contingents of French troops are still stationed in the country, more or less at the disposal of the local rulers, whose position has still to be ensured by foreign troops. The local army increasingly takes on the role of referee between rivaling political groups or is used by the politicians against their internal opponents. Such countercoups and purges, initiated by the rulers, exceed in frequency the successful ousting of a government. This tendency to move away from the legalized exercise of power toward the illegal use of force is only the most visible expression of a state of affairs in which intimidation, arrest, and exiling of opponents has become a routine daily occurrence. Even in supposedly democratic countries like Kenya the freedom of opposition constitutes a right on paper only.

Due to the weakness of the national institutions of the political center, the army and police acquire a key position although they are small in terms of numbers. Officers commanding not more than a few hundred persons frequently decide the fate of a state. Altogether, there are not more than 250,000 soldiers between the Sahara and Zambezi, and these are almost without sophisticated arms. In contrast to the North African countries, none of the tropical African states has an efficient air force or navy capable of decisive actions. South Africa, Rhodesia, and Portugal, on the other hand, maintain together 300,000 men under arms, equipped with modern armory and better trained in technological warfare. Nonetheless, the costs for the small armies in the tropical states are approximately double the amount spent on investments in industry and agriculture. Everywhere the salaries of the soldiers have been increased since independence so that in some states an ordinary soldier earns ten times as much as the average worker. In countries in which the army is used for collecting taxes, new possibilities for additional illegal soldiers' income have been opened. These factors alone raise doubts about the usual explanation for the prevalence of an army—that in developing countries military regimes are necessary for disciplining the backward population.

The lavishness or an obsession with status of many politicians has often been pointed out. African leaders such as Julius Nyerere in Tanzania, who demonstrate personal modesty and avoid wasting scarce resources on economically questionable prestige projects, are an exception. To be sure, lavishness has to be considered against the background of the syncretic social structure, in which the central institutions supposedly have to demonstrate their use and mask their weak power by grand gestures. What becomes evident after several years of independence is the broad gap between the expected and professed goals of modernization and the fading capacity for realizing such hopes. This failure became most obvious in states such as Mali, Guinea, or Ghana at the time of Nkrumah which were most committed to radical modernization, trying to mobilize the people with the help of a state party and economic planning along socialist lines. Subsequently, most of these partially successful attempts had to be cut down, as a result of internal pressure, and their complex dependence on foreign capital and terms of trade. Tanzania's much quoted declaration of Arusha means hardly more than an official admittance of this poverty and dependence, and, therefore, the solemn pledge to get out of the *circulus vitiosus* through her own efforts. In other supposedly socialist schemes for the nationalization of foreign business, the expropriation served more to fill the pockets of the ruling bourgeoisie than to promote the welfare of the average people. Barriers in the path of progress are also independent of the personal qualities and wisdom of political leaders. Politicians free from megalomania cannot abolish the neocolonial terms of trade because of their personal virtues. Even in the case of Nkrumah, personal failure contributed least to his ousting, when compared with the other factors involved. It seems necessary, therefore, to be acquainted with the deeper causes of the widespread corruption, which is, though, no higher than in feudal Asia.

Compared with their former situation, the takeover of the colonial administration constituted a rapid career rise for the new bureaucrats. In achieving this goal, they were backed by their clan, which through joint financial efforts was able to send its promising offspring to school. Now the former supporters expected gratefulness and the new politician, so much better off than his kin in the rural areas, could not afford to ignore their expectations. Another temptation for enrichment at the cost of the public was the example of the white predecessors. Indoctrinated with inferiority feelings by colonial education, the new elite in power frequently felt the need to demonstrate its equality by the same arrogance and style of life as the colonists. Today, African servants often prefer the paternalistic benevolence of the white expatriate to the treatment of the black capitalist. In the case of the civil servants, the adaptation of the colonial salaries proved to be particularly fatal. Salaries often constitute more than half of the annual government expenditure. The size and pomp of the diplomatic corps of many African states contrasts sharply with the poverty of the country: it can be viewed as an indirect travel service for a few top members of the new bourgeoisie.

As Andreski points out, the ratio between the average income of an unskilled worker and a higher civil servant is approximately 1:5 in Western Europe; in some of the African states, however, the ratio is as high as 1:40. In the absence of other opportunities, a position in the state service, therefore, appears to be the most promising or even the sole way to acquire wealth and prestige. The loss of such a position, on the other hand, or the defeat in an election, constitutes a severe downfall into the old poverty unless the temporary power has been abused to furnish protection against the unsafe future. This sort of legal collective graft of the political and administrative power elite is still further increased by various other illegal prerequisites. While the same corruption in a rich industrialized setting has hardly any significance in the total context, or at least does not constitute a strain on the economy, the scarce resources become still less accessible for the mass of the population under the conditions of poverty in Africa. A generally corrupt state administration constitutes particularly easy operational ground for neo-colonialism of the Western and the Eastern version alike. Under such circumstances, simple bribery more than any other means secures foreign influence. Amounts spent on advertising, public relations, and lobbying in Western countries flow in Africa directly into the pockets of the appropriate individuals who repay with the facility of special customs, tax exemptions, or state orders at the expense of the public. The mere existence of giant corporations with fantastic offers in the midst of poverty is seen by Andreski as the main reason for such widespread corruption. Capitalist and communist states alike compete to replace the former direct colonial rule by simply buying off the local power elite.

This situation, however, is always jeopardized by groups excluded from such opportunities. Among these are the growing numbers of graduates who find the expected administrative positions already occupied, and are also unable to find a niche in the foreign-dominated business appropriate to their high expectations. In addition to the absence of seniority in office, the present administrators are often not legitimized by better qualifications. In contrast to the first generation of African politicians who came to power mostly through political conditions, the subsequent claimants are indeed formally better trained.

To the discontented of this group must be added the growing young Lumpenproletariat in the shacks of the cities. The political potential of this underemployed *Jeunesse*, massed in the few cities, should not be underestimated and has already demonstrated its power in 1963 in Congo-Brazzaville. Together with the peasant masses in the neglected rural areas, in which 80 percent of the total population still lives on the traditional subsistence economy, these groups seem to support the prediction of Frantz Fanon that the real liberation of Africa has yet to come.

6

Revolutionary or
Evolutionary Change?

Implications of Economic Expansion

MOST MAJOR STUDIES ON SOUTH AFRICA REFLECT THE
assumption that an essential contradiction exists between an irrational race policy and the requirements of a rationally organized, expanding industrial society. Optimal productivity would
preclude racial restrictions. Historian L. M. Thompson states:
"It remains to be seen whether industrialization and pigmen-
tocracy are compatible."[1] A race policy against industrial interests is regarded as inevitably leading to explosive conflict, due
to the interdependence of the economic system. "The more economic interdependence there is, the less feasible Apartheid becomes. Two major elements in the social structure; namely the
polity and the economy pull in opposite directions, thereby creating rapidly mounting strains," writes Pierre van den Berghe.[2]
Similarly, Leo Kuper states: "Presumably, there must be some
point at which an equilibrium can no longer be maintained between continued economic growth and increasing political rigidity."[3]

1. Leonard M. Thompson, *Politics in the Republic of South Africa*
(Boston: Little, Brown, 1966) p. 150.
2. Pierre L. van den Berghe, *South Africa: A Study in Conflict* (Middletown: Wesleyan University Press, 1965) p. 274.
3. Leo Kuper, "The Political Situation of Non-Whites in South
Africa," in William Hance (ed.), *Southern Africa and the United
States* (New York: Columbia University Press, 1968), p. 103.

Implicit in many of these analyses is the assumption that the South African economy is inescapably bound to the pursuit of growing productivity, inferring that "economic rationality urges the polity forward beyond its ideology," as economist Ralph Horwitz puts it.[4] Heinz Hartmann names the contradiction by emphasizing "that the basic question about the future economic growth in South Africa is whether political restrictions will continue to act as obstacles in the path of business, or whether economic forces will require the government to go slow on its political schemes."[5] One of the basic requirements of a complex capitalist economy would seem to be disregarded in South Africa: namely, a freely mobile labor force responsive to labor demands. While the non-whites are largely confined to unskilled jobs, all technical and managerial positions are filled by whites, who are often overstrained and underqualified. Where the achievement principle with all its implications is so severely limited, increased inefficiency, it is maintained, is an inevitable consequence. Hartmann mentions additional economic disadvantages which, however, have subsequently been eliminated: the strained explosive internal situation that keeps potential immigrants away, encourages the emigration of professional people, and creates an unfavorable climate for foreign investment and thus thwarts the inflow of foreign know-how. "Neither the professionalism nor the 'human relations' philosophy of Anglo-American management are compatible with Apartheid."[6] In this conflict, most studies of Apartheid infer optimistically that economic considerations will weigh heavier and industrial pressure will keep a check on fanatic politicians forcing them to compromise sooner or later. Translated into Marxist categories, this means that the artifically chained forces of production are not allowed their full development within an outdated institutional frame of race laws and, therefore, must inevitably burst apart these modes of production.

Contrary to this dominating view stands the opinion of Her-

---

4. Ralph Horwitz, *The Political Economy of South Africa* (London: Weidenfeld & Nicolson, 1967), p. 427.
5. Heinz Hartmann, *Enterprise and Politics in South Africa* (Princeton: Princeton University Press, 1962).
6. Ibid., p. 84.

bert Blumer, derived from a general analysis of the relationship between racialism and industrialization.[7] Blumer argues that, according to all empirical evidence, a race order existing prior to industrialization could be taken over, continued, and if necessary, further cemented. "The picture presented in a racially ordered society is that industrial imperatives accommodate themselves to the racial mould and continue to operate effectively within it."[8] If an alteration or abolition of traditional race relations were to come as in the United States, not economic requirements but external political factors would have engendered such development. The accommodation of industry to a racially defined order can be considered rational insofar as it takes the established prejudices of the economic subjects into account. These would be rational decisions "which are guided just as much by the aim of efficient operation and economic return as if they took into account only the productive capacity of the individual racial member."[9] Thus the paradoxical situation could emerge in that while industrialization might thoroughly change the social order, the race system anchored within it would remain. In the case of South Africa, Blumer maintains: "There is no question that industry, like other areas of life, is being brought firmly under the control of the official Apartheid policy, despite the apparent disfavour shown by many industrialists to different portions of the programme."[10]

A decision in this controversy is easier if the South African economic situation and its development in the recent booming years is investigated in greater detail. First, it is readily apparent that the hypothesized friction between entrepreneurs and the government is grossly overrated. Empirical surveys indicate[11] that both groups agree on the basic principles of white rule and differ only on tactical measures. The interests of both coincide

7. Herbert Blumer, "Industrialization and Race Relations," in Guy Hunter (ed.), *Industrialization and Race Relations* (London: Oxford University Press, 1965), pp. 220–53.
8. Ibid., p. 238.
9. Ibid., p. 233.
10. Ibid., p. 252.
11.See H. Adam, "The South African Power Elite: A Survey of Ideological Commitment," in H. Adam (ed.), *South Africa: Sociological Perspectives* (London: Oxford University Press, 1971).

on the central issue of maintaining a cheap labor force as the single most important factor in the economic boom and high profit rates. The government realizes that the inequities between race groups can only be compensated for by a generally rising standard of living and the avoidance of severe recessions. Only economic strength enables the government to defy external pressure and to control the sounding board of internal opposition. The entrepreneurs on their part are aware that only the Apartheid order, and especially the prohibition of effective non-white unions, ensures a relatively cheap labor force. Any political advance of the non-whites would enable them to force economic concessions to the detriment of white profit rates. Thus far, Apartheid has not been an obstacle to the present boom, but one of its important prerequisites.

Rapid economic growth and a high degree of inefficiency—through a waste of talents and various other irrational measures deriving from race ideology—do not necessarily exclude each other. Even a racially limited industry achieves an acceptable rate of productivity and profit. Abundant cheap labor and South Africa's extraordinary wealth of scarce mineral resources have permitted an astonishing rate of expansion in spite of low individual productivity.

However, it remains questionable how long this situation can endure and whether future developments may have to take other factors into account, especially a decline in the significance of unskilled labor. Already the bottleneck of skilled labor, due to its reservation for whites only, is proving a severe problem. This conflict between the potential of expansion through use and training of qualified non-whites and its restriction through racial laws, is increasingly being resolved by financial compromise. By increasing the wages of the white workers, the permission of the unions has on occasion been secured to employ non-whites in hitherto "reserved" jobs. An inflationary trend was the consequence of this situation, and it is becoming increasingly evident that job reservation in the traditional form can no longer be maintained if a long-term crisis is to be avoided.

From the middle of 1970 there have been various indications that the government was adopting a more conciliatory attitude toward the use of non-white labor in urban areas. For the exchange of investments in the border areas and Bantustans under new financial incentives, the Minister of Finance Diederichs assured "every willingness on our part to ensure the greatest degree of development in the White areas."[12] While stressing that "the maximum use of labour resources takes place within a definite socio-economic structure and in a political context," Diederichs stated that he would not favor a slowdown in economic growth for "external and internal protection."[13] "It is not impossible that methods may be found whereby the establishment of industries in these areas can be encouraged and, at the same time, more non-White labour can be made available for those industries which remain in the White areas."[14] By the middle of 1970, 72 percent of the applications for additional African laborers, under the then relatively new Planning Act, had to be granted. All other evidence indicates that the traditional industrial color bar could be sustained only by large-scale exemptions and the deceptive redefinition of job descriptions to circumvent prohibitions attached to the employment of non-whites in skilled positions. *Die Burger* articulates the political aspect of this Afrikaner dilemma with the question: "The heart of the matter can be summed up in a few words: How is the full non-White labour potential of the country to be incorporated into the South African economy without producing in the White workers a feeling of being in danger and without arousing in them a spirit of resistance which could not only be eco-

12. *The Star*, 29 August 1970.
13. Ibid.
14. Ibid., 15 August 1970. In a survey of the manpower situation in commerce and allied services undertaken by the Association of Chambers of Commerce in 1970 the following vacancies as percentage of number employed in executive, clerical, sales, and other staff positions, were reported (*STATS*, October 1970, p. 1225): white male 6.6; white female 5.4; African male 3.5; African female 3.2; Coloured male 7.6; Coloured female 3.3; Asiatics male 3.5; Asiatics female 2.1. Almost half of the respondents reported a labor turnover beyond 25 percent per annum, in spite of an increase in labor costs of more than 5 percent. The survey attributes this phenomenon primarily to the shortage of white workers, who constitute a strained pool of skills too small to meet the demands of a growing economy. The entrepreneurs view the lack of competition for the white worker as the main cause of this high occupational mobility.

nomically disastrous but also disastrous for the relations between White and non-White?"[15] At the same time, the bitter
exchange over the ceiling for African miners in the reserves between the government and its press on the one side and the
Mine Workers Union on the other indicated that, in the name
of the moral credibility of separate development, industrial interests can increasingly disregard white worker protectionism
which no longer has the unanimous support of Afrikanerdom.
With the widespread underhand circumvention of job reservation, the only valid formula now generally applied in this realm
is that pertaining to role relationships: whites do not work under non-whites, in other words, non-whites are not allowed to
rise to supervisory and administrative positions, connected with
direct authority over whites.

The system of migratory labor provided an essential base for
the profitability of the gold mines. It was not worthwhile to in-
vest in the training of the temporary contract workers; as this
step together with social security measures such as providing
housing for the family members instead of the compound system, would have increased the labor costs and thereby affected
the profitability of the mines because of the fixed price of gold.
Increased wages under the conditions of tribal subsistence economy would lead to a greater shortage of labor rather than an
increase in productivity. Hence, in the gold mining industry the
lowest wages are paid to force the Africans, through poverty,
into the labor market. The average ratio between the income of
white and black workers is here about 16:1; in the secondary
industry, however, 5:1. At present, 65 percent of approximately
550,000 African mine workers come from territories outside of
South Africa.[16]

The labor constellation in the expanding secondary industry
differs considerably from this situation. While hitherto characterized by cheap and, therefore, unproductive work, the grow-

15. *Die Burger*, 19 August 1970.
16. The numerical ratio between whites and Africans is 1:8 in mining; 1:3 in secondary industry. Similar wage and working conditions
persist in the agricultural sphere, in which government presently attempts to counteract the trend toward a better paid urban industry
by a strict recruitment system in the reserves with financial gains for
the chiefs and headmen.

ing mechanization requires a new labor policy. With the increased need for skilled workers, industry has a vested interest in the schooling and living conditions of its workers. At present, of the economically active Africans, 60 percent have no schooling at all, only 8.3 percent have passed standard six, and 0.3 percent are matriculants. Approximately 65 percent of the Africans in urban areas are literate, as compared with 23 percent in the rural areas.[17] This low standard of education has to be increased with continuing bureaucratization and mechanization. The *Johannesburg Star* emphasizes this trend in mid-1970 by pointing to the hitherto ambiguous reactions on the government's part: "The Government has found itself obliged by economic imperatives and by its own industrial supporters tacitly to abandon the old rigid line between White work and what was so offensively called Kaffir's work. But it has not yet been able to bring itself to provide for the education and industrial training that non-Whites need in order to do their new tasks with full responsibility. And it sticks to an outworn doctrine that non-Whites must always get less money than Whites even for the same work, which is in the longer run perilous to the White worker."[18]

It is the political consequence of this trend that the government attempts to resist. The Apartheid planners calculate more realistically than their industrial opponents the political effects and power shifts of this economic integration. An editorial in *Die Burger* states their ambivalence toward the advocates of a more ample use of non-white labor:

> There are many considerations against it, but even if they should all be removed, there still remains the one big, predominant consideration that the planned greater use of the Black labour force would have many far-reaching social and political consequences which, in the long run, even its advocates would not be prepared to suffer. This more abundant use means that more and more Black people would be used for more than merely untrained labour—for the kind of work which can really only be done by people living permanently with their families, in the existing big cities of the country. Political rights in the White area cannot

17. E. G. Malherbe, quoted in *The Star*, 19 January 1969, and *STATS* (February 1969):905.
18. *The Star*, 8 August 1970.

indefinitely be denied them, because in their established urban existence, they would become increasingly alienated from the Bantu homelands wherein they must presently exercise their political rights. The only alternative to the granting of these political rights would be naked baasskap, and those who still think that the relations between White and Black in this country can be stabilized on a basis of baasskap, are wilfully deaf and blind.[19]

Since the Apartheid utopia is unlikely to succeed either economically or politically in the sense of African support for the scheme, economic growth can be expected to further undermine the political race restrictions as predicted in the editorial cited above. Furthermore, in order to create a consumer market for expanding production, African income cannot be allowed to stagnate. Finally, above all, the avoidance of conflict depends on a continual increase in wealth, and the fulfillment of low, but nevertheless rising, African aspirations.

In South Africa, too, direct exploitation in the form of long working hours and low wages as demonstrated by the history of industrialization elsewhere will be increasingly substituted by more intensive techniques of production, even though the abundant cheap labor has so far hampered the trends toward mechanization. In this process, the range of concessions, and the scope with which the owners can yield to pressure from below, increases at the same time. In contrast to the early phases of industrialization with a limited surplus, discontent can now be accommodated more easily through wage increases and other gratifications within the system. At the same time, however, this process increases the power of the antagonists of white rule in a sphere in which it is most vulnerable; it necessarily works toward its own abolition or at least modification. However, the historical experience of earlier industrialization in other countries indicates that this is not an automatic process: this direct association of democratization with industrialization reflects a sociologically naïve abstraction from historical conflicts. In a long struggle the European labor movement had to fight for the achievement of its present rights: it had to hasten the process of change through political actions. Similarly, the issue of an open confrontation between the race-classes in South Africa will only

19. *Die Burger*, 29 October 1968.

arise again when Africans are in a position to force the system to its knees by a long general strike. This constellation has so far not existed, even in the hypothetical case of a total African strike. In such a case, though under considerable stress, the whites would be capable of existence as an economically viable group for longer than the strikers could survive.

This, however, is no longer possible at a higher stage of industrialization that brings increased interdependence. The African sociologist Archie Mafeje states: "There is no doubt that if disruption of the South African economy were possible and could ensure the achievement of their political goals, the Blacks would have no qualms in implementing it. On the other hand, if it were possible, the Whites would not hesitate to do away with Black labour as shown by their desire to recruit more skilled labour from Europe instead of training Black South Africans."[20]

In summary it can be said that the analytical perspective which focuses on the essential compatibility between economic interests and white political power comes much closer to reality than the naïve belief in economic growth as the magic defeat of racial discrimination. It recognizes that the disputes between industrialists and the government's supporters are not about the abolition of white power but the distribution of its yields within a system of wage color bar and the suppression of labor organizations. However, while economic development may reinforce white supremacy in the short run, it also undermines it in the long run. The most serious shortcoming of the "collaboration theory," is its undialectical nature. The increase in the non-white proportion of the manufacturing labor force from 70 percent in 1960 to 75 percent in 1966 and 80 percent in 1971 signals a prerequisite for white vulnerability by non-white labor pressure. Given the white manpower shortage, economic growth makes it imperative that skilled positions be filled by non-whites. This requires giving adequate training to the formerly untrained. The investment in this training and the increasing dependency of an enterprise on its qualified workers necessitates a relatively stable labor force.

20. Archie Mafeje, *Race* (July 1967):115.

Thus an expanding economy built essentially on migratory labor, as the grand Apartheid envisages, is not compatible with this stage of technological development. Contract labor is the dominant feature of an economy based mainly on extractive industries and agriculture which requires only a small percentage of highly skilled individuals in supervisory positions. Even with a higher degree of mechanization—a development which has yet to overcome massive obstacles—South Africa's growing economy would still call for the transference of an increasing number of contract workers into skilled producers. This new type of qualified blue- and white-collar worker will be hard pressed for high individual productivity, a characteristic not essential in an economy with abundant contract labor. Individual productivity in turn cannot easily be commandeered. It is grounded in a mentality, basically not at odds with the surrounding social system. Individual productivity presupposes psychological incentives in terms of a more or less satisfied labor force, and it is difficult to see how the present system of white-controlled residential and political mobility can achieve this basic contentment among those on whom it increasingly depends.

This growing white economic dependency on political subordinates seems to be the only realistic base on which the latter can pressure their dominators into making substantial concessions, or achieve for themselves a more sudden change of political power on the basis of gradually acquired strategic positions in the expanding economy. South African whites are increasingly unable to fill these positions with members of their own group or immigrants. It is difficult to forecast when this threshold between white and non-white functional power in the economy will be reached. What is certain, is that at the present stage of technological development white power is still able to hold its grip on its material base even in the face of hypothetically united African refusal to continue to serve. The average African laborer, barely above the minimum subsistence level, cannot afford to be "endorsed out."[21] If anyone, it will be the

21. The Bantu Labour (Settlement of Disputes) Act. No. 48 of 1953 makes it unlawful for an African worker to take part in a strike,

top of a rising non-white labor hierarchy, professionals and independent members of a non-white middle class, who can risk
challenging imposed conditions, not those whose life chances
are entirely controlled by white power-holders.

Rumblings of intense dissatisfaction with political overtones
can already be detected among the colored teachers or African
students. Only as the ranks of the non-white skilled strata swell
can a challenge to their subordinate status as objects of white
power be successful. It seems unrealistic to assume that a non-
white middle class can be as easily integrated under present
South African conditions as in other industrialized societies.
While it is conceivable that resentment among the three subordinate ethnic groups could be fostered by various differential
rewards and competition, a growing awareness of such manipulation on the part of educated individuals can be expected to
militate against it. There is no inherent conservatism among
rising members of a subordinate class; on the contrary it was
this group which initiated and led most historical uprisings.

It is only meaningful for Africans to strike with the goal of
achieving political power, and not merely for an improvement
in material conditions as has been the tradition of the European
labor movement. The illegality of any strike in itself would not
permit a choice. Only the seizure of political power, the control
of the state's instrument of coercion together with the authority
to shape the economy of the country according to their concepts,
would seem sufficient to satisfy the opponents of white rule: in
South Africa, a strike is virtually synonymous with revolution.
In a settler colony, however, revolution cannot mean only the
exchange of the political leadership, as in the previous colonial
revolutions. A government under African leadership could
function only if economic control did not sabotage political decisions but provided their basis. Hence, a redistribution of the
accumulated wealth would be a necessary consequence of any
political change. It seems doubtful whether the non-white
masses, at this stage, considering their politicization through the

---

go-slow, or similar action. The punishment can be up to three years
imprisonment and/or a fine of 500 pounds.

long struggle, would be satisfied by a change through which a black bourgeoisie alone became the main beneficiary. The difference between the conservative role of middle-class leaders in other African countries and likely more progressive role of African intellectuals and professionals in South Africa would seem to result from the economic development and the extreme political polarity in the South African situation. No conservative middle-class group could take and hold control of an internal dynamic liberation movement for long. Speculation that South Africa, because of her political and economic preconditions, might thus develop into the first genuine socialist society in Africa, would seem not too far-fetched from this perspective.

The question is whether the white rulers will allow this final conflict to develop or whether their "rationality" is sufficient to prevent this clash, to channel it, and to compromise in their own interests. There is considerable evidence to suggest that the South African ruling class will not behave much differently than its European predecessor; but it is conceivable that it has learned from earlier experiences. The often asserted alternative for the South African whites, "to oppress or be oppressed,"[22] is too simple, although present statements of politicians would like to foster belief in this choice of the racially pure oppressor. It seems questionable, however, whether the famous slogan "rather poor but White than rich but Black"[23] will find the necessary support when put to the test. There is evidence that the majority of the English-speaking entrepreneurs accept the necessity for radical concessions.[24]

Much will depend on whether the whites will find an ally for the defense of a revised status quo in an, as yet, rudimentary African middle class. Although there are currently hardly any indications of such a coalition, and much indicates the opposite as pointed out earlier, the material advantages of the continuous boom filtering down to a few Africans could lead to such an alliance. Already, several members of the Indian and Coloured

22. Stanislav Andreski, *Elements of Comparative Sociology* (London: Weidenfeld & Nicolson, 1964), p. 268. Similarly, Pierre L. van den Berghe, *Race and Racism: A Comparative Perspective* (New York: John Wiley, 1967), p. 130.
23. Verwoerd 1963, Blaar Coetzee in Vereeniging, 18 October 1967.
24. See H. Adam, "South African Power Elite."

bourgeoisie have turned out to be supporters of the system that, on the social and political sphere, strongly discriminates against them. The growing class features of the race society are hinted at in the fact that this tiny non-white middle class, on the basis of their financial status, succeeds to a certain extent in avoiding some of the worst disadvantages of Apartheid order.[25] Just as the white rulers have learned to come to terms with foreign African dignitaries, they could change their attitudes toward the local non-white bourgeoisie. Such a coalition would coincide with the Bantustan concept that would add the traditional elements to this pact. With the same facility that the Afrikaner tycoon Anton Rupert can name a black vice-president of Kenya as a director of his tobacco empire, the internal race relations also could be oriented toward business interests in due time as the necessity for it develops. It is now already theoretically accepted among the Afrikaners that the non-white "must be able to become managers of business, industrial and other undertakings,"[26] although in separate branches since it is argued that white employees would not otherwise cooperate. It seems likely that it will be realized in practice even in the white enclaves un-

25. A more detailed example might illustrate this. The popular stereotype of the rich Indians appears grotesque compared with the fact that nearly half of his population group lives under or barely above the poverty level. On the other hand, there are a considerable number of Indian households of the upper middle class whose style of life allows them to stay away from the harsher experiences of separation. The car, sometimes chauffeur-driven, avoids usage of the public transport; their economic position frequently brings them into informal contact with members of the white bureaucracy who often buy certain goods cheaper from the Indian dealer. The Group Areas Act has not driven them indiscriminately into depressing substandard housing schemes such as Chatsworth, but some live in fashionable suburbs with African servants. Some avoid Apartheid during their holidays by traveling abroad since Indian businessmen do not normally encounter difficulties in getting a passport. Frequently, they also send their children to schools and universities abroad. The sole precondition for such a life, to be sure, is political passivity. With exceptions, this description applies also for the much smaller middle class of Coloureds and a gradual development in the same direction can be foreseen for some independent Africans even though the legal restrictions are much more severe in their case. It is the average African who really has to bear the worst brunt of Apartheid.
26. *Die Burger*, 20 January 1969.

der economic and political pressure, resulting in a cooptation of the useful non-whites rather than increased racial polarization.

It can be assumed that such tendencies would emerge first with regard to the Coloureds and later the Indians whose aversion against the African proletariat predestine them to be a useful ally of white domination. Even though there are thus far no signs of such a policy, it is officially conceded that "separate development," as far as the Coloureds are concerned, is in a dilemma. Not only is it impossible to construct a Coloured geographical "homeland," but the whole concept of a separate Coloured group is based not on cultural differences but on mere skin shades and political discrimination. The future solution, as occasionally painted, already reveals in its vague formulation the doubts of the nationalists. So, for example, *Die Burger* hopes: "What will definitely also grow is a group consciousness and a feeling of belonging together among what is now a very loose and fairly incohate collection of sections and classes of people. Group sentiment and group pride is after all encouraged by the White trustee. It could gradually become a national sentiment, so that one would have to speak with more justice than at present of a brown nation: thus, a brown nation alongside the white nation in a single state, economically interwoven, but socially apart and with separate administrative institutions at a local as well as at a national level."[27]

In contrast to the attitude toward the Africans, in which a material and political threat as well as cultural differences support white racialism, the official approach toward the Coloureds and Indians is exclusively based on racial obsession. Such a myth, however, is more easily jettisoned since a psychological change of mind has hardly any material consequences for the whites. On the contrary, an integration of the Coloureds would strengthen the white laager against more real threats, and some Afrikaners already informally advocate such a change. *Die Beeld*, expressing the minority view of the more liberal Afrikaner bourgeoisie in the Cape, urges the removal of "the source of bitterness among the Coloured people," especially "those who have reached a high rung of the ladder—an Afrikaans poet

27. Ibid., 10 February 1969.

of stature like Adam Small, teachers and other professional men."[28] The paper advocates "uplifting" the Coloured community "but also—and above all—that when they are uplifted, they will be accepted as such by the Whites. . . . There are daily contacts between Coloured and White within the accepted pattern of separation and contact situations will necessarily be multiplied and become more complicated. To put it bluntly, will the civilised White treat the civilised Coloured man as civilised people treat each other when they come into contact? . . . This period is decisive. It simply must provide the evidence that we can take the Coloured people in growing numbers with us and accept them as associates in determining our future."

The English-language press expresses similar pragmatic views more bluntly and without the frequent sentimental affinity of Afrikaners for "our children." "If the Coloured people now show decisively that despite the insult and injuries of the past 20 years they still repudiate separation, is it sane to go on trying to make them accept it? Is it sane to risk turning 2,000,000 people into enemies of the White group who could still be its most reliable allies in the whole world? Does the country's security position permit its racists to go on indulging in that luxury?"[29]

If such expectations were to be realized, however, a new dilemma would arise, since then the rigid race ideology can hardly be upheld with regard to Indians and "educated Africans." It seems that change, if at all, might be forthcoming in this sphere of racial obsessions among Afrikaners, as race relations have already been deideologized and streamlined during the sixties. Due to the growing strength of white dominance, its legitimating ideology has changed. As Die Burger has put it: "So that we no longer have to dream and to talk about a mission in Africa which we are now more and more able to discharge."[30]

Interracial Contact and Conflict Resolution

Paradoxically, "separate development" also has a tempering effect on racial discrimination. Increasingly, the leading mem-

28. Schalk Pienaar in Die Beeld, 28 September 1969.
29. The Star, 27 September 1969.
30. Die Burger, 9 May 1969.

bers of the white and non-white administration cooperate on an equal footing. Whether the contact occurs among faculty of the non-white universities,[1] or the "autonomous" non-white councils, or at other overlapping contact areas of an inextricably interwoven multiracial society, does not matter compared with the fact that leading Afrikaners meet members of their outgroup for the first time in a capacity other than the traditional master-servant relationship. There are signs that this administrative contact gradually leads to more equalitarian perceptions. Nowhere else than in South Africa are oppressors and oppressed so close,[2] so dependent on each other.

In a sensitive case study of white-African worker relationships in a South African bus company, K. G. Hahlo[3] found, for example, that paternalistic joking relationships of the master-servant type existed only in the lowest occupational category. On a higher skilled level, "sponsor-relationship" between European supervisors and African workers crosscut racial boundaries and created *mutual* rights and obligations. Both group members experienced difficulties in upholding in the interracial working contact, the social distance required by the overall political system and community pressure outside the work sphere.

Among all writers on South Africa, it is especially Leo Kuper's merit to have pointed to the complexity of the South African social situation and the simplicity of the notion of "irrecon-

---

1. At the three African university colleges, 200 faculty positions are occupied by white as against 47 Africans. At the Indian college, the teaching staff comprises 109 whites and 25 Indians, while the Coloured institution in Belville had only two non-white lecturers as against 83 whites in 1968. Muriel Horrell, *A Survey of Race Relations*, 1968 (Johannesburg: South Africa Institute of Race Relations, 1968), p. 255.
2. Mere contact across the race barriers alone, to be sure, does not mean very much. All depends on the kind of relationship. Intimate contact in a paternalistic relationship goes well with the most contradictory prejudices. The object of outraged hate is the black who supposedly does not know his prescribed place. Contact on an equal basis, in the restaurant, before the counter in the post office, or at the soccer field, is not tolerated. The racist, however, has no objections to the intimate contact with his African servants, the "Nannies," and frequently African females as sexual objects, if it remains secret.
3. K. G. Hahlo, "A European-African Worker Relationship in South Africa," *Race* 11 (July 1969):13–34.

cilable conflict."[4] By emphasizing the forces countervailing open racial warfare—above all economic interdependence in an advanced industrial society and crosscutting loyalties—Kuper indeed initiates fruitful "thought beyond the platitudes of violence."[5] Far from advocating a particular program or engaging in wishful thinking, Kuper describes realistically the trends in favor of and against evolutionary changes. He analyzes the frequently neglected "individuating interracial processes" in a seemingly polarized situation, in which initial racial solidarities become inevitably fragmented through necessary, though regulated, cooperation in new interracial structures and contacts. While these developments undermine the racial rigidity, the political system dominated by a white working class electorate insulates itself successfully against "liberal interracial influences."[6]

This then is the central dilemma of independent settler societies: their constitutional structure renders changes in the social structure politically ineffective by blocking even a qualified franchise and, hence, preventing the gradual upward mobility of individuals from the subordinate groups. This would seem to support the development of collective racial identifications, although Kuper points to the fragmentation of the Africans by their different life situations and perceptions of reality which limit their ability "to mobilize effectively even by means of racial violence."[7] In his conclusions, Kuper leaves as an open question whether "interracial association" is likely to determine the future of South Africa or whether the "probability of extreme violence" will finally prevail. "In any event, in the absence of

---

4. Leo Kuper, *An African Bourgeoisie: Race, Class, and Politics in South Africa* (New Haven: Yale University Press, 1965), p. 391.

5. Leo Kuper, "Political Change in White Settler Societies: The Possibility of Peaceful Democratization," in Leo Kuper and M. G. Smith (eds.), *Pluralism in Africa* (Berkeley: University of California Press, 1969), p. 169. See also these important articles: Leo Kuper, "Structural Discontinuities in African Towns: Some Aspects of Racial Pluralism," in H. Miner (ed.), *The City in Modern Africa* (New York: Praeger, 1967) and Leo Kuper, "Conflict and the Plural Society: Ideologies of Violence among Subordinate Groups," in Kuper and Smith, *Pluralism in Africa*, pp. 153–67.

6. Kuper and Smith, *Pluralism in Africa*, p. 189.

7. Ibid.

common political institutions, such as English and Afrikaners share, and in the absence of a mediating third power, the direct confrontation of organized racial groups with a long history of conflict and oppression between them seems likely to complete the transformation of South Africa into a garrison state or to precipitate holocausts of violence and destruction."[8] However, Kuper cautiously articulates the hope that the United Nations might perform the role of the decisive mediating Third Party, since "internal social processes would not be sufficient in and of themselves to transform the political structure of South African society."[9] This most sophisticated analysis of South African society confesses uncertainty in its final conclusion: *"Perhaps under certain creative* constitutional arrangements and in association with such a mediating power as the United Nations, acting in a role analogous to that of the metropolitan power in colonial society, the individuating interracial processes *may* provide a basis for *relatively* peaceful democratic change"[10] (emphasis mine). There is, however, no hint as to what the certain creative constitutional arrangements could be, whether they would be likely to receive minimal consensus, under which circumstances, nor is there a discussion of the limitations of the United Nations or its essential paralysis in the cold war competition.

More than merely describing tendencies that support an evolutionary or revolutionary change per se, it would seem necessary to show their significance and to weigh them against each other. Kuper is reluctant to abandon a rather vague and abstract academic discourse in favor of more concrete political analysis. The owl of Minerva still begins its flight at dawn. A sociological analysis which attempts to go beyond this stage would have to determine to what extent changing interest constellations among the dominant group result in gradually changing attitudes. The focus on the subjective aspects of individuating processes neglects their underlying objective structure: the changing class base of white racialism, and its superfluousness under conditions that make smoother preservation

8. Ibid.
9. Ibid., p. 190.
10. Ibid., p. 191.

of privileges more desirable and less embarrassing to friendly interests outside the settler society. It might be possible to formulate as a general hypothesis that the tenacity of social and political institutions or their resistance to change varies with the degree to which they materially benefit important social groups. More specifically, the strength of this resistance is proportional to: (1) the number of persons or groups who benefit, (2) the size and nature of this benefit, and (3) the social power which these groups wield relative to groups who do not benefit from this structural arrangement. These elements are permanently changing, especially with the rise of Afrikaner capitalism and the restricting of benefits by certain Apartheid regulations for the industrial pressure groups.

But even assuming the static, obstructive nature of the central political institutions, expressing the obsessions of the prejudiced majority among the hegemonic group, there is no reason why gradual political change in favor of the subordinates could only take place through their participation *within* the same political system, that is through franchise as common voters. After the rise of Black Power ideology and the general decline and mistrust of liberal democracy, it seems futile even to speculate that "the means to this fuller political participation may be a qualified franchise, acquisition of elements of the culture of the dominant group qualifying for citizenship and democracy extending through incorporation of acculturated individuals."[11] In the postcolonial period these concepts are unlikely to find support among the politically active non-white elite, even in such strongholds as independent settler societies. If some leading subordinates were to advocate such reformist solutions now, they would very soon be ousted from their position of leadership by more radical demands. The strength of Afrikaner nationalism lies in the fact that it had realized from the beginning that a common but differential participation of the colonized in the same political institutions as their masters would either lead to increased dissatisfaction among the politicized or to the rapid downfall of white rule.

11. Ibid., p. 170.

Indeed, political integration is most likely to take place through enforced segregation of the kind that the Afrikaner Nationalists pursue without recognizing its long range implications. Imposed separate political activity will not only function as a collective bond, heightening consciousness by sharpening the issues along the lines of racial stratification, but it will also bring the subordinates gradually into a greater position of power than their token political incorporation could produce. No longer can whites negotiate with "Uncle Toms" representing nobody; their "bargaining" partners are becoming equals according to political reality, short of the collapse of the entire system of white legitimacy. The political magazine *News/Check* summarized the white experience with government-approved Africans at the occasion of the Coloured elections: "South Africa has already had some experience of this sort of thing from the Transkei parliament, whose leaders have not hesitated to slate the government for things like the dumping of surplus Africans in the impoverished homelands. The lesson taught there is that toughness enhances the status of the institution from which it emanates, both in the eyes of its electorate, and also of White South Africa. Even the opposition no longer proclaims Transkei PM Kaiser Matanzima a 'government stooge.' "[12]

Given the history and current state of racial antagonism within South Africa, the neocolonial solutions which the government envisages for the local African population herded into Bantustans, will not work as easily as it did for the former colonial powers in the rest of Africa. The earlier quoted South African political magazine, generally sympathetic to the government, has articulated this inherent contradiction of separate development in the following way:

> On the whole, the National Party is making the same mistake that the colonial powers made—assuming that the transition to independence can be a slow and leisurely process and easily controlled. Ironically, at the same time it is fostering a national awareness among the Bantu which can only hasten the process. One could say that the Transkei, for instance, has progressed so far that Pretoria cannot withhold independence.[13]

12. *News/Check*, October 1969.
13. *News/Check*, 18 April 1969, p. 11.

The government has repeatedly committed itself to the utopian Apartheid ideas in spite of warnings from its right wing. It is difficult to assess how much of this commitment is mere propagandist rhetoric or genuinely believed expediency for dealing with the "African problem." In September 1970 Prime Minister Vorster repeated that any one of South Africa's black nations were free to ask the government for independence. Economic viability would not be made a prerequisite for these talks. "It is their inalienable right to exercise their powers of self-determination tomorrow, if necessary."[14] What seems relevant is not the sincerity or expediency of such statements but its impact on those to whom it refers. The political consciousness of the non-white politicians who are active within the Apartheid framework has never been a subject of intensive research and yet it seems crucial since it is this realm where gradual pressures and change are most likely to occur in the foreseeable future. Indeed, the "derived power" of the Bantustan politicians has to be seen in the context of their white source and growing base among their own supporters.

However, to flatly denounce such non-white politicians as sellouts, stooges, or mere "satraps" and to ignore them, as is frequently done by Apartheid opponents outside the country, is to overlook the dynamics of their limited activity. Even in the slave society of the American South, the slaves never were entirely powerless and the masters never were in absolute control. Eugene D. Genovese has argued that the view which sees the slave only as victim of oppression denies that he is capable of autonomous action, be it only the skill to survive.[15] Such a view is as elitist as the focus on the dominant political culture, which has been criticized as racialist by black scholars. The complex interaction in an interwoven network of mutual pressures and expectations of master and servant is the more important in a system of domination which needs to legitimate itself by alleged equality of collaboration in separate units of a common social order. The few reactions of subordinate activists do not reveal much about the future of this experiment. But they do indicate

14. *The Star*, 19 September 1970.
15. Eugene D. Genovese, "American Slaves and their History," *New York Review of Books*, 3 December 1970.

interesting ideological features and perhaps the direction in which the black–white controversy could develop if Apartheid were to be carried to its promised ends.

Not surprisingly, the white-dictated freedom has engendered a kind of black resignative defiance which rationalizes defeat as victory. In almost direct reflection of the white ideology of racially pure poverty, black Bantustan leaders glorify their rural simplicity as opposed to city prosperity. The less accessible the forbidden fruits, the more they must be rejected in theory to reconcile barren reality with the relics of former dreams. Typical of this mood is a speech by C. M. C. Ndamse to white students at the University of the Witwatersrand:

> The bright lights and imposing buildings of the White cities we have helped to build have less appeal for us than the barren land that gives us a sense of belonging, that gives us the opportunity to manage our own affairs—or even to mismanage them. At least we have the right to be wrong or the right to be right, and who among us would choose to be wealthy in captivity rather than poor in liberty. We would rather rule in hell than serve and sweep the streets in heaven. . . . [16]

White dominated reality has become so strong that "wealth in liberty" or "rule in heaven" is not even the alternative. With a pragmatic cynicism black politicians begin to test the limits of suppression and the scope of their granted rights. In the words of Zulu chief Gatsha Buthelezi:

> If we can get all these human rights and dignities through separate development, well, let's get on with it. Some people have accused me of switching allegiances because I've long been an opponent of the government. I don't think this is true. What I'm doing is working within the system—and I must try and get as much representation for my people as possible.[17]

There are hardly any illusions about power in this attempt to improve the survival chances within an oppressive system: "The government must set the pace—we are placed in a cleft stick that

16. C. M. C. Ndamse, manuscript of a speech at the University of the Witwatersrand, September 1969.
17. *News/Check*, 26 June 1970.

ultimately whatever I say does not matter—what matters is what they allow."[18]

Although voices have no power, they are allowed to be raised. From the perspective of those unaccustomed to opportunities to express their views, this means substantial progress, regardless of its effects on the objective situation:

> Some Africans have referred to the Transkei as an economic backwater, and it may well be so. But the big difference is that we now have the right to say so without being branded as agitators.[19]

While this non-white criticism has similarities to white liberal protest for its own sake or the individual conscience of the critics, it also differs with respect to its potential force. With its helpless articulation, the awareness of non-white subordinates is growing. While the white protest has no chance to transgress the boundaries of those few who can afford nonracial open-mindedness in the midst of firmly entrenched bigotry, black self-assertion gains confidence and a growing awareness of reality as a distribution of power. Token share in this power along traditional lines is no longer accepted. The powerless subordinate hopes for a situation of equal struggle: "We have no ambition to go to Cape Town any more—and if we ever did it would have to be under somewhat different circumstances, along the road that goes via Umtata."[20]

As in the United States the first victim in this growing black power nationalism seems to be its staunchest ally, not its polar opponent. The white liberal is despised as the phony representative of a perspective which harmonizes the antagonistic conflicts. A Coloured journalist, who advocates the shrewd and cunning use of separate development as "an important instrument to improve our peoples' condition," expresses at the same time a widespread suspicion of white dogooders:

> It is time we stood squarely in front of those Whites who are 'with us' and told them, 'we are not interested in what you say.

18. Ibid.
19. Ndamse, manuscript of a speech at the University of Witwatersrand, September 1969.
20. Ibid.

We want to know what you are doing.' For if there is one aspect
of our condition in this country that we should not delude ourselves about, it is that we will have a 'better' life under a 'liberal'
White government.[21]

Whether non-white medical students at the University of
Natal object to being called the negative of whites or the politically active African students break away from the last multiracial organizations left in South Africa, separate development
does assert a new awareness among the subordinates. It emanates from the gap between promise and reality. The claim of
white legitimacy is an additional weapon in the hands of those
who have, of course, never been completely helpless. Their dignity and symbolic power which separate development claims to
establish could well be an important educational step in the
transfer of real power, perhaps the only one realistically available for the opponents of Apartheid at present.

What the rulers had once granted with the intention of nomi-
nal concessions to growing demands of equality could outlive its
initial purpose and turn out to become the most powerful threat
the colonizers have faced. No initial dependency of the non-
white politicians on the white controlling agency can prevent
their subtle ascendancy to power, from the position of stooges
to challengers of white domination, once a base among their
own people and in the overall political system of white legitimation is sufficiently secured. It is likely that the evolutionary
change of white South Africa will take place through more concessions under the pressure of increasingly powerful challenges
that would otherwise jeopardize white interests altogether
through a structural change. The question of transfer of power
could develop into a problem of sharing power, not because
both antagonists have become less hostile toward each other,
but because they both would lose more by insisting on the final
solution of their hostility than by settling for mutual concessions on the basis of mutual strength. What would seem to be

21. Howard Lawrence, "Coloureds must face Apartheid in New
Way," *Sunday Times*, 23 August 1970. For a strong rejection of this
view in the name of a party mandate, see (Coloured) Labour Party
Leader David M. G. Curry, "Apartheid: Coloureds say No Compromise," *Sunday Times*, 30 August 1970.

decisive is whether this envisaged process of mutual concessions through power confrontations could be confined to the political sphere, or whether it might develop its own dynamic beyond basically "rational" politics.[22] There is evidence that power confrontations can be contained rather than moving toward an escalation of irrationality. The considerable investments of Third Party powers in South Africa underlies their interest in easing tensions on both sides of the color line. The Apartheid theory in its most pragmatic form does not dehumanize the subordinates and, therefore, might contribute to a climate of "deracialization" more than the focus on the traditional *baasskap* policy is able to recognize. South African whites do realize that they are the outcasts of the world and display strong collective narcissism as a result. Their desire for acceptance as "civilized" might also contribute to a process of psychological modernization when backed by the increasingly obvious necessity to de-emphasize racial prejudices in a context where they are no longer the sole determinants of their fate.

Political Consequences of Structural Changes in the Laager

It has been generally accepted that "the tragedy of the South Africans is that they never changed their minds."[1] Leonard Thompson summarizes this view with the statement that today the Afrikaners are themselves victims of their past. "So tyrannical is tradition over them that they are left with no room for effective manoeuvre, no means to genuine reconciliation."[2] Although such interpretations might have been correct in the ear-

22. "Rational" in the Weberian sense of achieving an end with the optimum means. Politics is indissolubly bound up with having a voice. Voiceless politics is violence. As Hannah Ahrendt says: "Organized violence—warfare—may be necessary to protect the political process but it must not be confused with it." If there is a long term solution of the South African race conflict, short of considerable genocide on both sides, it is only if politics becomes the continuation of war by other means and not, according to the Clausewitz Maxim, war the continuation of politics.
1. I. Bundury, in *International Affairs* (April 1967).
2. L. M. Thompson, "The South African Dilemma," in L. Hartz (ed.), *The Founding of New Societies* (New York: Harcourt, Brace & World, 1964), p. 216.

lier stage of Afrikaner rule when there was no need for a revision of traditional attitudes, they are now doubtful with respect
to the new foreign policy and the ideological debates in the formerly homogeneous laager.

The frictions and splits among the Afrikaners reflect, above
all, a changed social structure. One can hardly overestimate the
significance of Afrikaner economic advancement in their political battle with English capital. A byproduct of this has been a
growing stratification within the white camp as a whole, and no
longer simply between English and Afrikaners. The growth of
Afrikaner capital control in recent decades is one of the most
important internal developments. The active support of Afrikaner entrepreneurs by the government, and the activities of
state-controlled corporations in various branches, have considerably challenged the predominance of English capital. Although only limited information is available, the following figures in table 6 do give some indication of this development.[3]

TABLE 6

THE AFRIKANER SHARE OF INCOME IN THE
PRIVATE SECTOR OF THE ECONOMY

	1938/39	*1948/49*	*1954/55*	*1963/64*
		Percentage of Total		
Industry Division	1	1	1	10
Mining	3	6	6	10
Commerce	8	25	26	31
Transport	–	9	14	14
Liquor and services	–	20	30	30
Professions	–	16	20	27
Financial	5	6	10	21
Sundry	–	27	35	36
Agriculture, forestry, and fishing	87	85	84	83
Total	–	24.8	25.4	26.3
Total excluding Agriculture	–	9.6	13.4	18.6

3. Quoted from a speech by T. F. Muller, Managing Director of Gen-
eral Mining and Finance Corporation, as reported in *Volkshandel*,
August 1968. Quoted here from *STATS*, 15 December 1968, 874–75.
Muller's speech is reported to be based on research by Professor J. L.
Sadie of the University of Stellenbosch.

The small total of only 18.6 percent of income in the private economy when agriculture is excluded is misleading since it does not include the economic activities controlled by the state. According to this source, if these activities in which Afrikaners play the leading role were to be added, it would more than double the Afrikaner share. The same source shows a seventeenfold increase of the total assets held by Afrikaans companies between 1950 and 1960. During this period the economy of the country showed a fourfold increase. Between 1946 and 1960 the ratio between Afrikaner and English income changed from 100:180 to 100:125, although the importance of agriculture, as the main sector of Afrikaner economic activity, decreased in relation to other branches.

The Afrikaner backwardness, although gradually dwindling, still exists and this not only with respect to financial power. The percentage of English-speaking matriculants is still double that of Afrikaans-speaking students: 12.9 percent as compared with 6.4 percent. Only 1.5 percent of the Afrikaans-speaking whites have a university degree as compared with 3 percent of their English-speaking counterparts.[4] Nevertheless, new on the political scene of the last two decades is the emergence of an Afrikaner urban middle class, a moneyed rather than educated bourgeoisie, with a "white collar" orientation. An overview of the proportion of Afrikaners in selected occupations shown in table 7 indicates a trend away from less skilled occupations to more technical and better remunerated professions.

The leveling of the income gap and educational standard between Afrikaner and English groups is encouraging a parallel tendency to emphasize class differences rather than ethnic cleavages within the ruling group. Racial distinctions, though not less important, are now experienced in a different context of interests. On the one hand, the qualified expert and owner hardly has to be afraid of any decline in his status during his lifetime, and, therefore, tends frequently to a more openminded attitude in the racial dispute; but, on the other hand, the white worker and clerk, aware they can be replaced by cheaper and frequently more qualified non-whites, tend to react with in-

4. *News/Check,* 24 November 1967; *The Star,* 6 July 1968.

TABLE 7

AFRIKANER SHARE IN SELECTED OCCUPATIONS

	1946	1960	Percentage of Change
Increases:			
Administrative and managerial workers	.9	2.5	+178
Clerical workers	10.0	21.0	+110
Professional and technical workers	6.5	9.0	+ 38
Salesworkers	4.5	5.6	+ 24
Craftsmen, production workers, and labourers	20.7	25.0	+ 21
Decreases:			
Farmers, fishermen and lumbermen	30.0	16.0	− 47
Workers in transport and communication	13.1	9.0	− 32
Service workers	6.7	6.0	− 11
Unspecified	3.5	2.4	− 32

creased hostility toward the potential threat. As the level of the restricted non-whites is raised and the expanding economy becomes more dependent on the unrestricted use and training of this labor source, the more the competitive pressure in the lower white strata will be felt. This will probably lead to more frictions within the ruling group centered around the alternatives of further integration or extreme racialism retarding economic expansion. Indications of such tendencies could be seen long before the open split in the Nationalist Party. For example, in a strike of white mine workers in the Orange Free State in 1966, the government approved the attempt of the mining management to use black workers for hitherto reserved jobs underground. The spokesman for the discontented workers' Action Committee, Ras Beyers, declared: "If the government now intends to become the lackeys of the Anglo-Jewish capitalists, it had better get used to the idea of being rejected by the miners."[5]

Since the formal split of the Nationalist Party in 1969, the class differences within Afrikanerdom have become more pronounced. In the view of *Die Vaderland*: "Open clashes between the Government and a certain section of the money power seems unavoidable."[6] It is significant that this paper, which represents

5. *News/Check*, 21 November 1966.
6. *Die Vaderland*, 13 April 1970.

the traditional policy without being openly critical of the government, includes in its attack the "Afrikaans money power," which would have been inconceivable several years ago. The different class interests among white South Africans are stated as the "question of the maximum profit with the cheapest labour in the shortest possible time,"[7] on the one hand, and, on the other, the refusal to tolerate the logical corollary "that White workers should be replaced by non-White workers for the sake of greater profit."[8]

Any prediction about the likely future course of white settlers in southern Africa has to be based on an assessment of the strength of both conflicting groups. The April 1970 general elections revealed the weakness of traditional racialism and the growing appeal for a more moderate and less rigid form of white domination. Although many factors not related to this question have influenced voting behavior, one can safely assume that under conditions of economic prosperity the pragmatists in both party camps will pay further lip service to a white working class electorate but will be able to persuade the white majority to accept a gradual change from petty Apartheid to a policy of non-white advancement in *separate political* and *integrated economic* avenues. In this context the economic roles of the state and of the political parties, which decide about this critical area, need further elaboration.

Under conditions of potential racial disturbance and strategic efforts to offset structural discontinuities through economic planning, and the bureaucratic regimentation of three-quarters of the populace, the growing role of the state in economic affairs assumes a new quality. State intervention in private sectors of the economy as well as through state-controlled corporations is not merely balancing an unstable boom, as in other capitalist countries, but is the very prerequisite of the settlers' survival. While state economic activity initially aimed primarily at the protection and promotion of the Afrikaner proletariat, it has now assumed the role of guaranteeing rapid, though differential, material advancement for all groups, including the non-white proletariat. Severe legislative restrictions on private profit,

7. Ibid.
8. *Die Transvaler*, 14 April 1970.

which would probably not be tolerated by big business in Western countries, are accepted more easily in South Africa because of the potentially extreme instability of laissez-faire racialism. This has reconciled the English-speaking entrepreneurs, to a large extent, to the dominant political group. Leo Kuper notes that with the Afrikaner converting political power to wealth and prestige "many of the English elite of wealth have moved from disdain for the Afrikaner political leaders to deference."[9] Mutual dependency has led to a compromise of conflicting attitudes on both sides, if not to actual collaboration. This tendency, above all, has taken the sting out of the United Party's political objections to government policy.

The United Party policy could easily find common ground with the *verligte* branch of the Nationalists. The United Party race policy insists on "enlightened, just, but firm White leadership" as well as residential, social, and educational separation and the legal machinery to enforce it. Differences, however, still remain with respect to the implementation of racial domination, especially in the economic sphere. The United Party advocates that "these laws be administered humanely and realistically to meet the demand for labour to fit the right man to the right job."[10] The Party stands, above all, for a laissez-faire racialism, subordinating state interference in the economy to private profit interests. In an editorial in *The Star* before the 1970 general election, the voters choice was presented as "freedom to run your racial separation your own way; or having a compulsively meddlesome state on your neck all the time."[11] The paper praises the alternative to the Nationalist government as a "South Africa in which racial distinctions existed and were observed without being pressed so far as to imperil security or the economy; a South Africa in which, inter alia, employers were free to employ whom they needed and dismiss whom the exigencies of their trade made redundant or objectionable."[12] Nationalists and their opponents agree on human labor as a

9. Leo Kuper, "Structural Discontinuities in African Towns: Some Aspects of Racial Pluralism," in Horace Miner (ed.), *The City in Modern Africa* (New York: Praeger, 1967), p. 150, n. 12.
10. *The Star*, 4 April 1970, p. 1.
11. Ibid., p. 11.
12. Ibid., p. 12.

commodity for maximum exploitation, but they differ on their labor policies with respect to this end. The United Party entrepreneurs press for the creation of a stable, settled labor force—"the raising of their standards of living, their training and opportunities for productive employment."[13] But on the Nationalist side, stronger feelings of traditional differentiation, coupled with the fear of white workers, serve to block this modernizing process at least for the present. How long this can last will depend on the growing strength and skill of private Afrikaner capitalists to manipulate their less wealthy fellow Afrikaners in the name of traditional folk values, and to persuade them to accept less rigid and more pragmatic race relations. The right-wing movement of the Hertzog group against the sellout of Afrikaner capitalists indicates that this is not an easy task. However, given a continuing boom and an increasing Afrikaner stake in the expanding economy, the long-term alleviation of petty Apartheid and a less rigid state interference in the labor market can be expected.

Above all, in the interest of its own preservation, white policy will have to accept what de Villiers Graaf calls "actively fostering the emergence of a responsible (Bantu) middle class as a bulwark against agitators."[14] With its own class position firmly entrenched and no longer inferior to the English-speaking rivals, the Afrikaner leadership is likely to show itself more ready to follow the experience of other conflict-prone societies, which have been able to neutralize their explosive potential by fostering a rising middle class with a stake in the maintenance of the status quo. The transformation from a race society into a class society along Portuguese lines lies in the interest of continued white privileges, which would be considerably strengthened by a policy of deracialization. If the perspective which views racialism basically as an expression of fear of competition, bolstered by a psychological need to create inferior outgroups, is a valid one, then there is no reason why Afrikaner nationalism could not undergo this vital change.

The growing political heterogeneity of Afrikanerdom as a consequence of socio-economic changes and its long political

13. Ibid., p. 1.
14. Ibid.

hegemony is not merely reflected in the *verligte-verkrampte* dispute. Afrikanerdom has always had its extreme right-wing ideologists and its few prominent dissenters on the other side, such as Leo Marquard, Uys Krige, Beyers Naudé, Braam Fischer, and, among the younger writers, André Brink and B. Breytenbach. The politically relevant change is the emerging criticism of sacred Afrikaner traditions and beliefs by its own loyal supporters who are not on the fringe of the *Volk*. For the first time the Afrikaner press criticizes the government for the refusal of passports,[15] the imposition of censorship, as well as the idiosyncracies of petty Apartheid. Sacred institutions, such as the once powerful *Broederbond*, are being questioned. "Has the bond still a right of existence?" asks Dirk Richard, the editor of *Dagbreek*.[16] His explanation of the waning role of this influential lobby is revealing: "It no longer acts like a powerful entity from its influential hiding place, for the same quarrels, differences of opinion and gradual division which Afrikanerdom is experiencing in the open have also penetrated into the Broederbond."[17] Even though the Afrikaner press is far from giving up its major role as a government propagandist versus the English press, it indicates at the same time the slow emergence of more sophisticated readers who appreciate the cautious questions by pragmatic critics. There is the possibility that this trend could lead to the formation of liberal political pressure groups within Afrikanerdom, similar to the foundation of the dissident Christian Institute in the religious sphere.

A number of Afrikaner intellectuals, considered to be innovative opinion leaders in their cautious attempts to come to grips with postcolonial trends, have already voiced frequent warnings. Their platform in the fifties was mainly the South African Bureau for Racial Affairs (SABRA), until Verwoerd in the early sixties brought pressure upon the organization to oust its progressive elements, such as Stellenbosch's Nic Olivier. However, the issues of these early disputes—the future of the Coloureds, the pace of "homeland" development, and the aboli-

15. See *Die Beeld*, 14 June 1970 in the case of playwright Athol Fugaard.
16. *Dagbreek*, 13 September 1970.
17. Ibid.

tion of petty Apartheid—continued to find relatively enlightened public advocates, not least in the spiritual center of Afrikaner-dom. Potchefstroms' Wimpie de Klerk or *Die Burger*'s editor Piet Cillie appear to represent the trendsetting intellectual voice of Afrikanerdom much more than *Hoofstad*'s editor Andries Treurnicht, let alone the extreme right, such as represented by the former director of the African Institute P. F. D. Weiss. Afrikaner sociologist Nic Rhoodie, although hardly influential in government circles, represents perhaps most typically the new emerging pragmatism among the ruling elite. Reporting about the American reaction to South Africa, he suggests that they do not "wish us to plunge headlong into ethnic suicide through biological amalgamation," but "they are adamant that colour and race per se should not be so manifestly institutionalized."[18] While "a country can still commit the sin of having a totalitarian political system," it would be considered "a lesser sin than a formalised colour differential."[19] Rhoodie concludes: "I now feel more strongly than ever before that White South Africa should make certain realistic adjustments and sacrifices for the sake of expediting its policies while it is still in a position of strength."[20]

Some sociologists have speculated that the main obstacle to this pragmatic accommodation, the Afrikaner working class, can be brought to place their economic interests ahead of their racialism. A tightening of the economic screws "might cause them to look for assistance in a labour struggle at least to those thousands of Africans and other non-Whites who are their fellow workers. . . ."[21] Nothing seems further away from a reality in which white labor aristocracy is the staunchest defender of racial extremism. Whether their group loyalty is strong enough to be manipulated into accepting racial concessions as advocated by some Afrikaner intellectuals and politicians seems an important question for the cohesiveness of white power.

Given the widely divergent outlooks and attitudes among

18. *News/Check*, 8 August 1969.
19. Ibid.
20. Ibid.
21. Austin A. Turk, "The Futures of South Africa," *Social Forces* 45 (March 1967):402–12.

these groups and individuals who are considered the intellectual spokesmen of the Afrikaner, it is questionable whether the notion of an ideologically or politically homogeneous Afrikanerdom continues to have much meaning beyond the obvious cultural characteristics of this group. In the absence of strongly felt internal or external pressures, the former unifying emotional bond among Afrikaners has certainly given way to a diluted ethnocentrism and nationalism, to be revived periodically in election campaigns or memorial days. The growing secularization of Afrikaners in the religious sphere has been paralleled by a lessened emphasis on the ideological basis in the political realm. It is indicative that the Nationalist Party in 1970 felt it necessary to appoint a public relations officer to improve its image. In South Africa too, political programs have to be advertized and sold successfully and can no longer be presupposed as a kind of inherited group disposition. To be sure, these trends among the ruling group of the country have so far hardly influenced its basic racial policies but would seem to be a prerequisite for any realistic perception of Afrikaner self-interest.

The South African political commentator Stanley Uys has stressed the decisive psychological function of the Nationalist Party's split for the group-consciousness of the Afrikaner.[22] The *broedertwis* has broken the magic spell of Afrikaner solidarity by demystifying the leadership and exposing on a large scale its political role rather than its divine function of preserving an Afrikaner identity that did not allow for dissent. Under a charismatic leader like Verwoerd, a challenge to his policies became immediately an attack on a prophet, "who could with credibility even invoke divine authority when it was required."[23] After the split the sacred meaning of Party unity was lost, and politicians became mortal. The demystification of the Party has increased the possibilities of less emotional and more pragmatic political responses toward threats against white privileges. While the emergence of a small group of "true Afrikaners" has

22. *Sunday Times*, 18 January 1970.
23. Lawrence Schlemmer, *Political Policy and Social Change in South Africa: An Assessment of the Future of Separate Development and of Possible Alternatives to the Policy* (Johannesburg: South African Institute of Race Relations, 1970).

undoubtedly immobilizing influences on the policy of the ruling Party, it not only paralyzes nontraditional initiative but also frees the pragmatists from stumbling blocks. The power of the more dogmatic group lies primarily in "its latent capacity to rouse Afrikanerdom to action if its leaders go too far,"[24] but the split over policy strategies (and no longer group loyalties) allows experimentation with new alignments for the first time. As in accord with other industrial societies, party organizations in South Africa will be less prone in the future to dictate political blueprints based on the inspirations and credentials of a superior leadership, but will instead respond more directly to various pressures and conflicting interest constellations among the electorate. This opens a new avenue for the most powerful lobby, the industrial interests, thus decreasing the contradictions between polity and business demands.

Summarizing these trends, it seems evident that the historical friction between the English- and Afrikaans-speaking populace is gradually being replaced by class contradictions within the two groups. As an entrepreneur, an Afrikaner has more in common with his English-speaking counterparts than with his poorer fellow Nationalists. The debates within the Afrikaner circles mirror these changing economic conditions and styles of life. With their growing economic control over a relatively powerful industrial state, with increased urbanization, and diminishing isolation—in both external and internal respects and through the smoother control of the African threat—the dominant interests of the political rulers have come to resemble those of the formerly hated industrialists. Both groups, no longer the Anglo-American Corporation of Harry Oppenheimer alone, now have a direct financial interest in a pragmatic race policy that regards ideological traditions as secondary and that will not confine itself much longer to the political securance of Afrikaner survival. A South African journalist has described the characteristics of this still small but influential group: "Whatever its members may be, they are bilingual and proud of it, they are self-confident; hold international values in their life-styles; believe progress comes from economic advancement; and are prepared

24. Stanley Uys, *Sunday Times*, 18 January 1970.

to reconsider critically sacred assumptions about White/Black relations that may hold up greater prosperity."[25]

This transcendence of old lineups through a common involvement in business will increase rather than decrease. The relatively cautious tactics of the Pretoria government toward the regime in Rhodesia, which jeopardized the intended reconciliation of South Africa's imperial interests with her markets to the North, can be viewed as a further sign of this new policy.[26] As long as the government represents such trends, and can at the same time secure the privileged position of the white workers and farmers by raising wages and subsidies, it is in an unchallengeable position. At the same time, the number of Afrikaners, so far restricted to only a few writers and clergymen, who dissociate themselves completely from the racialist implications of their nationality, is likely to increase. *Die Burger* complains that "among young Afrikaners, there seem to be many who would like to escape from the loaded sectional and exclusive associations of what is actually a fine and proud name."[27]

Even though the majority of Afrikaans-speaking whites, particularly those in the state bureaucracy, can expect economic security mainly from the patronizing policy of the National Party, there is an increasing number of them whose security is no longer dependent on an unquestioned allegiance to the *Volk*, and whose interests, therefore, do not necessarily coincide with the program of the government.[28] This social stratification is

25. *News/Check*, 6 December 1968.
26. The dramatic dispatch of South African anti-guerrilla forces to the Northern areas of Rhodesia in 1967 seems to contradict such a policy. This decision, however, only illuminates the dialectic of the conflict. When it comes to strategic considerations, South Africa has no choice but to put her strength on the side of her weaker allies, thereby defeating her own interests. There is probably no other single factor which will more greatly undermine the political strength of South Africa in the long run than her necessary alliance with the weak Portuguese and Rhodesian remnants of colonialism.
27. *Die Burger*, 21 February 1969.
28. Afrikaners not only staff the upper governmental positions but can rely on rank and file support in civil service of the country as well. Of its members, 71 percent are originally Afrikaans-speaking, compared with 58 percent in the whole population. This composition

accompanied by the steady dissolution of the once solid, ideologically homogeneous block of Afrikaners in the role of underprivileged whites.

The differences between *verligte* and *verkrampte* would seem in the long run to be more severe and persistent than their common ethnocentric frame would suggest. The debates about "true Afrikanerdom" derive their significance from the fact that they reflect these distinct economic interests. How far the expansion of South African capital to the north can be facilitated by ideological concessions depends both on the outcome of the controversy between the traditional racialists and the pragmatists, and also on the economically required political changes with respect to the internal attitudes of whites on petty Apartheid.

This does not mean that the present policy of the *verligte* is likely to change basically. What can be expected is only that for such a policy, ideological considerations will not be decisive, but that it will remain sufficiently flexible to adapt itself to new conditions and, if necessary, to compromise. This elastic, "rational" race-nationalism is capable of internal liberalization, in contrast to the irrational National Socialism in Europe. Such a development does not preclude the outbreak of violent conflicts, but it makes them less likely. Above all, the rational racial domination is most likely to falsify the assumption that mounting internal tension will make a violent revolutionary change inevitable. The South African whites, who at present determine the racial policies of their country, have almost perfected their domination over the non-white labor potential, and they will continue to do this in their own interests. They are not, as often viewed by the outside world, blindly fumbling toward their inevitable end. They are effective technocrats, who are establishing an increasingly unshakeable oligarchy in a society where the wealth of an advanced industrialization in the hands of the few whites coexists with the relative deprivation of the non-whites. If this is to be cemented by a gradual deracialization and

---

becomes more distinctive in specific sectors: 87 percent of the white policemen are Afrikaners. Of the 4,294 employees of the prisons department in 1966, only 63 are English. *Hansard,* cols. 2185–2195, 16 September 1966.

economic concessions, South Africa's white elite is capable of achieving this in spite of internal contradictions.

In concluding, it has to be stressed, however, that deracialization will not be the automatic outcome of changes in the occupational structure, but will have to emanate from pressures originating in the political realm. The pace of deracialization, especially, will depend on how much the white rulers are forced to give in. Changes in the economic sphere make Afrikaners more susceptible to certain kinds of African advancement and profit considerations in general, but above all bring Africans into a position of growing strategic strength. The mounting importance of manufacturing—as compared with the declining role of agriculture and mining—requires more job dilution and the admission of more and better trained Africans into semi-skilled and skilled positions of crucial significance for the functioning of an industrial society. The widespread flouting of "job reservation" by means of downgrading skilled work, pay-offs to white workers or simple official exemptions indicate this trend. As emphasized earlier, a necessary corollary of non-white occupational incorporation must be stability of the labor force, if a sufficient productivity rate is to be achieved. Manufacturing capital interested in a domestic market for its products presupposes also purchasing power of the local workers in contrast to the foreign market-oriented mining capital.

These trends bring the subordinates finally into a position from which they can exercise pressure more successfully than as completely dependent unskilled migratory workers. However, the crucial weakness of the African workers is their lack of organization in the absence of trade unions or urban political parties, which could channel individual frustrations into collective behavior. Consequently, strike action is hardly possible for such atomized and fragmented groups. In this respect, the growing withdrawal of the most politicized and sophisticated Africans from the few remaining multiracial organizations into their own groups within the Apartheid framework could function as a catalyst. The fate of the civil rights movement in the United States appears to repeat itself ten years later in South Africa. "Whites might talk about the erosion of freedom, but for the blacks there was no freedom anyway and the topic was futile."[29] All the more so could the homeland concept serve as a union substitute even for the urban worker, a rallying point and organizational platform for emerging nations of black power and a new African nationalism in Azania. Independence is not necessarily a prerequisite for this kind of homeland power. On the contrary, having pressed for independence, some African politicians are now holding back. They feel that formal independence would finalize the white-dictated distribution of land and the world would be unlikely to support claims for lost land after independence.

In whatever form the latent conflict eventually crystallizes, only by having asserted their own identity will the subordinates be able to overcome their inferior status. Thus, South Africa's political dynamics dialectically strengthens the antagonists of white domination by the very process of their separation and exclusion until the subordinates themselves have accumulated sufficient power for their own liberation.

29. One of the African justifications for withdrawal from NUSAS and founding of SASO in 1970. Quoted in Muriel Horrell, *A Survey of Race Relations*, 1970, p. 245.

Selected Bibliography

ENGLISH-LANGUAGE PUBLICATIONS ON THE GENERAL South African socio-political situation or relevant aspects of it, regardless of the professional perspective of the author, are included in this bibliography, with the focus on more recent works, published since 1960. For a more detailed bibliography, which also includes titles in Afrikaans and other languages, see H. Adam (editor), *South Africa: Sociological Perspectives*, London: Oxford University Press, 1971.

Attention should be drawn to the various useful articles and pamphlets published in South Africa, especially by the Johannesburg Institute of Race Relations and the South African Bureau for Racial Affairs. Most of these titles, concerned with actual or specific political questions, are not included here; the same applies to most of the regular publications of international and private organizations, parties, and churches which could be considered primary material, while this bibliography emphasizes more its interpretation in the social science literature. Therefore, the vast body of literary writing with political connotations has had to be largely excluded.

Adam, Heribert. "The South African Power Elite: A Survey of Ideological Commitment." In *South Africa: Sociological Perspectives*, edited by Heribert Adam. London: Oxford University Press, 1971.

Adam, Kogila. "Dialectic of Higher Education for the Colonized: The Case of Non-White Universities in South Africa." In *South Africa: Sociological Perspectives*, edited by Heribert Adam. London: Oxford University Press, 1971.

Andreski, Stanislav. "Aspects of South African Society." In *Elements of Comparative Sociology*, edited by Stanislav Andreski. Pp. 263–81. London: Weidenfeld & Nicholson, 1964.

————. "Reflections on the South African Social Order from a Comparative Viewpoint." In *South Africa: Sociological Perspectives*, edited by Heribert Adam. London: Oxford University Press, 1971.

Archibald, Drew. "The Afrikaners as an Emergent Minority." *British Journal of Sociology* 20 (1969):416–25.

Arrighi, Giovanni, and John S. Saul. "Nationalism and Revolution in Sub-Saharan Africa." *The Socialist Register*, 1969, pp. 137–88.

Asheron, A. "Race and Politics in South Africa." *New Left Review*, January/February 1969, pp. 55–68.

Austin, Dennis. *Britain and South Africa*. London: Oxford University Press, 1966.

————. "White Power?" *Journal of Commonwealth Political Studies* 6 (1968):95–106.

Ballinger, Margaret. *From Union to Apartheid*. Cape Town: Juta, 1969.

Banton, Michael. "White Supremacy in South Africa." In *Race Relations*, pp. 164–92. London: Tavistock Publications, 1967.

Benson, Mary. *The African Patriots: The Story of the African National Congress of South Africa*. London: Faber and Faber, Ltd., 1963.

————. Revised as: *South Africa: The Struggle for a Birthright*. London: Penguin, 1966.

Bloom, Leonard. "Self Concepts and Social Status in South Africa: A Preliminary Cross-Cultural Analysis." *Journal of Social Psychology* 51 (1960):103–12.

————. "Some Problems of Urbanization in South Africa." *Phylon* 25 (1964):347–61.

Bloom, Leonard, A. C. De Crespigny, J. E. Spence. "An Interdisciplinary Study of Social, Moral and Political Attitudes of White and Non-White South African University Students." *Journal of Social Psychology* 54 (1961):3–12.

Brett, E. A. *African Attitudes: A Study of the Social, Racial and Political Attitudes of Some Middle-Class Africans*. Johannesburg: S.A. Institute of Race Relations, 1963.

————. "African Attitudes to South African Society: The Reactions of Some Middle-Class Africans to Their Position in South Africa." *Race* 6 (1964):52–62.

Brookes, Edgar H. *Apartheid*. New York: Barnes & Noble, 1968.

————. *Apartheid: A Documentary Study of Modern South Africa*. London: Routledge and Kegan Paul, 1968.

Brown, Douglas. *Against the World: A Study of White South African Attitudes*. London: Collins, 1966.

Bull, Theodore. *Rhodesia: Crisis of Colour*. Chicago: Quadrangle Books, 1968.

Bunting, Brian. *The Rise of the South African Reich*. London: Penguin, 1964.

Carstens, Peter. *The Social Structure of a Cape Coloured Reserve: A Study of Racial Integration and Segregation in South Africa.* New York: Oxford University Press, 1966.

Carter, Gwendolen M. *The Politics of Inequality: South Africa Since 1948.* New York: Praeger, 1962.

――――. "African Concepts of Nationalism in South Africa." In *South Africa: Sociological Perspectives,* edited by Heribert Adam. London: Oxford University Press, 1971.

Carter, Gwendolen M., Thomas Karis, Newell M. Stultz. *South Africa's Transkei: The Politics of Domestic Colonialism.* Evanston: Northwestern University Press, 1967.

Cawood, Lesley. *The Churches and Race Relations in South Africa.* Johannesburg: South African Institute of Race Relations, 1964.

Chilcote, Ronald H. *Emerging Nationalism in Portuguese Africa: A Bibliography.* Stanford: Hoover Institution Press, 1969.

Clemens, Frank. *Rhodesia: The Course to Collision.* London: Pall Mall Press, 1969.

Cole, Ernest. *House of Bondage.* New York: Random House, 1967.

Cowen, Denis Victor. *The Foundations of Freedom with Special Reference to Southern Africa.* Cape Town, New York: Oxford University Press, 1961.

Dale, Richard. "South Africa and the International Community." *World Politics* 18 (1966):283–96.

Danziger, Kurt. "Ideology and Utopia in South Africa: A Methodological Contribution to the Sociology of Knowledge." *British Journal of Sociology* 14 (1963):59–76.

――――. "The Psychological Future of an Oppressed Group." *Social Forces* 42 (1963):31–40.

――――. "Modernization and the Legitimation of Social Power." In *South Africa: Sociological Perspectives,* edited by Heribert Adam. London: Oxford University Press, 1971.

Davis, J. A., and J. K. Baker. *Southern Africa in Transition.* London: Pall Mall Press, 1966.

De Kiewiet, C. W. "Loneliness in the Beloved Country." *Foreign Affairs* 42 (1964):413–27.

――――. "South Africa's Gamble with History." *The Virginia Quarterly Review* 40 (Winter 1965):1–17.

――――. *A History of South Africa: Social and Economic.* London: Oxford University Press, 1966.

――――. "The World and Pretoria." *Africa-Report* (February 1969): 46–52.

De Ridder, J. C. *The Personality of the Urban African in South Africa.* London: Routledge & Kegan Paul, 1961.

Dickie-Clark, H. F. *The Marginal Situation: A Sociological Study of a Coloured Group.* London: Routledge & Kegan Paul, 1966.

――――. "The Dilemma of Education in Plural Societies: The South

African Case." *South Africa: Sociological Perspectives,* edited by Heribert Adam. London: Oxford University Press, 1971.

Doxey, G. V. *The Industrial Colour Bar in South Africa.* Cape Town: Oxford University Press, 1961.

————. *The High Commission Territories and the Republic of South Africa.* London: Oxford University Press, 1963.

————. "The South African Problem: A Conflict of Nationalism." *International Journal* 18 (1963):501–12.

————. "Enforced Racial Stratification in the South African Labour Market." In *South Africa: Sociological Perspectives,* edited by Heribert Adam. London: Oxford University Press, 1971.

Doxey, G. V., and M. P. Doxey. "The Prospects for Change in South Africa." In *The Year Book of World Affairs, 1965.* Pp. 69–88. London: Stevens & Sons, 1965.

Dugard, C. J. R. "The Legal Effect of United Nations Resolutions of Apartheid." *South African Law Journal* 83 (February 1966):44–59.

Duncan, Patrick. "Toward a World Policy for South Africa." *Foreign Affairs* (October 1963):38–48.

————. *South Africa's Rule of Violence.* London: Methuen, 1964.

Du Toit, Brian M. "Politics and Change in South Africa." *International Journal of Comparative Sociology* 7 (1966):96–118.

————. "Colour, Class and Caste in South Africa." *Journal of Asian and African Studies* 1 (1966):197–212.

Evans, G. "Partition and South Africa's Future." *Journal of International Affairs* 18 (1964):241–52.

Feit, Edward. *South Africa: The Dynamics of the African National Congress.* London: Oxford University Press, 1962.

————. "Conflict and Cohesion in South Africa: A Theoretical Analysis of 'Separate Development' and its Implications." *Economic Development and Cultural Change,* July 1966, pp. 484–96.

————. *African Opposition in South Africa: The Failure of Passive Resistance.* Stanford: Hoover Institute, 1967.

————. "Community in a Quandary: The South African Jewish Community and 'Apartheid'." *Race* (April 1967):395–408.

————. "Urban Revolt in South Africa: A Case Study." *The Journal of Modern African Studies* 8 (1970):55–72.

Ford, Richard B. "The Urban Trek: Some Comparisons of Mobility in American and South African History." In *South Africa: Sociological Perspectives,* edited by Heribert Adam. London: Oxford University Press, 1971.

Frye, William. *In Whitest Africa: The Dynamics of Apartheid.* Englewood Cliffs: Prentice Hall, 1968.

Gibson, Richard. "A Hard Look at Africa's Liberation Movements." *Race Today* 1, no. 4 (1969).

Gross, Ernest A. "The Coalescing Problem of Southern Africa." *Foreign Affairs* 46 (1968):743–57.

Hahlo, H. G. "A European-African Worker Relationship in South Africa." *Race*, July 1969, pp. 13–34.

Hahlo, H. R., and E. Kahn. *The South African Legal System and its Background*. Toronto: Carswell, 1968.

Hall, Richard. *The High Price of Principles: Kaunda and the White South*. London: Hodder and Stoughton, 1969.

Hance, William A., ed. *Southern Africa and the United States*. New York: Columbia University Press, 1968.

Harrigan, Anthony. *The New Republic*. Pretoria: van Schaik, 1966.

Hartmann, Heinz. *Enterprise and Politics in South Africa*. Princeton: Princeton University Press, 1962.

Hellmann, Ellen. *Soweto: Johannesburg's African City*. Johannesburg: South African Institute of Race Relations, 1968.

——. "The Effects of Industrialization on Social Structure and Family Life." In *Council Papers on Industrialization and Human Relations*. Johannesburg: South African Institute of Race Relations, 1968.

——. "Urban Bantu Legislation." *New Nation*, September 1969, pp. 9–11.

——. "Social Change Among Urban Africans." In *South Africa: Sociological Perspectives*, edited by Heribert Adam. London: Oxford University Press, 1971.

Hepple, Alexander. *South Africa: A Political and Economic History*. London: Pall Mall Press, 1966.

——. *Verwoerd*. London: Penguin Books, 1967.

Hill, Christopher R. *Bantustans: The Fragmentation of South Africa*. London, New York: Oxford University Press, 1964.

Horrell, Muriel. *South African Trade Unionism: A Study of a Divided Working Class*. Johannesburg: South African Institute of Race Relations, 1961.

——. *Action, Reaction and Counteraction: A Review of Non-White Opposition to the Apartheid Policy, Counter-Measures by the Government and the Eruption of New Waves of Unrest*. Johannesburg: South African Institute of Race Relations, 1963.

——. *A Decade of Bantu Education*. Johannesburg: South African Institute of Race Relations, 1964.

——. *Reserves and Reservations: A Comparison of Plans for the Advancement of Under-Developed Areas in South Africa and the United States, Including Information about the Development of the African Reserves in South Africa as at June, 1965*. Johannesburg: South African Institute of Race Relations, 1965.

——. *Group Areas: The Emerging Pattern with Illustrative Examples from the Transvaal*. Johannesburg: South African Institute of Race Relations, 1966.

——. *Legislation and Race Relations: A Summary of the Main*

South African Laws Which Affect Race Relationships. Johannesburg: South African Institute of Race Relations, 1966.

———. *South West Africa.* Johannesburg: South African Institute of Race Relations, 1967.

———. *The Rights of African Women: Some Suggested Reforms.* Johannesburg: South African Institute of Race Relations, 1968.

———. *Terrorism in South Africa.* Johannesburg: South African Institute of Race Relations, 1968.

———. *South Africa's Workers: Their Organization and the Patterns of Employment.* Johannesburg: South African Institute of Race Relations, 1969.

Horrell, Muriel, ed. *Bantu Education to 1968.* Johannesburg: South African Institute of Race Relations, 1968.

Houghton, Desmond Hobart. *The South African Economy.* Cape Town: Oxford University Press, 1967.

Hudson, W., G. F. Jacobs, and S. Biesheuvel. *Anatomy of South Africa.* Cape Town: Purnall, 1966.

Hutt, W. H. *The Economics of the Colour Bar.* London: Andre Deutsch, 1964.

Johns, Sheridan W., III. "The Birth of Non-White Trade Unionism in South Africa." *Race* 9 (October 1967):173–92.

Johnstone, Frederick A. "White Prosperity and White Supremacy in South Africa Today." *African Affairs* 69 (April 1970):124–40.

Kahn, Ely Jacques. *The Separated People: A Look at Contemporary South Africa.* New York: W. W. Norton, 1968.

Kepple-Jones, A. *South Africa: A Short History.* London: Hutchinson, 1966.

Kruger, D. W. *The Making of a Nation: A History of the Union of South Africa 1910–1961.* New York: Humanities Press, 1970.

Kuper, Leo. (1957) *Passive Resistance in South Africa.* New Haven: Yale University Press, 1960.

———. "The Heightening of Racial Tensions." *Race* 2 (1960):24–32.

———. *The College Brew.* Durban: Privately published, 1960.

———. "Racialism and Integration in South African Society." *Race* 4 (1963).

———. "The Problem of Violence in South Africa." *Inquiry* 7 (1964): 295–303.

———. *An African Bourgeoisie: Race, Class, and Politics in South Africa.* New Haven: Yale University Press, 1965.

———. "Structural Discontinuities in African Towns: Some Aspects of Racial Pluralism." In *The City in Modern Africa,* edited by H. Miner. New York: Praeger, 1967.

———. "The Political Situation of Non-Whites in South Africa." In *Southern Africa and the United States,* edited by W. A. Hance. Pp. 85–104. New York: Columbia University Press, 1968.

———. "Political Change in White Settler Societies: The Possibility of Peaceful Democratization." In Leo Kuper and M. G. Smith, *Pluralism in Africa*. Berkeley: University of California Press, 1969.

———. "Conflict and the Plural Society: Ideologies of Violence Among Subordinate Groups." In Leo Kuper and M. G. Smith, *Pluralism in Africa*. Berkeley: University of California Press, 1969.

———. "Continuities and Discontinuities in Race Relations: Evolutionary or Revolutionary Change." *Cahiers d'Etudes Africaines* 10 (1970):361–83.

———. "Nonviolence Revisited." In *Protest and Power in Black Africa*, edited by Robert J. Rotberg and Ali A. Mazrui. Pp. 788–804. New York: Oxford University Press, 1970.

———. "Stratification in Plural Societies: Focus on White Settler Societies in Africa." In *Essays in Social Stratification*, edited by Leonard Plotnicov and Arthur Tuden. Pp. 77–93. Pittsburgh: University of Pittsburgh Press, 1970.

Laurence, John. *The Seeds of Disaster*. New York: Taplinger, 1968.

Legum, Colin, and Margaret Legum. *South Africa: Crisis of the West*. New York: Praeger, 1964.

———. *The Bitter Choice: Eight South Africans' Resistance to Tyranny*. Cleveland: The World Publishing Company, 1968.

Legum, Colin. "Colour and Power in the South African Situation." *Daedalus* (Spring 1967):483–95.

Leiss, Amelia Catherine, ed. *Apartheid and the United Nations Collective Measures: An Analysis*. New York: Carnegie, 1965.

Leistner, G. M. E. "Foreign Bantu Workers in South Africa: Their Present Position in the Economy." *South African Journal of Economics* 35 (March 1967):30–56.

Le May, G. H. *British Supremacy in South Africa*. London: Clarendon Press, 1965.

Lever, H. "Reducing Social Distances in South Africa." *Sociology and Social Research* 51 (July 1967).

Lever, H., and Wagner, O. J. M. "Ethnic Preferences of Jewish Youth in Johannesburg." *Jewish Journal of Sociology* 9 (June 1967): 34–47.

Lewin, Julius. *Politics and Law in South Africa*. London, Merlin Press, 1963.

———. *The Struggle for Racial Equality*. London: Longmans, 1967.

Lombard, J. A., J. J. Stadler, and P. J. Van der Merwe. *The Concept of Economic Cooperation in Southern Africa*. Pretoria: Bureau for Economic Policy and Analysis, 1969.

Loubser, Jan J. "Calvinism, Equality and Inclusion: The Case of Afrikaner Nationalism." In *The Protestant Ethic and Modernization*, edited by S. N. Eisenstadt. Pp. 367–83. New York: Basic Books, 1968.

Luthuli, A. *Let My People Go: An Autobiography*. New York: Mac-Graw-Hill, 1962.

MacCrae, Norman. "The Green Bay Tree." *The Economist* 29 (June 1968).

———. "What Will Destroy Apartheid?" *Harpers*, March 1970, pp. 30–42.

Magubane, Ben. "Pluralism and Conflict Situations in Africa: A New Look." *African Social Research* 7 (1969):529–54.

Malherbe, E. G. *Need for Dialogue*. Johannesburg: South African Institute of Race Relations, 1967.

———. *The Nemesis of Docility*. Johannesburg: South African Institute of Race Relations, 1968.

Malhotra, R. C. "Apartheid and the United Nations." *Annals of the American Academy of Political and Social Science* 354 (July 1964): 135–44.

Mandela, Nelson. *No Easy Walk to Freedom*. London: Heinemann, 1965.

Mann, J. W. "Race-Linked Values in South Africa." *Journal of Social Psychology* 58 (1962):31–41.

———. "Rivals in Different Ranks." *Journal of Social Psychology* 61 (1963):11–27.

———. "Attitudes Towards Ethnic Groups." In *South Africa: Sociological Perspectives*, edited by Heribert Adam. London: Oxford University Press, 1971.

Manning, Charles A. W. "In Defense of Apartheid." *Foreign Affairs*, October 1964, pp. 135–64.

Marcum, John A. *The Angolan Revolution, Vol. I: The Anatomy of an Explosion*. Cambridge: Massachusetts Institute of Technology Press, 1969.

Marquard, Leo. (1955) *The Story of South Africa*. London: Faber and Faber, 1960.

———. *Liberalism in South Africa*. Johannesburg: South African Institute of Race Relations, 1965.

———. *The Peoples and Politics of South Africa*. London: Oxford University Press, 1969.

Mason, P. "South Africa and the World: Some Maxims and Axioms." *Foreign Affairs*, October 1964, pp. 150–64.

Mathews, A. S., and R. C. Albino. "The Permanence of the Temporary: An Examination of the 90 and 180 Day Detention Laws." *South African Law Journal*, February 1966, pp. 16–43.

Mathews, A. S. "Security Laws and Social Change in the Republic of South Africa." In *South Africa: Sociological Perspectives*, edited by Heribert Adam. London: Oxford University Press, 1971.

Mayer, Philip. *Townsmen and Tribesmen*. Cape Town: Oxford University Press, 1961.

———. "Migrancy and Study of Africans in Towns." *American Anthropologist* 64 (1962):576–92.

———. "Religion and Social Control in a South African Township."

In *South Africa: Sociological Perspectives,* edited by Heribert Adam. London: Oxford University Press, 1971.

Mbeki, Govan A. M. *South Africa: The Peasant's Revolt.* Baltimore: Penguin, 1964.

Meer, Fatima. "African and Indian in Durban." *Africa South* 4 (1960): 30–41.

—————. *Portrait of Indian South Africans.* Durban: Avon House, 1969.

—————. "African Nationalism—Some Inhibiting Factors." In *South Africa: Sociological Perspectives,* edited by Heribert Adam. London: Oxford University Press, 1971.

Minty, Abdul S. *South Africa's Defense Strategy.* London: The Anti-Apartheid Movement, 1969.

Morlan, Gail. "The Student Revolt Against Racism in South Africa." *Africa Today* 17 (May–June 1970):12–20.

Muller, A. L. *Minority Interests: The Political Economy of the Coloured and Indian Communities in South Africa.* Johannesburg: South African Institute of Race Relations, 1968.

Muller, C. F. J., F. A. Van Jaarsfeld, and Theo Van Wijk, eds. *A Select Bibliography on South African History.* Pretoria: University of South Africa, 1966.

Munger, Edwin S. *Notes on the Formation of South African Foreign Policy.* Pasadena: The Castle Press, 1965.

—————. *Afrikaner and African Nationalism: South African Parallels and Parameters.* London: Oxford University Press, 1967.

—————. "New White Policies." In *Southern Africa and the United States,* edited by W. A. Hance. New York, London: Columbia University Press, 1968.

—————. "South Africa: Are There Silver Linings." *Foreign Affairs,* January 1969, pp. 375–86.

Ngubane, Jordan K. *An African Explains Apartheid.* New York: Praeger, 1963.

—————. "South Africa's Race Crisis: A Conflict of Minds." In *South Africa: Sociological Perspectives,* edited by Heribert Adam. London: Oxford University Press, 1971.

Niddre, David L. *South Africa: Nation or Nations?* Princeton: von Norstrand, 1968.

Nielsen, Waldemar A. *African Battleline: American Policy Choices in Southern Africa.* New York: Harper and Row, 1965.

Orlik, Peter B. "Divided Against Itself: South Africa's White Policy." *The Journal of Modern African Studies* 8 (July 1970):199–212.

Paton, Alan. *The Long View.* New York: F. A. Praeger, 1968.

Patterson, Sheila. *The Last Trek: A Study of the Boer People and the Afrikaner Nation.* London: Routledge and Kegan Paul, 1957.

Pauw, B. A. *The Second Generation: A Study of the Family Along Urbanized Bantu in East London.* Cape Town: Oxford University Press, 1963.

Pettigrew, Thomas F. "Social Distance Attitudes of South African Students." *Social Forces* 38 (1960):246–53.

Pienaar, S. and A. Sampson. *South Africa: Two Views of Separate Development*. London: Oxford University Press, 1960.

Ramparts. "Southern Africa: A Smuggled Account from a Guerrilla Fighter." *Ramparts*, October 1969, pp. 8–18.

Ransford, Oliver. *The Rulers of Rhodesia*. London: John Murray, 1969.

Reader, D. H. *The Black Man's Portion*. London: Oxford University Press, 1961.

Rhoodie, N. J., and H. J. Venter. *Apartheid: A Socio-Historical Exposition of the Origin and Development of the Apartheid Idea*. Amsterdam: De Bussy, 1960.

Rissik, Gerard. "The Growth of South Africa's Economy." *Optima*, June 1967, pp. 52–60.

Robson, Peter. "Economic Integration in Southern Africa." *Journal of Modern African Studies* 5 (December 1967):469–90.

Rose, Brian, ed. *Education in Southern Africa*. London: Collier-Macmillan, 1970.

Roux, Edward. *Time Longer Than Rope: A History of the Black Man's Struggle for Freedom in South Africa*. Madison: University of Wisconsin Press, 1964.

Sachs, E. S. *The Anatomy of Apartheid*. London: Collet's, 1965.

Sachs, Benjamin. *South Africa: An Imperial Dilemma; Non-Europeans and the British National, 1902–1914*. Albuquerque: University of New Mexico Press, 1967.

Samkange, Stanlake. *Origins of Rhodesia*. New York: Praeger, 1969.

Schlemmer, Lawrence. *Political Policy and Social Change in South Africa: An Assessment of the Future of Separate Development and of Possible Alternatives to the Policy*. Johannesburg: South African Institute of Race Relations, 1970.

Segal, Ronald Michael. *Into Exile*. New York: MacGraw-Hill, 1963.

––––––. *The Race War*. London: Jonathan Cape, 1966.

Segal, Ronald Michael, ed. "Sanctions Against South Africa." International Conference on Economic Sanctions Against South Africa. Baltimore: Penguin, 1964.

Shingler, John, and Martin Legassick. "Students in South Africa." In *Student and Politics in Developing Nations*, edited by D. K. Emmerson. Pp. 103–45. New York: Frederick A. Praeger, 1968.

Simons, H. J., and R. E. Simons. *Class and Colour in South Africa 1850–1950*. Harmondsworth: Penguin, 1969.

Snellen, I. Th. M. "Apartheid: Checks and Changes." *International Affairs* 43 (April 1967):293–306.

Solomon, Larry. "The Economic Background to the Revival of Afrikaner Nationalism." In *Boston University Papers in African History*, I, edited by Jeffrey Butler, 1964.

Spence, J. E. "The Political Implications of the South African Bantustan Policy." *Race* 3 (May 1962):20–30.

———. "Prospects for Change in South Africa." *World Today* 20 (September 1964):365–72.

———. *Republic Under Pressure: A Study of South African Foreign Policy.* London: Oxford University Press, 1965.

———. "The Origins of Extra-Parliamentary Opposition in South Africa." *Government and Opposition* 1 (October 1965):55–84.

———. *Lesotho: The Politics of Dependence.* London: Oxford University Press, 1968.

———. "South Africa's 'New Look' Foreign Policy." *World Today,* April 1968, pp. 137–45.

Spottiswoode, Hildegarde, ed. *South Africa: The Road Ahead.* London: Bailey Bros. and Swinfen, 1960.

Stacey, R. D. "Some Observations on the Economic Implications of Territorial Segregation in South Africa." *South African Journal of Economics* (Johannesburg) 34 (March 1966): 50–67.

Steyn, Anna F., and Colin M. Rip. "The Changing Urban Bantu Family." *Journal of Marriage and Family,* 30 (1968):499–517.

Stone, Julius. "Reflections on Apartheid After the South-West Africa Cases." *Washington Law Review* 42 (June 1967):1069–82.

Stultz, Newell M. "Creative Self-Withdrawal in the Transkei." *Africa Report* 9 (April 1964):18–23.

———. "The Politics of Security: South Africa Under Verwoerd, 1961–6." *The Journal of Modern African Studies* 7 (1969):3–20.

Stultz, Newell M., and Jeffrey Butler. "The South African General Election of 1961." *Political Science Quarterly* 78 (March 1963): 86–110.

Sundkler, B. G. *Bantu Prophets in South Africa.* New York: Oxford University Press, 1961.

Suttner, Sheila. *Cost of Living in Soweto.* Johannesburg: South African Institute of Race Relations, 1966.

Tabata, I. B. *Education for Barbarism in South Africa.* London: Pall Mall Press, 1960.

Thompson, Leonard M. *The Unification of South Africa, 1902–1910.* Oxford: Clarendon Press, 1960.

———. "Afrikaner Nationalist Historiography and the Policy of Apartheid." *Journal of African History* 3 (1962):125–41.

———. "The South African Dilemma." In *The Founding of New Societies,* edited by Louis Hartz. Pp. 178–218. New York: Harcourt, Brace and World, 1964.

———. *Politics in the Republic of South Africa.* Boston: Little, Brown, 1966.

Thompson, Richard. *Race and Sport.* London: Oxford University Press, 1964.

Times, The. "Anatomy of Apartheid, 1960." Articles from *The Times.* London: The Times Publishing Co., 1960.

———. *The Black Man in Search of Power.* London: Nelson, 1968.

Tiryakian, Edward A. "Apartheid and Politics in South Africa." *Journal of Politics* 22 (1960):682–97.

———. "Sociological Realism: Partition for South Africa?" *Social Forces* 46 (December 1967):208–21.

UNESCO. *Apartheid—Its Effects on Education, Science, Culture and Information.* Paris: UNESCO, 1967.

United Nations. *Unit on Apartheid. Military and Police Forces in The Republic of South Africa.* New York, 1967.

van den Berghe, Pierre L. "Miscegenation in South Africa." *Cahiers d'Etudes Africaines* 4 (1960):68–84.

———. "Some Trends in Unpublished Social Science Research in South Africa." *International Social Science Journal* 4 (1962).

———. "Apartheid, Fascism and the Golden Age." *Cashiers d'Etudes Africaines* 8 (1962):598–608.

———. "Race Attitudes in Durban, South Africa." *Journal of Social Psychology* 57 (1962):55–72.

———. *Caneville: The Social Structure of a South African Town.* Middletown: Wesleyan University Press, 1964.

———. *South Africa: A Study in Conflict.* Middletown: Wesleyan University Press, 1965.

———. "Racial Segregation in South Africa: Degrees and Kinds." *Cahiers d'Etudes Africaines* 6 (1966):408–18.

———. *Race and Racism: A Comparative Perspective.* New York: John Wiley, 1967.

———. "Language and Nationalism in South Africa." *Race* (July, 1967).

Vandenbosch, Amry. *South Africa and the World.* Lexington: University of Kentucky Press, 1970.

van der Horst, Sheila T. "The Economic Implications of Political Democracy." *Optima* (June 1960).

———. *African Workers in Town: A Study of Labour in Cape Town.* Cape Town: Oxford University Press, 1964.

———. "The Effects of Industrialization on Race Relations in South Africa." In *Industrialization and Race Relations,* edited by G. Hunter. Pp. 97–140. London: Oxford University Press, 1965.

van der H. Schreider, D. M. "History on the Veld: Towards a New Dawn?" *African Affairs* 68 (April 1969):149–59.

van der Merwe, W. "Stratification in a Cape Coloured Community." *Sociology and Social Research* 46 (1962):302–11.

———. "The Economic Influence of the Bantu Labor Bureau on the Bantu Labor Market." *South African Journal of Economics,* March 1969, pp. 4–54.

van Rensburg, Patrick. *Guilty Land.* London: J. Cape, 1962.

Vatcher, William Henry. *White Laager: The Rise of Afrikaner Nationalism*. London: Pall Mall Press, 1965.

Vilakazi, Absolom. *Zulu Transformations: A Study of the Dynamics of Social Change*. Pietermaritzburg: University of Natal Press, 1962.

Walshe, A. P. "The Changing Content of Apartheid." *Review of Politics* 25 (July 1963):343–61.

————. "The Origins of African Political Consciousness in South Africa." *The Journal of Modern African Studies* 7 (1969):583–610.

————. "Black American Thought and African Political Attitudes in Southern Africa." *The Review of Politics*, January 1970, pp. 51–77.

————. *The Rise of African Nationalism in South Africa*. London: C. Hurst, 1970.

Weisbord, Robert G. "The Dilemma of South African Jewry." *Journal of Modern African Studies* 5 (1967):233–41.

Wellington, J. H. *South West Africa and Its Human Issues*. London: Oxford University Press, 1967.

Welsh, David. "Urbanization and the Solidarity of Afrikaner Nationalism." *The Journal of Modern African Studies* 7 (1969):265–76.

————. "Capital Punishment in South Africa." In *African Penal Systems*, edited by A. Milner. New York: Praeger, 1969.

Wilson, Monica. "South Africa." *International Social Science Journal* 13 (1961):225–44.

Wilson, Monica, and Archie Mafeje. *Langa: A Study of Social Groups in an African Township*. Cape Town: Oxford University Press, 1963.

Wilson, Monica, and Leonard Thompson, eds. *The Oxford History of South Africa, I. South Africa to 1870*. London: Oxford University Press, 1969.

Worrall, Denis. "Partition: An English-Speaking Point of View." *Journal of Racial Affairs* 18 (January 1967):14–23.

Index